Also by Robert McKee

*Story: Substance, Structure, Style, and
the Principles of Screenwriting*

*Dialogue: The Art of Verbal Action for Page,
Stage, and Screen*

Storynomics

CHARACTER

*The Art of Role and Cast Design for Page,
Stage, and Screen*

ROBERT McKEE

TWELVE

NEW YORK • BOSTON

Twelve
Hachette Book Group
1290 Avenue of the Americas, New York, NY 10104
twelvebooks.com
twitter.com/twelvebooks

First Edition: May 2021

Twelve is an imprint of Grand Central Publishing.
The Twelve name and logo are trademarks of Hachette Book Group, Inc.

The publisher is not responsible for websites (or their content) that are not owned by the publisher.

The Hachette Speakers Bureau provides a wide range of authors for speaking events. To find out more, go to www.hachettespeakersbureau.com or call (866) 376-6591.

Library of Congress Cataloging-in-Publication Data has been applied for.

ISBNs: 978-1-4555-9195-4 (hardcover), 978-1-4555-9194-7 (ebook)

Printed in the United States of America

LSC-C

Printing 1, 2021

To Mia,
my wife, my life.

CONTENTS

PART THREE:
THE CHARACTER UNIVERSE

PART FOUR:
CHARACTER RELATIONSHIPS

Characters are not human beings. A character is no more human than the Venus de Milo, Whistler's Mother, and Sweet Georgia Brown are women. A character is a work of art—an emotive, meaningful, memorable metaphor for humanity, born in the mind-womb of an author, held safe in the arms of story, destined to live forever.

INTRODUCTION

For most writers, what's past is past, and so they focus on future trends, hoping to improve their chances for production or publication by adapting to what's current. Writers should indeed stay in tune with their times, but while cultural and aesthetic vogues come and go, there are no trends in human nature. As evolutionary science has shown in study after study, humanity has not evolved for eons. The guys and gals who stenciled their handprints on the walls of caves forty thousand years ago were doing then what we do today—making selfies.

For thousands of years, artists and philosophers portrayed and studied human nature, but then, beginning in the late nineteenth century, science focused on the mind behind that nature. Researchers evolved theories of human behavior ranging from psychoanalysis to behaviorism to evolutionism to cognitivism. These analyses labeled and catalogued traits and flaws by the dozens, and without question their perceptions stimulate the writer's creative thinking about characters and casts. This book, however, does not favor any single school of psychology. It gathers concepts from many disciplines to trigger the imaginings and intuitions that inspire and guide the talented.

Character's primary purpose is to enrich your insights into the nature of the fictional character and sharpen your creative techniques as you invent a complex, never-seen-before cast of personalities, starting with your protagonist, then moving outward through your first, second, and third circles of supporting roles, ending with the nameless passing at the far edges of episodes. To that end, expect reworkings. Chapter by chapter, refrain by refrain, certain primal principles will echo inside new contexts. I reiterate ideas because each time an artist rethinks the familiar in a new light, her comprehension deepens.

In the chapters that follow, the principle of contradiction underpins virtually every lesson in character design. I play opposites against each other: characters versus human beings, institutions versus individuals, traits versus truths, the outer life versus the inner life, and so on. You and I know, of course, that along any spectrum strung between polar extremes, shades of possibility blur into overlaps and admixtures. But for clear, facile perception of character complexity, a writer needs a sensitivity to contrast and paradox, an eye for contradiction that unearths the full range of creative possibility. This book teaches that skill.

As always, I will call on current examples, both dramatic and comic, taken from award-winning films and screen series, novels and short stories, plays and musicals. To those contemporary works, I will also add characters created by canonical authors from the past forty centuries of literacy—Shakespeare first among them. Some of these titles may be unread or unseen by you, but hopefully you'll add them to your personal program of study.

Characters taken from all eras serve two purposes: (1) The task of an illustration is to exemplify and clarify the point at hand, and, as it happens, the sharpest example is often history's first. (2) I want you to take pride in your profession. As you write, you join an ancient, noble, truth-telling tradition. Brilliant casts from the past will set the stage for your future writings.

Character has four parts. **Part One: In Praise of Characters** (Chapters One through Three) explores sources of inspiration for character invention and lays out the foundational work that shapes your talents toward creating superbly imagined fictional human beings.

Part Two: Building a Character (Chapters Four through Thirteen) pursues the creation of never-met-before characters, beginning with methods from the outside in, followed by the inside out, expanding into dimensionality and complexity, ending with roles at their most radical. As Somerset Maugham expressed it, "The only inexhaustible subject is human nature."

Part Three: The Character Universe (Chapters Fourteen through Sixteen) contexts character by genre, performance, and reader/audience/character relationships.

Part Four: Character Relationships (Chapter Seventeen) illustrates the principles and techniques of cast design by mapping the dramatis personae of five works taken from prose, cinema, theatre, and longform television.

All told, I will parse the universe of character into its galaxies, galaxies into solar systems, solar systems into planets, planets into ecologies, ecologies into the life force—all in order to help you uncover creative meanings in the human mystery.

No one can teach you *how* to create story, character, or anything else. Your processes are idiosyncratic, and nothing I teach will do the writing for you. This book is not a how-to but a what-is. All I can do is give you aesthetic principles and examples to illustrate them, laying out parts, wholes, and their relationships. To this course of study, you must add your brains, taste, and long, long months of creative work. I cannot take you by the hand. Instead, I offer knowledge to leverage your talent. To that end, I suggest you read this book slowly, stopping and going to absorb what you've learned and give thought to how it applies to your work.

Character strives to deepen your insight into character complexity, sharpen your eye for expressive traits, and in those dark days when inspiration needs a friend, shepherd you through the configuration of an entire cast.

THE PRONOUN PROBLEM

The mind-stubbing word-jams of *s/he, he/she, her/him, he-and-she,* and *her-and-him,* along with the mind-numbing pronoun *one* and the plural pronouns of *their, they,* and *them* used to neutralize gender, well intentioned as they may be, slow the read. The singular pronoun *he* may pretend to be gender neutral, but he is not. So, in odd-numbered chapters, unspecified persons will be female; in even-numbered chapters, they will be male.

PART I

IN PRAISE OF CHARACTERS

Characters shape our lives in ways our fellow human beings do not. Our upbringing sets forces inside us in motion, but once we start to absorb stories, characters become equally important guides and models—far more than our parents and society dare admit. Invented beings enlighten us, help us make precious sense out of ourselves and those around us.

The first three chapters take a deep dive into the elements of human nature, as well as the principles of the storyteller's art, that form the basis of the fiction writer's profession. Chapter One opens this study with a look at the differences between imagined and actual human beings.

1

CHARACTERS VERSUS PEOPLE

A human being is an evolving work-in-progress; a character is a finished work-in-performance. Real people impact us directly and explicitly; characters slip into our imaginations and touch us implicitly. Human beings have social lives; characters live in the cast their author invented. People represent themselves; characters symbolize the human spirit.

Once in performance on page, stage, or screen, however, these metaphors become person-like, singular and unique. Unlike the opaque natures of people, brilliantly dramatized characters are clearer yet more complex, intriguing yet more accessible, than anyone you may know. What's more, once fixed within the parentheses of her story, she stays who she becomes and never changes beyond her story's climax.

When a human being spills out of reality, it's into a grave, but when a character spills out of a story, it's into another story. Jimmy McGill, for example, went from *Breaking Bad* to inspire the prequel *Better Call Saul*; Jesse Pinkman did the same for the sequel *El Camino*.

You don't have to look far to glimpse the divide between characters and people. Just compare actors to their roles. The finest performers rarely inspire the people in their daily lives the way their characters compel the world's audiences. Why? Because people experience far more than they express, while characters express everything they experience. A character enters a story as a canister of the past and a sponge for the future, written and performed to express her nature in full, to be known to the core and remembered indefinitely. Great characters are therefore more layered, more dimensional, more involving than the human stuff of their making.

Human beings exist twenty-four hours a day; characters exist between curtain up and curtain down, fade-in and fade-out, first page and last. A person has a life yet to live and it finishes when death decides; a character is finished when her author decides. Her life begins and ends when readers open and close a book or audiences enter and exit a theatre.[1]

If a character had access to our reality, she would walk out of her story and never come back. She would have other, more pleasant things to do than suffer her fictional life.

CHARACTER AND INSIGHT

Compared to those around us, characters, because of their willingness to stand still while we study them, fill us with insight. As a character talks and acts in front of us, a psychic power seems to take us through her words and deeds, down to her unspoken thoughts and desires, then even deeper into the silent currents in the ultimate subtext, her subconscious mind. When we turn our gaze on ourselves, however, our subconscious stays stubbornly sub. For that reason, the truth of who we really are always remains something of a mystery. As Robert Burns put the problem, "Oh, would some power the gift to give us, to see ourselves as others see us." We baffle ourselves at times, but a cast of characters offers a kind of group therapy.

Characters lean into their futures, focused on personal goals, their awareness narrowed by their pursuit. But when we pick up a book or buy a ticket, we first lean back to survey the 360-degree world that encircles the cast, and then forward to peer into psychological depths. Thanks to these aesthetic angles, we can gain insights into characters and their societies often better than we see into ourselves and our own. I often wish I understood myself and the United States as well as I understand Walter White and *Breaking Bad*.

CHARACTER LIMITS

Relentless contradictions crosscut human nature—good and evil, love and cruelty, generosity and selfishness, wisdom and stupidity, and so on down an endless list of opposites. But in the everyday world, few explore their inner paradoxes to the breaking point. Who of us has dared pursue our fragmented self into the dark depths suffered by Sethe in Toni Morrison's *Beloved*? Who has navigated as many points on the moral compass as *Better Call Saul's* two-souls-in-one, Jimmy McGill / Saul Goodman? Did William Randolph Hearst live his everyday life with anything like the fatal passions of his cinematic avatar in *Citizen Kane*?

Even the renowned—Marcus Aurelius, Abraham Lincoln, Eleanor Roosevelt—are remembered more as characters than people because biographers novelized them, writers dramatized them, and actors gave them life after death.

CHARACTER AND FOCUS

People wear masks; characters invite intrigue. We often meet people either too difficult to understand or too irrelevant to bother with, but an author can turn an annoying persona into a personality puzzle. The finest fictional characters demand rigorous concentration and psychological acumen from the writer. Just as we grapple with the difficult people in our lives, we gravitate toward characters who make our brains work. That's why, with a delicious twist of irony, characters who demand effort feel so very real. The more specific, dimensional, unpredictable, and difficult to understand, the more fascinating and more real a character seems. The more generalized, more consistent, more predictable, and easy to understand, the less real, less interesting, and more cartoonish she seems.[2]

CHARACTER AND TIME

From a character's point of view, a river of time pours out of her half-remembered past and spills into an ocean of unknown futures. But from our point of view, storytelling spatializes time within the parentheses of first and last images. Because an author has frozen time's flow, the observing mind of the reader/audience skates freely back and forth through days, months, years, tracing story lines to their roots, unearthing causes buried in the past, prophesizing future outcomes before the character's fate arrives.

A story is a metaphor for life that expresses the nature of being; a character is a metaphor for humanity that expresses the nature of becoming. A story unfolds, event by event, but once told it stands, like a work of temporal sculpture, in a state of permanent being. A multifaceted role, on the other hand, changes and reshapes the character's inner and outer selves through conflict, until the climax sends her into a future beyond the story's climax, altered in substance and circumstance—an arc of becoming.

Ideas have a life span, often short. That's why stories tend to rust, and the more era-bound their meanings, the shorter their existence. For even the greatest of stories to survive, their themes need constant, up-to-the-now reinterpretation.

What lasts is character. Homer's Odysseus, Shakespeare's Cleopatra, James Joyce's Leopold Bloom, Arthur Miller's Willy Loman, Mario Puzio's Michael Corleone, Margaret Atwood's Offred the Handmaid, and the Charles brothers' Frasier and Niles Crane will live in the world's imagination long after their stories have faded from memory.[3]

CHARACTER AND BEAUTY

When a character's traits and depths align seamlessly, she emanates beauty. Beauty is not prettiness. Pretty is decorative; beautiful is expressive. This quality has been described as harmony (Plato), radiance (Aquinas), sublimity (Elijah Jordan), clarity and repose (John Ruskin), a deedless calm (Hegel)—all attempts to define the feeling that emanates from fine art, no matter how turbulent or dark the work. A character may be villainous, even Horror-film ugly, but when her traits harmonize into a meaningful whole, she radiates a kind of beauty, however grotesque. And as Plato taught, our response to beauty feels much like love, and so the pleasure we take in a superbly crafted character is more than a matter of judgment—it's a sense of affection. Beauty amplifies our inner life; kitsch deafens it.[4]

CHARACTER AND EMPATHY

Empathy with a character calls for refined sensitivity. Vicarious identification excites our senses and energizes our minds. Characters empower us to reflect, to know ourselves from within and without. They show who and why we are who we are in all our strangeness, inconsistency, duplicity, and hidden beauty.[5]

Henry James said the only reason to write fiction is to compete with life. In the same vein, the only reason to create a character is to compete with humanity, to conjure up someone more complex, more revealing, more magnetic than anyone we might meet. If stories and characters didn't compete with reality, we wouldn't write them.[6]

What do we want from a well-told story? To live in a world we could never experience. What do we want from a well-told character? To experience a life we would never live through a person we could never forget.

Memorable characters find a home in our minds by drawing us into a shared humanity. Linked by empathy, a character takes us through the vicarious yet dynamic experiences of someone else's emotional life. A memorable character can be separated from her story and then held in the imagination, encouraging us to send our thoughts into the spaces between her scenes, into her past and future.

Unlike us, characters get a lot of help. On the page, vivid prose descriptions and dialogue ignite our mirror neurons and give characters their heightened presence. Onstage and on-screen, actors bring the writer's creations to life. As audience members, we deepen, refine, and seal each performance with our personal perspectives. As a result, every character acquires unique shadings while she works her way into our psyche. Indeed, like images in dreams, well-written characters are more vivid than their real-life counterparts because, no matter how naturalistically they're portrayed, at heart characters symbolize the human spirit.

CHARACTER AND AUTHOR

Although characters seem to live in fictional worlds the way people exist in reality, a story's cast is as artificial as a ballet troupe—a society choreographed to meet an author's purpose.[7] And what is that purpose? Why do writers do this? Why create human facsimiles? Why not spend our days with friends and family, content in their company?

Because reality is never enough. The mind wants meaning, but reality offers no clear beginnings, middles, or ends. Stories do. The mind wants unfettered insight into itself and the secret selves of others, but people wear masks, inside and out. Characters do not. They enter barefaced and exit translucent.

Events, in and of themselves, have no meaning. Lightning striking a vacant lot is pointless; lightning striking a vagrant matters. When an event adds a character, suddenly nature's indifference fills with life.

As you create your characters, you naturally gather pieces of humanity (your sense of self, your sense of people like you yet not like you, personalities around you that are sometimes strange, sometimes trite, attractive one day, repulsive the next) to create fictional creatures. Yet you know full well that the characters you compose are not their real-life inspirations. Although the people in a writer's life may spark ideas, like a mother who loves her children in ways she never loves her husband, an author knows she loves the characters that grew in her storied garden in ways she never loves their seeds.

And what do characters need from their creator? Here's a short list of ten faculties that equip the writer.

1. Taste

Learning to discriminate between bad and good in other people's writing is not difficult, but to see it in your own calls for guts and judgment powered by an intrinsic disgust with banality and an eye for the vital versus the lifeless. An artist, therefore, needs a keen sense of distaste.[8]

Bad writing festers with flaws more grievous than clichéd roles and on-the-nose dialogue. Hackwork suffers from the moral failings of sentimentality, narcissism, cruelty, self-indulgence, and, above all, lies that originated in the writer. Tough-mindedness not only inspires truthful writing but a truthful life as well. The more you spot these faults in your own pages and trash them with the repugnance they deserve, the more you avoid them in life.

Sharp-eyed fictions express the gap between the fantasies that distract us and the realities they obscure, between illusion and fact.[9] Such works render insights into life as if illuminated from a distant, unseen wisdom.

So, the more you read superior writers and watch excellent films, screen series, and theatre, the more you widen and deepen your taste.

2. Knowledge

To pen a superior work of fiction, an author must acquire a godlike knowledge of her story's setting, history, and cast. Character creation, therefore, demands a writer's constant observations of herself and the humanity around her—all she knows of life. When she senses a lost past, she can access her most vivid memories. To fill in the blanks between, she can research the life sciences of psychology, sociology, anthropology, and politics. When those don't teach enough, she can buy a ticket to travel, discover, and explore the unknown firsthand.[10]

3. Originality

Creative originality calls for insight. An observation may inspire an author, but to enrich what's on the surface, she adds her unique way of seeing what's not there, what's beneath, a hidden truth no one else has spotted before.

More often than not, what's mistaken for originality is simply the recycling of a forgotten influence. The notion "This has never been done before" is rarely true. Rather, it's a symptom of the writer's ignorance of everything other writers have done before she decided to try it herself. Too often the urge to do something different results in a difference that's not only trivial but worsens the telling. Most stabs at innovation fail because they have in fact been tried before and found hackneyed.

Originality and adaptation are not contradictory, although awards for original versus adapted work perpetuate this myth. With the exception of *The Tempest*, all of Shakespeare's plays adapt a found story into a new play.

Genuine innovation is a what, not a how—a new thing, not a new way of doing an old thing. In any medium or genre, a story must generate expectation, escalate stakes, and create surprising outcomes. That's given. Modernism and postmodernism were powerfully original because they exposed previously unseen subject matter, inverted accepted wisdoms, and refocused the way we looked at life. Those days are gone. Despite the stylistic excesses of transformational special effects in film, fragmentation in literature, and audience participation in theatre, recent decades have seen no revolutions. Techniques that savage art forms lost whatever teeth they had long ago. Today, the avant-garde spirit rips into content, not form, using story to expose the lies the world has learned to live with.

4. Showmanship

Storytelling combines a tightrope walker's daring with a magician's gift for deft concealment and surprising revelation. An author, therefore, is first and foremost an entertainer. She gives her reader/audience the dual excitement of the true and the new: first, face-to-face encounters with dangerous truths; and second, never-seen-before characters who confront them.

5. Awareness of the Reader/Audience

Fiction and reality cause experiences that differ in quality but not in kind. A reader's/audience's response to a character calls on the same attributes of intelligence, logic, and emotional sensibility that people employ in their daily lives. The chief difference is that an aesthetic experience has no purpose beyond itself. Fiction calls for long-term, uninterrupted concentration that ends with meaningful, emotional satisfaction. Therefore, the writer must craft all characters with an eye to their moment-by-moment impact on the reader/audience.

6. Mastery of Form

To want to create a work of art, you have to have seen one. Your original source of inspiration is not the lives of others, not your life, but the art form itself. A story is a metaphor for life, a massive symbol that expresses maximum meaning from minimal material. Your first experience of story form moved you to fill it with character content—the humanity you find in yourself and others, the dynamic values you sense in society and culture.[11]

The problem is this: Form is the conduit for content, but ultimately they interlock. As we will see in the next chapter, story is character, and character is story. So before you can master either, you must unlock them. Characters can be taken out of a story and examined psychologically and culturally and given a stand-alone meaning. Walter White, for example, symbolizes corrupt entrepreneurship. But once back inside their story, their meaning may change greatly. So to begin writing, it seems to me, story holds the key.

7. Hatred of Clichés

A cliché is an idea or technique that when first invented was so good—so great, in fact—that people have recycled it again and again and again for decades.

Knowledge of your art form's history is a basic necessity; an eye that spots a cliché when you see one and, more important, when you write one is an artistic imperative.

For example, the idea that beautiful, young jet-setters enjoying unlimited cocaine and sex are in fact depressed and miserable is not a revelation. Thousands of plays, films, novels, and lyrics have sung that tune. The emptiness of indulgence has been a cliché in both high art and pop culture ever since F. Scott Fitzgerald's Daisy and Gatsby.[12]

If the rich are your subject matter, investigate the multitude of characters created not only by Fitzgerald but Evelyn Waugh, Noel Coward, Woody Allen, Whit Stillman, and Tina Fey, and all the films, plays, or television dramedies that featured songs by Cole Porter sung by Frank Sinatra, up to and including the HBO series *Succession*.

8. Moral Imagination

By moral, I mean more than good/evil or right/wrong. I mean all the positive/negative binaries of human experience, from life/death to love/hate to justice/injustice to rich/poor to hope/despair to excitement/boredom and beyond, that sculpt us and our society.

By imagination, I mean more than daydreaming. I mean an author's full knowledge of time, place, and character powered by her creative vision. When a writer imagines the peoplescape of her story's world, her vision of values must guide her sense of what is vital, what is trivial.

A writer's values shape her unique vision of life, of the global landscape of positive versus negative charges that surround her. What is worth living for? What is worth dying for? Her answers express her moral imagination, her ability to mine the binaries of human experience to envision deeper, more nuanced characters.

My concern is not with Sunday school morality but the value-sensitive imaginations of writers who create and hone characters. You will find yours in the core of being that shapes your humanity. What drives you will in turn drive the creatures you create.

9. An Ideal Self

When not writing, an author can be what writers so often are: a flawed, troubled soul that others find annoying and difficult. But when an author sits down to write, a transformation takes place. As she puts her fingers on the keyboard, she becomes her most intelligent, most sensitive. Her talent, concentration, and above all honesty are at their maximum pitch. This best possible self authors her truest insights into character.

10. Self-Knowledge

Here's how a trio of renowned writers reacted to Socrates's dictum "Know thyself": " 'Know thyself?' If I knew myself, I'd run away," Johann Wolfgang von Goethe. "A caterpillar who wanted to know itself would never become a butterfly," Andre Gide. "Everything I know about human nature I learned from me," Anton Chekhov. All three, I'm sure, knew themselves in depth, but Chekhov was the least cynical and the most clear-eyed. He knew that we spend our lives essentially alone.

Despite our relationships with the people we love or hate, despite our observations and researches into society, the solitary truth is that we never know anyone the way we know ourselves. Until science invents a technology that lets us live in the consciousness of another human being, we will always spend our days at a distance, reading the signs in other people's faces, sitting behind our eyes in the company of one, essentially alone.

All fine character creation begins and ends in self-knowledge. No matter how a writer pictures her essential self—as a secret ego lurking behind a gallery of social personae or as a never-changing core at the center of reality's flux—she is self-contained and unique. From her core of self-awareness, the writer must extrapolate the inner mutability of the characters she creates. In other words, each of us owns the only mind we will ever meet unmasked. Therefore, all fine character creation begins and ends in self-knowledge.

Yet irony smiles on us, for despite the clear differences between people—disparities of age, gender, genes, culture—we are far more alike than different. We all live through the same essential experiences: the joy of love, the dread of death. So you can be certain that whatever thoughts and feelings run through your mind, they run through the minds of everybody else coming down the street toward you, each in their own time, their own way.

The more you penetrate the mysteries of your own humanity, the more you perceive the humanity in your characters, and the more they express your insights into human nature. As a result, your characters echo in the empathetic reader/audience. What's more, as people read and watch, they make discoveries about themselves because your characters grew out of qualities of you, qualities new to them.

In Chapter Five we'll explore writing in-character, a technique that turns your inner life into your character's inner life, so that your character becomes someone you know as well as you know yourself.[13]

A LAST NOTE

Badly written characters show us who other people are not; clichéd characters show us who other people prefer; unique characters show us who we prefer; empathetic characters show us who we are.

Because our daily lives don't permit dangerous satisfactions such as revenge, we devour the gratifying satisfactions of story. We call on story to transport us to countless worlds, but the drivers who take us beyond our mortal reach are characters, and the fuel that powers our imagined travels is empathy.

The variety of complex characters that centuries of fiction provide greatly exceeds the range of people we will ever meet and enriches our insights into those we do. And because we know characters better than people, we love them in ways we rarely love people. Of course, we don't know people, even those closest to us, very well to begin with, so we shouldn't be surprised. If, on the other hand, you don't believe what I just said, if you don't feel that the fictional betters the factual, you may want to reconsider your profession.

2

THE ARISTOTLE DEBATE

Plot Versus Character

The terms *plot-driven* and *character-driven* were invented by film critics in the mid-twentieth century to mark the difference between Hollywood movies and European cinema—or in their view, between mass entertainment and artistic sophistication. Soon after, book reviewers began writing in a similar vein about literary novels versus best sellers. Off-Broadway originally served as a proving ground for Broadway, but in the 1960s the New York theatre world drew the line between art and money along Forty-Second Street. This pattern repeated in the English theatre between tradition-bound stages in the West End of London and the avant-garde on the Fringe. Years later, U.S. television divided into subscription- versus advertisement-funded programming, pitting streaming's character-driven art for adult audiences against the commercial networks' plot-driven entertainment for family viewers.

ARISTOTLE'S RANKINGS

This divide has an ancient pedigree. In his *Poetics*, Aristotle ranked the six components of dramatic art from top to bottom in terms of their creative difficulty and importance to the work as (1) Plot, (2) Character, (3) Meaning, (4) Dialogue, (5) Music, (6) Spectacle.

He believed that events demand greater artistry to create and impact audiences with greater power than do characters. His opinion held sway for two millennia, but beginning with *Don Quixote*, the novel evolved into the dominant storytelling medium, and by the end of the nineteenth century writers about writing reversed Aristotle's top two, declaring that what the reader really wants is memorable characters. A plot's string of events, they claimed, is simply the writer's clothesline to display his characters.

This theory conceives of plot as actions and reactions on the physical and social planes, while it confines character to thoughts and feelings in the conscious and subconscious spheres. In fact, these four domains are mutually influential.

When a character witnesses an event, his senses convey it to his mind instantly, so that the event happens to him internally at virtually the same moment it happens externally in his world. The reverse is also true: When a character makes a decision, this internal event becomes external as he puts it into action. External and internal events flow fluidly through the senses from level to level, inside to outside and back, each affecting the other. Restricting the definition of plot to external actions misses the vast majority of what happens in a human being's life. The plot-driven versus character-driven debate is specious and always has been since Aristotle made his list.

Questioning which is creatively more difficult and aesthetically more significant, plot or character, commits a categorical error. It's illogical to ask which of the two is more than the other because they are, in essence, the same: Plot is character; character is plot. The two are back-to-back sides of the same storied coin.

A role does not become a character until an event brings his actions and reactions to life; an incident does not become a storied event until a character causes and/or experiences its change. A person untouched by events is a stand-alone, unlived, static portrait best hung on a wall. An activity without a character is like a rainy day on an ocean—a repetitious, trivial, uninvolving nonevent. To understand this distinction in depth, we need to define terms.

CHARACTER, PLOT, EVENT

Character names a fictitious being who either causes events to happen or reacts when someone or something else causes them, or both.

Plot names a story's arrangement of events. A plotless story, therefore, does not exist. If it's a story, it has a pattern of events, aka a plot; if it's a plot, it lays out a pattern of events, aka a story. No matter how brief the tale, all storytellers plot what happens to whom and thus design events.

As a work of fiction performs through time, it can be told in countless variations and departures from the classic form: shifts in point of view, events clustered thematically, events progressed causally, stories within stories, flashbacks, repetitions, ellipses, the believable, the fantastic—all depending on what best expresses the writer's vision. But no matter how a story's event design entices curiosity, readers and audiences are ultimately anchored to the telling through its characters.

The term shared by both definitions is *event*, so let's define it with precision: The dictionary definition of an everyday event is something that happens. In a story, however, if what happens changes nothing of value, the event has no meaning. If, for example, a passing breeze rearranges leaves on a lawn, things change but that event is meaningless because it's valueless.

For the storyteller, *value* is defined as a binary of human experience that can change its charge from positive to negative or negative to positive: Life/Death, Justice/Injustice, Pleasure/Pain, Freedom/Slavery, Good/Evil, Intimacy/Indifference, Right/Wrong, Meaningful/Meaningless, Human/Inhuman, Unity/Disunity, Beautiful/Ugly, and on goes the virtually endless list of the polarized changes that charge life with significance. The art of story, therefore, makes an event meaningful by imbuing it with a value.

For example, if something happened that caused one character to change his feelings toward another from love (+) to hate (−), that event becomes meaningful because the value of Love/Hate changed its charge from positive to negative. Or the reverse: If an event caused a character's finances to pivot from poor (−) to rich (+), that change becomes meaningful because the value of Poverty/Wealth underwent a movement from negative to positive.

A *storied event*, therefore, is a moment of value-charged change in a character's life. The cause of this change is either an action taken by a character, or a reaction by a character to an event outside his control. In either case, the event reverses the charge of a value at stake in his life.

TWO SIDES / SAME COIN

An event's two-sides/same-coin double effect becomes vividly clear when turning points swivel around either revelations or decisions.

By revelation: In the Act Two climax of *Chinatown*, the protagonist, J. J. Gittes (Jack Nicholson), accuses Evelyn Mulwray (Faye Dunaway) of murdering her husband. In reaction, she confesses, not to committing murder but to incest with her father and giving birth to their daughter. Gittes instantly realizes that her father, Noah Cross (John Huston) killed his son-in-law because he wants illicit possession of his granddaughter/daughter. This revelation of the true killer suddenly reverses the plot from negative to positive. At the same time, we get a rush of insight into Evelyn—all she has suffered and her courage to battle her lunatic father.

By decision: At this point Gittes could call the police, give them his evidence, and stand back while the cops arrest Noah Cross. Instead, he decides to go after the killer on his own. This choice turns the plot dangerously negative for the protagonist and simultaneously spotlights his fatal flaw: blind pride. Gittes is the kind of man who will risk his life rather than ask for help.

The terms *event* and *character* simply name two angles on turning points. Looking at story from the outside in, we see them as events; from the inside out we experience them as character. Without events, nothing is done by or happens to the characters; without characters, no one causes or reacts to events.

As Henry James put it, "What is character but the determination of incident? What is incident but the illustration of character? It is an incident for a woman to stand up with her hand resting on a table and look out at you in a certain way. If not an incident, I think it hard to say what it is. Character, in any sense in which we can get at it, is action and action is plot."[1]

Suppose you were writing a story that contained a Henry James–ian incident: Your protagonist, in great personal jeopardy, knowing that a lie will save him, stands up, puts his hand on a table, and looks at a woman in a certain way that expresses a dark, painful truth. His decision and action spin his life from positive to negative as he suffers the consequences. At the same time, his choice, his action, and its outcome express his true character: courageously honest man.

Let's say that this is the best scene in your story, but, powerful as it is, a problem arises downstream. As you finish the telling, you realize that your last act's climax falls flat, and because your ending fails, all your creative work from the beginning ultimately fails with it. What to do? You will find a saving solution in one of two places: character or event.

Event design: You could reverse the turning point. Instead of having your protagonist tell the truth, he lies to gain power and money. That rewrite may set up a satisfying climax, but at the same time it radically reverses his moral core. He's now a rich but corrupted man. If you like that character change, problem solved.

Character design: When you step back to study your protagonist's psychology, you realize that your climax lacks impact because your character is so sweet and innocent your ending is unconvincing. So you darken him morally, and then rewrite him into a tough survivor. How do you express this change of true character? Redesign events to dramatize his new shrewd, duplicitous self. If these new turning points set up a strong payoff at the climax, problem solved.

Once again, for clarity's sake: A plot event turns a value charge in a character's life; a character either acts to cause these events or reacts when external forces do the same. So to change a character's nature, you have to redesign events to express who he has become; to change events, you have to reinvent your character's psychology so he will make convincing new choices to take new actions. Therefore, neither plot nor character can be more creative or more important.

Why didn't Aristotle see this? One possible answer may lie in his admiration for Sophocles's play *Oedipus Rex*. Oedipus investigates a horrific crime only to discover that he is both its victim and its villain. Events beyond his control, events he does everything to escape but cannot, ruthlessly propel his fate and crush him.

Gripped by the tragic beauty of *Oedipus Rex*, far and away the finest play of his era, Aristotle implored other playwrights to equal its sublime power. So it's possible that Sophocles's portrayal of the irresistible force of fate moved the philosopher to overvalue events and undervalue character.

A second and more likely reason, however, is aesthetic convention: The playwrights of Athens did not write with an awareness of subtext. In fact, actors wore masks to express their character's essence. If one character lied to another, the audience would of course sense an unspoken subtext, but for the most part, characters said what they meant in full. Aristotle, therefore, gave what happens more weight than to whom it happens.

Today's authors, guided by centuries of psychological insights, separate true character from Characterization.

CHARACTERIZATION VERSUS TRUE CHARACTER

Characterization: All observable traits and outer behaviors—the composite of age, gender, race, speech and gestures, job and home, dress and fashion, attitudes and personality—in short, the masks or personae a character wears as he carries out his relationships with other people. These details provide clues to a character's identity, but readers and audiences know that appearance is not reality, that characters are not who they seem to be.

True character: A role's unseen, inner nature—his deepest motivations and rock-bottom values. When confronted by life's greatest pressures, this core reveals itself in the choices he makes and the actions he takes in pursuit of his most consuming desires. These decisions and deeds express his core identity.

Outer traits of characterization anchor a character's credibility, while the inner qualities of the true character shape the character and his future. If the reader/audience does not believe that he would do the things he does, say the things he says, pursue the desires he pursues, the storytelling fails. His essential self makes the choices and takes the actions that act out a story's happenings and set up its future events. True character and characterization combine to create a believable role in a believable telling—true in ancient times as well as today. But because the *Poetics* did not separate their functions, the plot versus character debate became an apples/oranges fallacy.

Characters are designed to either solve or fail to solve the problems they face; stories are designed to express the traits and qualities of characters as they struggle with their problems. A plot's events are what its characters do; characters are the vehicles who cause and/or carry out a plot's events. When we weigh the two, they balance each other perfectly. For well over a century, author-scholars from Henry James to David Lodge have proclaimed this logical interdependence. So why has the character-driven/plot-driven argument dragged on into the twenty-first century?

Because what looks like an aesthetic debate actually masks the cultural politics of taste, class, and, most of all, money. The phrase *character-driven* is code for "a superior work of art, made not for profit but love, best interpreted by academic critics, appreciated only by an intellectual elite, and ideally financed by public funds," versus *plot-driven* as code for the opposite: "a trivial work, written by hacks, laced with clichés, aimed at the undereducated, too trite to be of critical interest, and made for corporate profit."

The belief that giving more emphasis to what happens than to whom it happens causes second-rate art is, quite obviously, absurd. Homer's *Odyssey*, Shakespeare's *A Midsummer Night's Dream*, Ernest Hemingway's *The Old Man and the Sea*, Stanley Kubrick's *A Clockwork Orange*, and (if we lower the snobbery volume) Michael Frayn's farce *Noises Off* are all plot-driven masterpieces. On the other hand, how many superficial, overwritten, underexpressed, characterization-thick tortures on page, stage, and screen have you suffered through? In truth, neither tack guarantees anything.

Politics aside, the deep difference between these two components lies in the story's primal source of cause and effect. The terms *character-driven* and *plot-driven* make creative sense only when they name a story's dominant causality, not its aesthetic value. When your work-in-progress stalls, you will find a creative solution by asking the big question: What makes things happen?

Plot-driven stories put major turning points, especially the inciting incident, beyond the characters' control. More often than not, these happenings deliver a negative impact and come from one of three levels of conflict: (1) natural causes: dire weather, disease, fire, earthquakes, alien invasions, and other "acts of God"; (2) social causes: crime, war, manmade disasters, private and public corruption, acts of racial, gender, or class injustice, and the like; (3) chance: a winning lottery ticket, an automobile accident, the genes one is born with, and, most of all, blind luck—all the coincidences, good or bad, that flow through these levels.

Character-driven stories do the opposite: They put major events in the characters' hands. In these tellings, the choices and actions the characters make and take cause what happens. Not chance, not overpowering global or natural forces, but personal choices, powered by a free will, drive the telling.

Therefore, the six key differences between plot-driven and character-driven stories are:

1. Causality

In the plot-driven story, the forces that trigger key turning points emanate from outside or beyond the characters' reach: Criminals commit crimes, dictators declare war, plagues sweep the world, aliens invade the earth, the sun falls from the sky.

The character-driven story reverses that. Its dominant causalities stem from conscious and subconscious energies that move a character to want what he wants, choose what he chooses, and act the way he acts: He falls in love, commits a crime, blows the whistle on his boss, runs away from home, believes someone's lie, searches for the truth.

2. Identity

As we'll see in chapters that follow, desire helps shape a character's identity. A plot-driven story calls for a protagonist driven by a desire that originated outside of himself; a character-driven story favors a protagonist who follows a desire that originated within himself.

3. Values

In a purely plot-driven story, the protagonist struggles to give the world what it lacks, expressed in values such as Peace/War, Justice/Injustice, Wealth/Poverty, Brotherhood/Selfhood, Health/Disease, and the like. In a purely character-driven story, the protagonist struggles to fulfill what he personally lacks, expressed in values such as Love/Hate, Maturity/Immaturity, Truth/Lie, Trust/Distrust, Hope/Despair, and the like.

4. Depth

Plot-driven genres rarely develop the subconscious or irrational in their characters. Ethan Hunt, for example, obeys one conscious, logical desire: to repair a broken, unjust world. He and his IMF team therefore invent a plan, cleverly execute its steps, fix what's wrong, and restore justice. If in the midst of all this, Ethan were also haunted by an unresolved childhood trauma, his high-speed fun would sour faster than old milk.

Plot-driven stories enrich the telling with details drawn from their social and physical settings. Imagery from mountaintops to tuxedos, sounds from birdsongs to machinery fascinate the eye and ear.

Character-driven genres layer their tellings with psychological contradictions. They bury unknown desires within a character, and then bring these impulses into conflict with his rationalizations. As these character-focused tales reach into the depths, they at least touch, if not invade, the subconscious.

In Tennessee Williams's *A Streetcar Named Desire*, the play's protagonist, Blanche DuBois, repeatedly says that all she wants is to live happily in this world. But the brutality and ugliness of her ghetto life make that impossible. In truth, she subconsciously wants the opposite and ultimately achieves that deep desire at the play's climax as she escapes from reality into insanity.

Depth of character is a measure of inner complexity, but a character cannot have greater complexity than the forces of antagonism he confronts in life. How can we sense his depths if his conflicts don't expose them?

5. Curiosity

Character-driven works minimize physical and social conflicts to focus on personal wars within and between characters. The question "What will this character do?" grips the reader's or audience's curiosity. The answer, when well written, is unpredictable and delivers sudden surprise.

Shakespeare, the grand master of psychological realism, breathed a spirit of unpredictability into the hearts of all his principal characters. His romantic couples, for example, range in tone from the clownish Touchstone and Audrey (*As You Like It*) to the sophisticated Beatrice and Benedick (*Much Ado About Nothing*) and the tragic Antony and Cleopatra, and yet all these lovers jolt our expectations and amaze even themselves.

Touchstone doesn't understand why he wants to marry Audrey but does so on impulse; Beatrice shocks Benedick when she asks him to commit murder; the heroic Marc Antony, in the midst of a raging sea battle, suddenly turns coward and chases after the woman he loves. Whether comic, romantic, or tragic, stunned by their own impulsiveness, they all look at themselves and ask, "What have I done?"

Because plot-driven works eliminate inner conflicts, they must instead polarize their principals socially: Action heroes right injustices and save victims; action villains commit atrocities and kill the innocent. Because we know who they are and what they will do, these works compel curiosity by inventing radical weaponry that makes us wonder, "How will they do it?"

DC and Marvel superheroes, such as Wonder Woman, Superman, Spider-Man, and Storm, command either magical or biological powers in unique and fascinating ways to save or protect life; antiheroes, such as Deadpool, Loki, Black Widow, and Catwoman, also command unique powers, but to rule over or destroy life.

6. Freedom Versus Fate

Freedom and Fate are elusive but ever-present beliefs. Belief in *Freedom* suggests a future that's unknown, a mysterious terminus, one of many possible destinations that will always be hidden until life's last moment. *Fate* or *Destiny*, on the other hand, feels as if an invisible, inevitable, karmic force shapes our lives to an unavoidable event at the end point of our days. To the ancient Greeks, Fate seemed so real they personified it into three goddesses. To this day, people still use the phrase "the Hand of Fate."

The concepts of fate and freedom intertwine with the crafting of story in fascinating ways. When a story begins, the reader/audience looks toward a future where everything seems possible; the telling seems free to travel in a thousand, even random, directions in pursuit of its destiny. But once a story climaxes and we look back to the beginning, we realize that the path the telling took was inevitable, fated. These two viewpoints play out differently in plot-driven and character-driven stories.

At the inciting incident of an exclusively plot-driven action story, characters pursue either a positive or a negative destiny. At the climax, now that readers and audiences grasp the characters' natures and tactics, they see that the telling had to happen exactly the fated way it did. Predetermined people collide in predetermined ways. Heroes do selfless deeds to satisfy a need for altruism: It's who they are. Villains do sadistic deeds to feed their lust for power: It's who they are. The rigid natures of these monocharacters drive them to their fate.

Contrary-wise, when a purely character-driven work begins, we sense that the future hinges on contradictory forces dueling within complex characters as each struggles to make choices and take actions in the pursuit of desire.

In Hernan Diaz's *In the Distance*, for example, the novel's protagonist, Hakan, spends a lifetime searching for his lost brother in every way humanly possible. At the story's climax, as we look back to the beginning, we once again sense inevitability, but in this case, it was due to contradictory forces at war within the central character. His choices during pressure-filled turning points express his essential nature, but the sense of fate seems less inevitable. The telling could have gone a hundred different ways because Hakan was always free to choose a different path.

In all stories, the sense of fate versus freedom depends on where we stand in the course of the telling. At the inciting incident, we imagine the freedom of countless possible destinies; at climax, we sense inevitability . . . to a greater or lesser degree. In truth, nothing has any plans for us; fate has no goddesses, no hands. It's simply the mirage that appears when we gaze back on events through retrospective time.

MELDING PLOT AND CHARACTER

These two treatments of fate and freedom are at the extremes of plot-driven and character-driven tellings. Life, on the other hand, flows through a complex of reasons. Fine storytellers seldom choose one source of causality exclusively over another.

BALANCED CAUSES

Most authors seek a balance that mixes motivated choices with unmotivated happenstance. They blend events from both inside and outside the characters' control because no matter what causes what to happen, when it does, characters must react to change. Once an accident smashes into life, it immediately becomes a test of character for the survivors.

Shakespeare began his every play plot-driven. He worked either from histories recorded by English, Greek, or Scandinavian chroniclers such as Holinshed, Plutarch, and Saxo Grammaticus, or from fictional plots invented by other playwrights, most often Italians. As a result, sword fights and suicides, ghosts and witches, shipwrecks and wars, as well as boy-meets-girl-disguised-as-boy were among his favorite motifs. He then reshaped these tales into his own unique event designs, inventing brilliant protagonists and supporting casts to act them out.

The same was true, for example, of Joseph Conrad, who created grand, plot-driven adventures—*An Outcast of the Islands*, *Heart of Darkness*, *Lord Jim*, *Nostromo*, *The Secret Agent*—but by the final page they feel, like Shakespeare's plays, character-driven.

In his novel *Wilhelm Meister's Apprenticeship*, Johann Wolfgang von Goethe warned his fellow fiction writers that random external forces are just as vital to the artist as thought-provoked conflicts storming inside a character's mind. He urged a balance of causalities, hoping to offset the German *Sturm und Drang* propensity to reduce all storytelling to the emotional extremes of abnormal psychology.[2]

Consider the problem of causal balance in the most plot-driven genre of all: the war story. Homer's *Iliad*, progenitor of all combat epics, tilts the balance toward enormous military and physical forces, lashed by the whims of bickering gods; whereas Nicholas Monsarrat's World War II classic, *The Cruel Sea*, leans in the opposite direction, focusing on psychology. As naval battles on the raging North Atlantic pound their ship, captain and crew war with fear and must choose, moment by moment, how to react and act in the face of death. More recently, Karl Marlantes's Vietnam War novel, *Matterhorn*, strikes a horrific balance between furious jungle combat that rips the mind apart and the power of moral character to counterattack, survive, and hold the mind together.

Character-driven stories do not necessarily dramatize complex psychologies, nor do plot-driven stories require clichéd heroes and villains.

For example, *Boys Don't Cry* features a one-dimensional protagonist surrounded by hard-asses in pickup trucks, and yet the film is decidedly character-driven because no matter how narrow-minded they may be, the antagonists control what happens. On the other hand, Joseph Conrad laced his protagonist of *Lord Jim* with psychological complexity, but then lets the social forces surrounding Jim infect his guilt-ridden angst, limit his reactions, and eventually overwhelm him.

However balance is struck, at the end of the day the answer to all plot questions is found in character. Never ask open-ended questions such as "What happens?" Rather, "What happens to my character? How will it happen to him? Why does it happen to him and not to her? What changes his life? Why does it change in that particular way? What will happen in his future?" Direct all plot questions into your characters' lives. Otherwise, they're pointless.[3]

UNIFIED CAUSES

No matter a story's balance of outer and inner causality, the ideal outcome unifies character and plot in the mind of the reader/audience. A character's change of mind about whom he loves could deliver an impact equal to or surpassing a soldier betraying his comrades in battle. In both cases, the event not only turns a value charge but simultaneously reveals the role's true character.

In fine writing, no matter the genre, external events cause inner changes that expose and alter true character; inner desires drive choices and actions that cause external events. The two, character and plot, become a seamless one.

A LAST NOTE

If you're wondering where your story stands in the Aristotle debate— plot-driven, character-driven, or a balance of the two—simply list all your scenes and divide their turning points into those caused by character choice versus those caused by forces beyond their reach. Whichever way your telling leans, no one source of causality is more inspirational than another. Eventually, the way things happen will argue it out somewhere in the middle of your mind.

3

AN AUTHOR PREPARES

Before we delve into character creation, let's use this chapter to examine the foundational beliefs that underpin a writer's creative work. How do you view the nature of humanity? The influence of culture? The responsibility of authorship?

AN AUTHOR'S VISION OF CREATIVITY

Creativity as Madness

The ancients often portrayed creativity as a trancelike state verging on madness. Modern comedies, such as Tom Stoppard's satire of James Joyce in *Travesties,* abet these myths when they characterize artists as neurotics caught between the obsession to act out their fantasies and the embarrassments they trigger.

Creativity as Fantasy

In Freud's more compassionate view, creativity begins with the need to escape reality. Because pleasure is constantly contradicted by its consequences; because cake tastes sweet but rots your teeth; because romance puts a smile in your heart, then breaks it; because hopes rarely come true, human beings fantasize. In childhood, we learn to escape life's frictions by retreating into our imaginations, dreaming up adventures starring ourselves. In adulthood, these daydreams become rather luxurious. All human beings do this. Creativity, however, takes fantasy a critical step further.

Artists also dream *as if* scenarios, but then transport them out of their imaginations and into films, novels, plays, and streaming series. Although their tellings often portray hurtful experiences, the fictional realm poses no actual threat, so character pain simply transfigures into reader/audience pleasure.

Creativity as Discovery

Neuroscience, in a step toward divining creativity, has mapped the brain's hemispheres and identified their separate powers: The left brain executes the logics of deduction and induction, linear thinking, mathematics, pattern recognition, and language. The right brain commands the logics of causality and analogy, visualization, auditory imagination, nonverbal expression, intuition, rhythm, feelings, and moods.[1]

Consider, for example, Carl Sandburg's poem "Fog":

> *The fog comes*
> *on little cat feet.*
> *It sits looking*
> *over harbor and city*
> *on silent haunches*
> *and then moves on.*

When imagining this poem, images of "cat" and "fog" floated through Sandberg's mind. While his left brain saw two unrelated examples of biology and weather, his right brain noted a connection only a creative mind would spot and suddenly merged the two into an utterly new third thing, linked by a sense of stillness. As we read the poem, the poignant beauty of his metaphor enriches our inner life with a never-felt-before sensation. The unearthing of an unseen likeness is the most beautiful gift one mind can give another.

Creativity is, in essence, the discovery of the third thing. Talent is a duality-seeking sensor that spots hidden analogies between things that already exist. Then, in a creative flash, artists change the known into the new, melding two things into a never-seen-before fusion.

In which direction does creativity flow to discover the third thing?

Right brain to left or left brain to right? Particular to universal or universal to particular? Answer: Genius flows in both directions—at times alternating slowly, at others instantaneously—as reason and imagination inspire each other.[2]

For example, consider Fantasy. When creating magical characters, writers often begin with archetypes (Wise Man, Warrior, Earth Mother), then bring them down to earth to walk and talk among the common folk (a movement from conceptual to actual). Or when writing a Social Drama, a writer might start with an actual case taken from the news, then design a cast to express the battle between Justice and Injustice on a grand, symbolic scale (a progression from actual to conceptual). Compare, for example, two films from 2017: *Wonder Woman*, in which a goddess descends from heaven to fight in a human war, and *Three Billboards Outside Ebbing, Missouri*, in which a gift shop owner's revenge for her daughter's murder becomes a symbolic act.

Like the god Hermes, creativity is a wing-footed messenger that flies back and forth between two worlds—rational/irrational, left brain / right brain—taming real-life chaos with aesthetic order.

Like a child going out to play, creativity leaves reason at home and saddles up free association for long galloping rides. When two random thoughts suddenly collide and merge into a third idea, the right brain seizes this gem and hands it over to the left, so the writer can use her conscious skills to fit this shiny piece of originality inside a sketch-in-progress, reshaping it into a memorable character.

TWO THEORIES OF CHARACTER CREATION

How this process unfolds is subject for debate. Do writers invent characters or give them birth? Are characters conscious creations or subconscious manifestations?

Invention

Some writers start with an inspiration for a story, then brainstorm and improvise characters with traits and dimensions that fulfill the promise of their original vision.

Here's Suzanne Collins, author of *The Hunger Games*: "One night I was lying in bed, very tired, channel surfing. I flipped through images of reality shows where young people competed for a million dollars or a bachelor or whatever. Then I saw footage from the Iraq War. These two things fused together in an unsettling way, and that was the moment I got the idea for Katniss's story."

Novelist Patrick McGrath often finds his story spark in intriguing real-life behaviors, perhaps something as simple as an odd tone of voice or a hat worn at an eye-catching angle. He then asks the question: "What kind of person would talk in that voice and wear their hat that way?" Fingers on his keyboard, he merges his creative talents with a lifetime of observations and personal knowledge of human impulses, transforming the intrigue of a trait into a psychologically compelling character and story.

Giving Birth

Other writers see themselves as a kind of bystander, a conduit for personalities finding their way into a yet-to-be-written story. Their characters seem to live an independent existence in another realm, then pass through a mental birth canal into the author's awareness.

Elizabeth Bowen, in her book *Notes on Writing a Novel*, says that notion of character creation is misleading. Characters, she feels, preexist. They reveal themselves slowly to the novelist's perception—as might a fellow traveler chatting in a dimly lit railway carriage.

Elizabeth Strout, author of the Pulitzer Prize–winning novel *Olive Kitteridge*, said that her characters never echo her personal experiences, as readers often assume. Rather, they come to life mysteriously, organically, in stray scenes or bits of dialogue and then, through a process she finds difficult to explain, eventually coalesce. She scribbles snippets on scraps of paper and lets the scraps accrue. Discarding some, keeping others, she waits until "characters do their little things and I keep what's truthful."

Novelist Anne Lamott noted, "I've always believed that these people inside me—the characters—know who they are and what they're about and what happens, but they need me to help get it down on paper because they don't type."

For most writers, the day-in-day-out work of role creation calls on both modes—surprises from the subconscious (giving birth) and improvisation while pacing a room (invention). With each new character, the writer juggles all sources of inspiration, trying to get the balance just right.

There's mystery in creativity, no doubt, but the claim that a character refuses to do what her writer wants her to do strikes me as literary narcissism. Would a composer claim that a chord she wants to play refuses to sound itself? Would a painter claim that the color red has a mind of its own? Certain writers, hoping to make themselves mysterious, want us to believe that writing is dreamlike, that authors simply surrender to native impulses, that they are conduits for instinctive forces beyond their control. This romance has always sounded a bit phony, a bit pretentious.

Suppose, like a character created by Woody Allen or Luigi Pirandello, one of your roles stepped out of your telling and into reality. I don't mean into the fantastic realities of *The Purple Rose of Cairo* or *Six Characters in Search of an Author*; I mean into actuality. Suppose this character wanted to write her story. Suppose she took over your keyboard. Then suppose this gal discovers that she has no talent. Where would you go from there?

Characters are works of art, not artists. They manifest in an author's mind and will do exactly what she imagines them doing, although in often surprising ways. Being surprised by your own ideas is a daily experience for the talented writer. The subconscious mind absorbs an artist's direct experience of life and factual researches, as well as the artist's dreams and imaginings, then stirs all this material into new forms to be sent back to the conscious mind. This work goes on out of sight until suddenly, unexpectedly, insights into behavior and radical fusions of character traits take the writer by surprise. These flashes of genius result from subconscious churnings that go on behind the artist's awareness while she strains against the harness of craft.

Like the Lamaze method, creativity gives birth in a wide-awake world. No mystical spirit, no daughter of Zeus will descend from Olympus to inspire you. Writing will be what it always has been: giving breath to what you already know.

CREATIVE HUNGER

An artist amasses scraps and smidgeons of knowledge over a lifetime of learning, experiencing, and imagining, all swirling in the subconscious mind. A talented right brain gathers random bits, spots links between them, unites two into one, and then passes these creations to the left brain for use. With that, however, arises the artist's persistent problem:

Because you can create only from what's already in your mind, your work is strictly limited by the contents of your unthought thoughts.

The less you know and experience, the less likely your talent will generate originalities; contrariwise, the greater your understanding and insight, the more likely your talent will discover new ideas. An ignorant but talented writer may manage pieces of brief beauty, but authorship of complex full-length works demands a breadth and depth of knowing.

The moment your inspiration provides an intriguing but unfamiliar character, you suddenly realize that what you know is not enough. It never is. For your talent to fight above its weight, it needs to bulk up on knowledge. An author is not a pretender, not a literary fake, but someone with wide, deep awareness, someone with the cerebral power to punch home the truth. For that reason, writers of one-of-a-kind characters underpin their creativity with research.

Suppose one night you had this dream: A family dressed in white lab coats feverishly frets over tables filled with a dazzling array of test tubes. Something about this scene wakes you in a sweat. The next morning you start making notes in pursuit of this mysterious family. And what's in your notes? Questions demanding answers:

Who are these characters? Mother? Father? Son? Daughter? Are they scientists or saboteurs? What is their specific task? To create or destroy? Or do figures in lab coats symbolize something so personal it has nothing to do with science? Whichever way you answer, new questions will rise up to demand answers you may or may not have. Without a reservoir of unique knowledge, you can only imitate other writers. So how can you create a fascinating cast of original characters?

Start by filling files with everything you know about the characters and their world. You may think you know, but you don't know you know until you can write it down. Words spelled out on a page pull you out of self-deception and into reality, pointing the way to creative investigation. For if you find you cannot put your knowledge on paper, it means only one thing: It's time to learn.

THE FOUR RESEARCHES THAT FEED CREATIVITY

Research travels down four roads: personal, imagined, factual, and actual.

1. Personal Research

Your memory collects all the meaningful emotional experiences you have undergone in both reality and fiction. Over time, the origins of these two sources begin to blur because memory stores them in the same mental vault. That's why we often act as if what actually happened to us were a story and as if stories actually happened to us. The result? We know far more than we think we know…if we take pains to explore our past.

Inventorying memory is the first and most fundamental form of research. When you struggle to bring truth to light, simply ask, "What do I know directly from life that would help me create these characters?"

Let's say that you're a female writer composing a story that revolves around a patriarchal family, and you envision the son rebelling against his punishing father. How could memory help you create these characters and make this rebellion scene surprising, revealing, and cliché free?

Think back to your childhood. You were no doubt disciplined but perhaps never severely. Nonetheless, you reacted against your parent's rules. The dynamic of punishment and rebellion, with its core emotions of pain and anger, is universal. Ask yourself: What's the worst emotional pain I've ever suffered? What's the angriest I've ever been? What did I do in pain? In anger?

Re-create these scenes from your past and write them down in a vivid, diary-like way. Focus on the inner sensations of your emotions and their manifestations in physical behavior—what you saw, what you heard, what you felt, and, most important, what you said and did. Express these images and actions in language that makes your palms sweat and your heart pound as if it were happening again.

Now go back to your characters. Using your remembrances as a guide, imagine how your past experience might transfer, transform, or even reverse into theirs.

2. Imaginative Research

Memory takes whole events from the past and re-creates them in the present. Imagination, on the other hand, takes something that happened to you when you were five and couples it with something that happened to you when you were twenty-five. It takes an item you read in the news and pairs it with a dream you had one night, blends both of them with words you heard on a street corner, and finally ribbons all three inside an image you saw in a film. Your imagination uses the power of analogy to invent today's wholes out of bits of the past.

So, before your father and son begin to defy and dominate each other, simply bring them to mind. See them, hear them. Walk around them 360 degrees. Don't make lists of their traits, analyze their motives, or put words in their mouths. Not yet. Instead, take them for a long walk through your imagination.

In this early stage you're trying to gain an overall impression, the kind you might take away after chatting with someone at a party. But once you decide that a character deserves creation, you will have to submerge your imagination in much deeper waters.

3. Book-Bound Research

If you were to write about a conflicted father and son, you could draw on families you've lived in, families you've observed, and all those you might imagine. But no matter how familiar the subject, you will soon find that memory and imagination take you only so far. The knowledge you have at the beginning of a project is rarely enough to finish it. To that you must add book-bound learning.

If you read penetrating works on the psychology and sociology of the parent-child relationship, taking notes as if you were doing a thesis, two powerful things would happen:

1. You would discover your family in all the families under study, confirming the truth or untruth of everything you know. You would see that parents and children in differing cultures undergo common pressures and move through similar stages. Each family reacts and adapts in its own special way, but human beings are far more alike than different. Therefore, if your writing rings true, your particular will become universal as people recognize their personal household in your fictional clan. In other words, your writing will find its readers or audiences.

2. Insights you could never discover on your own will leap off those pages. As what you learn melds with what you know, creative choices flood the mind, one-of-a-kind choices that help you win the war on clichés.

4. Grounded Research

Your father-son showdown needs a setting. You may imagine them as equestrians, bickering as they practice for a dressage competition; or under their horse trailer, arguing as they fix a broken hitch; or on the highway home, yelling about who's to blame when the trailer comes loose. Three promising scenes, but you've never witnessed any of them.

Now, like a documentary filmmaker, locate these scenes in the real world so you can watch what happens, talk to people who live these events, and take notes until you master your subject. Never finish writing anything until you feel that you have gone deeper into your subject than anyone who has written about such things before, that you have become an absolute authority on your characters and their settings.

AN AUTHOR'S VISION OF HUMAN NATURE

Original characters grow out of an original perception of humanity, and so every fine writer develops her personal theory of what makes people do the things they do in the ways they do them. There is no recipe for this; artists are not necessarily orderly or disciplined. So every writer must piece her concepts into a singular vision her own way.

Your personal theory will then flow into your characters, influencing their sense of meaning and purpose, what they ought to do, what they must never do, what they ought to strive for or against, what they may hope to build or destroy, what vision of love and the relationships they work toward, what social changes they want to make, what choices and actions they want to take.

How your theory takes shape will depend on how you see mankind. Do you believe in a primal human nature shared by all or a plasticity that's molded by parental, economic, and cultural forces? Does human nature stay the same from person to person, or differ from men to women? Culture to culture? Class to class? Self to others?

To help you test your personal theories against some of history's more prominent beliefs, the following section is divided into two opposite points of view on one grand question, "Why do human beings do the things they do?"

This duality argues the nature-versus-nurture debate: What matters most? The genes and capacities a person was born with—her intrinsic nature? Or the way she was raised and acculturated—her extrinsic nurturing? In other words, who gets credit for humanity's successes? And who takes the blame for its relentless failures?

THE TWO GRAND THEORIES

When humankind began to think in depth about itself, it developed beliefs to make sense of chaos. These master creeds tend to split into two contradictory points of view on why human beings do the things they do. They take either the inside-out subjective, intrinsic view of the self, or the outside-in objective, extrinsic angle of society. In other words, nature versus nurture.

Indian

Let's start with two beliefs from India:

Intrinsic

Buddhism teaches that no unchanging soul or permanent identity exists within a human being. Rather, when we hear our thoughts, what we mistake for the "me" who thinks them, for a conscious self, is in fact a mirage, a nonself. In short, reality exists but the self is an illusion.

Extrinsic

Hinduism proposes the opposite belief: The self exists but reality is an illusion. The ground for what is is unknown and unknowable. Maya, the power of illusion, gives form to formlessness but conceals and distorts the source. The world we experience with our senses exists but as a pale imitation of the ultimate reality that hides behind Maya's illusions. This realm is unexplainable because language itself is a by-product of Maya.

Greek

Greek philosophy, developing at about the same time, contradicted both of these beliefs:

Intrinsic

Socrates, in contradiction to Buddhism, argued that the self, far from being an illusion, sits at the center of existence. "The unexamined life is not worth living," he taught, therefore, "know thyself." How can we hope for wisdom of the world that surrounds us until we come to terms with the world inside us? How can we understand other human beings until we perceive the humanity within ourselves?

Extrinsic

Aristotle, in contradiction to Hinduism, believed that the world is both real and knowable. At heart, we are political animals and our natural home is society. Fulfillment consists in the active, public exercise of our finest faculties aimed at the betterment of others. The well-lived life displays virtue, excellence, and distinctively rational thought in a like-minded community, extended over a lifetime.

Chinese

Chinese philosophy parallels both the Greek and the Indian:

Intrinsic

Taoism, like Socrates and Buddha, looked out on reality from within the self. This philosophy emphasizes living in harmony with the substance and patterns of the natural, rather than social, world. Taoism does not call for elaborate public rituals, but rather simplicity, spontaneity, compassion, and humility—behavior in accordance with the inner spirit of nature. Taoism teaches that mastering others requires force, while mastering the self requires strength; knowing others is wisdom, while knowing yourself is enlightenment.

Extrinsic

Confucius, like Aristotle and Hinduism, believed that well-being depends on a well-ordered society. Confucianism takes society's point of view to emphasize public morality, family loyalty, ancestor veneration, and a strict hierarchy in which elders are respected by their children, husbands by their wives, and in all cases, justice prevails.

Nineteenth Century

Two thousand, five hundred years later, philosophy remained split along the same divide:

Extrinsic

Karl Marx, like Aristotle, believed that social forces determine consciousness. Like Buddha, Marx felt that a fixed self does not exist: "All of history is a continuous transformation of human nature."

Intrinsic

Sigmund Freud reversed Marx. In his theory, the subconscious mind commanded the center of the universe; social structures beyond the family are irrelevant. His model of inner life comprised three components: id (the source of life's energy or libido), ego (the self or sense of identity), and superego (the conscience). Psychoanalysts since Freud have argued about which, if any, of these three components is the true self.

Twentieth Century

Extrinsic

In the mid-twentieth century, anthropologist Joseph Campbell invented his radical theory of myth. He took Carl Jung's belief in subconscious primordial archetypes and cast them as roles in an all-purpose story. Campbell claimed that his monomyth had been passed through the ages from culture to culture, when in fact it was more invention than legend.[3] Belief in this monomyth led many writers to reduce action characters to dimensionless clichés.

Intrinsic

Psychologist William James viewed inner life as an ongoing contradiction: At times the private self seems like a solid inner awareness, but then daydreams and confusions liquefy consciousness into ever-changing streams of images and impressions. James wondered, "How can it be that each of us has both a sense of an ongoing singular identity, plus a sense of the very different selves we used to be?" How can we be the one person we know and all the former selves that litter our memories? These Jamesian paradoxes help inspire the authorship of complex characters.

Twenty-First Century

In the most recent decades, the polarized dialogue on human nature took this form:

Extrinsic

Critical Theory, aka postmodernism, is a nurture-based system that sees the mind as a socially conditioned organ. Therefore, the use of one culture's subjective beliefs to judge another culture's behaviors and values is bigoted. This conviction went so far as to reject the scientific method itself—evidence gathering, experimentation, rational deduction—as biased and culturally skewed.

Intrinsic

Cognitive Science, the counterpoint to Critical Theory, grew out of linguistics, IT, and computer research. In this nature-based theory, the mind is a biological computer designed by evolution. CS believes that once we decipher the brain's codes and networks, the ultimate causes of human behavior will, thanks to science, be completely understood.

My sense of this intrinsic/extrinsic debate is that life always stirs some of both, but the quality and quantity of influence between genes and culture varies widely. More importantly, however, none of history's belief systems contemplates the impact of coincidence.

Consider the research done on identical twins: Two people born genetically the same will in time take on distinctively different personalities. Whether they are raised together in the same family or apart in different families, they keep certain similarities but do not remain identical.

From twin to twin, therefore, neither nature nor nurture makes the key difference. What does? Randomness.

Beginning with the accident of birth, haphazard collisions of worldly forces become a way of life for every human being: A child's genes interplay with the often impulsive behaviors of parents and siblings; a culture not of her choosing bends and shapes her; she is at the mercy of her teacher-by-teacher education; the same is true of her religious life service by service; games won and lost; her personal one-of-a-kind encounters with corporate politics, sending her career up and down the pyramid of power; and finally the physical environment up to and including the weather. Sun-browned kids left to run wild under blue skies are not the same as sun-starved kids raised in a rainy clime, watching nature programs on TV.

Which direction her life takes—up, down, or neither—turns on luck as much as any other factor. Once chance has done its thing, the character reacts. In reaction to coincidence, the forces of nature and nurture finally come into play.

THREE KEYS TO AUTHORSHIP

Take from this survey of beliefs what you will or reject them all. It matters not so long as your insights into humanity go deeper than common experience and routine schooling. To develop your personal theory, focus on a trio of faculties within yourself: Moral Imagination, Logical Implication, and Self-Knowledge. The final, fundamental preparation for writing is to focus your unique talents on these three conundrums. Solving them will give you a broader, more reflective understanding of why your characters do the things they do.

1. Moral Imagination

Moral Imagination means a sensitivity to life's values, an ability to recognize shifting charges (positive versus negative), shifting levels (conscious versus subconscious), shifting intensities (subtle versus overt)—the changing qualities that compel and propel people as they decide and act (or vacillate and procrastinate) in their efforts to confront (or evade) conflict.

To create a complex character, a writer's moral imagination peers into a character's inner realms to identify and measure the values at play in her personal and private lives—Maturity versus Immaturity, Honesty versus Dishonesty, Generosity versus Selfishness, Kindness versus Cruelty—all the dynamic charges of human nature.

To create a complex setting, a writer clashes the positive and negative charges of its social and physical environment—what's good versus what's evil, vital versus trivial, just versus unjust, meaningful versus meaningless, and so on down life's multitudinous values.

Without conflicting values, a story's social setting amounts to little more than a board game; without an author's moral imagination to align trait against trait, a role adds less than a Monopoly token. So, whether a writer starts with a setting and draws characters out of it or starts with characters and wraps a setting around them, she must ultimately charge both with her perception of life's values.[4]

2. Logical Implication

A storyteller must be blessed with the kind of mind that given a fingertip takes an arm, given an arm takes an army. In the same way that a composer hears a chord and creates a melody, a painter sees a swath and fills a canvas with wonder, a writer takes a hint and imagines a human.

You will never meet everyone you would need to know to fill multiple casts over a lifetime of storytelling. So instead, develop your power of deductive and inductive implication: Learn to work forward from piece into whole—see a child and imagine her tribe; work back from a whole to a piece—dream of a teeming city and find a lost soul.

3. Self-Knowledge

All writing is autobiographical. Every nugget of improvisation from within yourself and every trigger of inspiration from outside yourself finds its way to the page through you, filtered through your mind, your imagination, your feelings. This does not mean your characters are alter egos, but rather that self-knowledge is the taproot of character creation.

You are the only human being you will ever know in depth and breadth. Yours is the only subjectivity you will ever view objectively. Yours is the only inner voice you will ever converse with self to self. You live in the prison cell of your own mind, and so no matter how long your intimate, personal relationship with another person may last, you will never really know what goes on in her inner world. You can guess at it but never know it.

The only self you ever know is yours, and even then there are limits. Because self-deception distorts self-awareness, you never know who you are as well as you think you do. Self-knowledge is imperfect and in many ways fallacious. Nonetheless, it's all you have.

So, if you know yourself only in part and other people even less, how can you create original, complex characters? By asking this question, "If I were this character in these circumstances, what would I think, feel, do?" Then listen for the honest answer because it's always correct. You would do the human thing. The more you penetrate the mysteries of your own humanity, the more you're able to understand the humanity of others.

Despite clear differences between people—differences of age, gender, race, language, culture—we are all far more alike than we are different. We are human beings having the same fundamental human experiences. Therefore, if you are thinking and feeling it inside yourself, you can be certain that every person coming down the street toward you, each in her own way, is thinking and feeling it, too.

When we realize that the key to character creation is self-knowledge, and then watch the parades of characters, numbering into the hundreds, who have marched out of the minds of the world's greatest writers— William Shakespeare, Leo Tolstoy, Tennessee Williams, Toni Morrison, William Wyler, Vince Gilligan, Ingmar Bergman, and many, many others—characters that are so individual, so fascinating, so memorable, and all the product of one imagination, it dazzles.

PART 2

BUILDING A CHARACTER

My characters are conglomerations of past and present stages of civilization, bits from books and newspapers, scraps of humanity, rags and tatters of fine clothing, patched together as is the human soul.

—August Strindberg[1]

What's the best angle on character creation? Outside in or inside out? Should a writer first create a setting and then populate it with a cast? Or begin by imagining a cast and then building a world around them?

In either case, once a particular character comes into focus, the same questions apply: Should the writer invent surface traits and backtrack to the character's inner core? Or start at the core and work out to his traits? The next two chapters examine these contrasting techniques.

4

CHARACTER INSPIRATION: OUTSIDE IN

Inspiration rarely blazes into a finished, fully cast story. An artist's instincts usually spark just a sliver of intuition or a hint of mystery. These intriguing fragments send chain reactions of free association spiraling through the imagination. At first, what seems like a breakthrough usually dead-ends in a cul-de-sac of clichés, but in time precious insights trace a winding trail to success.

Inspiration can erupt from any of the many realms that surround an author, so picture the storyteller's universe as five concentric spheres nested one inside the other:

1. The outermost shell comprises actuality—time and place, people and things, past and present.
2. Inside the actual world rotates the fictional media of page, stage, and screen.
3. Within that sphere orbit the storytelling genres with their various conventions.
4. Each story houses a backstory reaching back to the characters' births, turning points that happen during the telling, and themes that unite all these events.
5. At the epicenter stands the author's creative self, looking out, in search of inspiration.

Let's begin on the outside and work our way in to the writer.

REALITY AS INSPIRATION

An impulse for character creation often sparks when the density of reality (objects, images, words, sounds, odors, flavors, textures) collides with a boundless imagination. Any random sensation or experience could trigger a cascade of freewheeling impressions that ultimately matures into a complex character. For the storyteller, however, the most frequent inspiration comes from other people.

People are to writers what sounds are to musicians. When an author improvises a character, human nature supplies the notes that the writer composes into a symphony of behaviors. As a result, fictional characters and real people divide into two very different genera of humanity.

A real person is enigmatic and incomplete—a life yet to be lived; a character is an artwork—a complete and expressive version of its original inspiration. People exist, yet characters often seem more intensely real. When people sail directly at us, we alter course to avoid collisions. Characters just glide on by, busily unaware that we watch their every turn. People confront us; we affect them. Characters intrigue us; we absorb them.

Early-twentieth-century authors such as Henry James and Luigi Pirandello felt that although characters could be known in godlike ways (as their novels and plays demonstrated), they had little confidence in objective observations of real people. Since they could witness only gestures and traits, they doubted they could ever know people in depth. They felt that the diagnosis of hidden motives is, at best, a guess—an educated guess, perhaps, but subject to error and prejudice.

And they were right. If you're writing a memoir, for example, your cast will naturally include people you know, but an acquaintance turned into a character can be as superficial as a snapshot. When you draw directly from life, look beneath the surface, uncover silent truths, surprise us with your insights. Do not copy. Rather, reimagine real people into intriguing characters we can believe in.

In other words, finding inspiration in a real person does not guarantee credibility. If a writer doesn't trust or believe in someone, he doesn't feel compelled to write him. But if, trait after trait, credibility grows in his mind, deepening his belief, then the work begins. Often, one unique facet suddenly implies an entire humanity, and this "telling detail" lifts an interesting inspiration out of the what is and into the what could be.

Writers with limited knowledge of their character's setting, society, and traits generalize and thus shrivel their belief and with that, their power to invent. Writers with a global purchase on reality generate unique characters in one-of-a-kind settings that instantly involve readers and audiences.

MEDIUM AS INSPIRATION

Choice of medium, the second source of inspiration, not only influences the shape of an author's stories but the traits and behaviors of the characters who live in them. To please the camera, for example, screen characters tend to act more visually than verbally. Screenwriters, therefore, tend to create characters who can express themselves with looks and gestures. To please theatre audiences, stage characters act more verbally than visually. Playwrights, therefore, tend to endow their characters with expressive dialogue.

Stage and screen characters perform in the present tense, aiming verbal and visual actions at their future desires. Prose voices usually narrate in the past tense, recalling events, retrospectively interpreting what happened in detail. Prose writers, therefore, often give their first-person narrators keen memories, discerning eyes, and sensitivity to subtext.

Beyond characterizing roles, choice of medium also impacts a writer's personal sense of identity. Who am I? A playwright? Showrunner? Screenwriter? Novelist? Each of these titles has a noble tradition, but I urge writers to move freely back and forth from page to stage to screen. Shrinking your writerly identity to a single medium limits your creative range.

If, for example, no one offers to produce your screenplay, why not rework it in another medium? Stage it as a play or publish it as a novel. Put your characters in public and watch how readers and audiences react. The insights you gain can never be glimpsed alone at your desk. Air your stories, field responses, and watch your skills grow. Flex your talents and give yourself an all-media title: writer.

To take your identity a level deeper, ask: "Am I in love with the art in myself or myself in the art?"[1] Do you write because the life inside you demands expression? Or because you dream of living an artist's life?

Many novices nurture crushes on Hollywood or Broadway or the writer-infested countryside of Connecticut. After a few rejections, their dream implodes and they quit. So make certain that whichever medium inspires you harmonizes with more than a lifestyle.

GENRE AS INSPIRATION

Most writers, I suspect, find inspiration in reality far less than they think and in fiction far more than they know. A true first spark rarely flashes from something seen on a street corner or glimpsed online. More often than not, it's a phrase of dialogue or beautifully turned image found in a novel, play, film, or series written in the genre they love.

The major media contain numerous genres (see Chapter 14), each with various subgenres, all of which can be combined or merged into an endless variety of story designs. So when in search of a new, original subject, pay attention to your own story-going habits. What screen series do you binge on? What films and plays do you run to see? Which novels do you read? What genre do you love? Let your passions inspire your early inspirations for character.

EVENTS AS INSPIRATION

Konstantin Stanislavsky, the Russian stage director, taught his actors a technique to unlock their talents that he called the "Magic If"—the shift to a hypothetical way of thinking that opens the imagination. To create a true-to-character moment, the actor asks the open-ended question "If XXX happened, what would I do?" then imagines his reaction.

So, for example, if the cast were rehearsing a family argument scene, an actor might silently ask himself, "What would happen if at this moment I were to punch my brother? How might he react? How might I react to his reaction?" With these hypothetical questions, these ifs, his imagination leaps to an unexpected yet truthful behavior.

Character creators do the same. As the Magic If floats through a writer's imagination, he improvises an inciting incident that in turn triggers the events that follow: If a shark ate a vacationer, what kinds of characters would go after the shark?[2] If a woman discovered that throughout nearly five decades of marriage her husband was secretly in love with his first love, his long-deceased fiancée, what kind of wife would let that revelation destroy her happiness?[3]

The question "What would happen if...?" often inspires a story's inciting incident; that in turn inspires the characters who react to it; that then determines whether the telling is plot-driven or character-driven. Stephen King says his novels always begin plot-driven. To launch a telling, he magic-ifs an inciting incident beyond his protagonist's control. From that point on, however, he hopes his characters will take over and make decisions he didn't see coming, so that by the last page, his tales feel character-driven.[4]

THEME AS INSPIRATION

Writing is an exploration of life. Like a seafarer, an author sails into his story, never quite sure where he's headed or what he will find when he gets there. In fact, if nothing on the horizon surprises him, he's steering a timeworn passage and needs a new compass point.

Eventually, as characters and events merge in climactic turning points, the writer discovers his story's meaning. In other words, the story surprises the writer with this insight; the writer does not dictate meaning to the story. And what is that meaning?

All well-told stories, from ancient myths to modern satires, express one essential idea: How and why life changes. This meaning arises out of deep causes that arc a story's core value from negative to positive or positive to negative—for example, from hate to love or the reverse, or from freedom to slavery or the reverse, or from a meaningless life to a meaningful life or the reverse, and so on through the myriad values at stake in humanity's countless tales. As a writer works in search of story, hidden causes from beneath the surface of society or within a character's subconscious mind suddenly reveal themselves, delivering insights into character an author can discover only through improvisation.

However, when writers move in the opposite direction, when they start with a belief and then concoct a plot and cast to demonstrate it, spontaneity hardens and the unforeseen is never discovered. Belief-fixated writers, in their burning zeal to prove their point, reduce stories to illustrated lectures and characters to mouthpieces. This practice is as old as medieval morality plays that cast a universal human being or Everyman as protagonist and then surrounded him with players who acted out his encounters with ideas such as Virtue and Vice, Mercy and Mischief, Beauty and Knowledge, Birth and Death—all in an effort to educate the morally illiterate.

Today, the practice of working backward from idea to story is the unfortunate tendency of Social Drama. This genre takes its themes from the many maladies that infect society: poverty, sexism, racism, political corruption—injustices and sufferings in all their guises.

A writer, for example, may come to believe that although drug dependency is a terrible social ill, it can be cured by love. So starting with the theme "Love cures addiction," he first creates a last-act climax in which an act of love turns an addict from decades of enslavement to a lifetime of sobriety. Knowing his ending, he then strings turning points back to a pill-popping inciting incident, filling events in between with characters who enact his theory. The good people become very very good people; the bad people very very bad people; and all the dialogue argues on-the-nose explanations of the power of love to cure addiction. The plastic results change no one's mind about love or addiction.

Meaning discovered while exploring character creation is always more insightful than belief used to mechanize a plot.

CHARACTER BIOGRAPHY AS INSPIRATION

Every character has a life history trailing back to the family that gave him birth. Does this past matter to the writer? Novelist Philip Roth thought yes. For him, the past was a cache of motivational catalysts and jeweled dimensions. That was why he devised five thousand or more biographical bits and pieces per protagonist.

Playwright David Mamet thought not. For him, inventing childhoods, with or without the usual traumas, seemed a waste of time.

These conflicting views have as much to do with the author's media choices as his work habits. Novels (with exceptions) speak in the past tense and project their characters' lives over spans of time; the theatre (with exceptions) runs its scenes along the cutting edge of the now. In fact, to get biographical exposition onstage playwrights call on novelistic devices such as reminiscing monologues and flashbacks, as did Edward Albee in *Who's Afraid of Virginia Woolf?* and *Three Tall Women.*

I side with Roth. Although few of his five thousand pieces of character biography found their way to the page, they gave him the foundational knowledge that set off fireworks of creative choices.

As you compile a character's past, look for patterns rather than singularities. Redundant emotional experiences deposit residues. Repeated traumas cause PTSD; daily coddling produces egoists. Imprints left by recurring emotions affect motivations (what to seek/what to avoid), temperaments (calm/nervous), dispositions (optimistic/pessimistic), personalities (charming/irritating), and other such traits.

Movements in the subconscious inspire qualities of behavior, and qualities of behavior mirror subconscious movements. Once these patterns take root, they drive lifelong strivings. A character rarely abandons his childhood traits in the face of adult conflicts. Instead, he will often react to a person in the present as if he were someone from his past. Groundwork laid in biography, therefore, will determine the tactics a character uses in later life.

As you build out a character's years prior to the story's inciting incident, focus on early adolescence. It's in these preteen days that he first dreams about the future, testing and formulating possible meanings and purposes. If he's lucky, he'll have a positive experience—an inspirational teacher, a personal epiphany—that commits him to the goal he pursues for a lifetime. Or his first glimpse of a life purpose may turn sharply negative. He suffers confusion, doubt, fear, shame, sadness, anger, depression—any combination or all of these at once. In other words, he becomes a teenager.

He then spends who knows how many years in an identity crisis of minor or major magnitude, trying to figure out who he is, where he came from, where he's going, and how he will fit in when he gets there. At some future point, for better or worse, a workable identity solidifies. He matures into a historian of his personal past and a prophet of his personal future, poised to enter your story.

While doing this research, the writer often comes to value the richness of the past over the void of the future. The remembered comes with textures and tensions, scents and shapes; the imagined offers possibilities without subtleties, blanks to be filled. From a character's point of view, he can only hope that the future will repeat a pattern he's coped with in the past.

THE SELF-STORY AS INSPIRATION

As a final tack from the outside in, do this: Sit your character down in a chair across from you, introduce yourself, and ask him to tell you his self-story. Your character is, of course, nonexistent, so when he speaks, it will be in a voice only your imagination can hear. In effect, you and your creative self have a conversation.

Self-stories express how people think about their life and see the reality around them. Elicit your character's self-story by asking questions about high points, low points, turning points, successes, failures, and other moments of stress. The story a character tells about himself, although rarely factual, expresses who he thinks he is. You have to decide if his version is true or false or some of both.

As he tells his tale, bear in mind that all statements of self are self-serving. It's impossible for human beings to do otherwise. All lines of dialogue, for example, that start with the pronoun *I* are followed, to some degree, by a deceit or exaggeration, no matter how profound or petty. Even when a character confesses to terrible deeds, a whisper from his subtext implies a bit of self-congratulation to the effect, "Aren't I sensitive, honest, and clear thinking to see these faults in myself and courageous to admit them in public?" When Hamlet curses himself with "Oh what a rogue and peasant slave am I," a certain pride in self-awareness rolls through his subtext.

In any case, self-descriptions do not mean what they seem to mean; they always have a purpose beyond the literal. So it's up to you to sense the difference between truth and BS, between self-awareness and self-deception. Always compare what a character says with what you feel when he says it.

No one is who he seems to be. Everyone wears a persona of characterization, the masks they've evolved to get through their day with as little friction as possible. To see behind his mask, question your character about his greatest dilemmas, the crisis choices he's made, and the actions he's taken in the face of high risk.

A self-story, for example, that matches cause with effect and organizes consistent values around persistent goals suggests a character with a well-organized psychology. Whereas an incoherent, inconsistent self-story that disconnects cause and effect and aims at multiple, contradictory goals suggests the opposite.[5]

Contradictions within a character form his dimensions. (See Chapter 9.) So, as you listen to your character's self-story, be alert to his inner oppositions. People often seek two things that cannot coexist. While he claws his way up the corporate ladder, for example, he expects pats on the back from coworkers. Doubtful. When he tells you about the various things he wants out of life, do they seem consistent or incongruous?

Find his whys. Your character's true motivations will be subconscious to him, but nonetheless, he will offer steadfast rationalizations for wanting what he wants. You, like an annoying five-year-old, must repeatedly ask why. Why does he do what he does? How does he explain his actions? His desires? And what's his plan to reach these desires? Has he mapped out a life strategy, or does he improvise day by day?

Finally, ask about his beliefs. Beliefs create the context for every action a human being takes. Does he believe God exists or not? That romantic love exists or not? In his mind, what's good? Evil? What institutions does he trust? Private? Public? None? What would he risk his life for? His soul for? What deep beliefs hold his world together?

Although beliefs mold behavior, they can change…sometimes on a dime. Fanatics, for example, often reverse ideologies and join the opposition side—communists become fascists, fascists communists. For the true believer, the passion of believing is more important than the meaning of belief.[6]

Let the insights you gain from all these levels inspire your development of character dimensionality and inner complexity.

5

CHARACTER INSPIRATION: INSIDE OUT

To project yourself into the consciousness of a person essentially your opposite requires the audacity of great genius.

—Henry James[1]

The second grand source of inspiration places the writer not at the center of her universe but at the heart of her character's universe. An adventurous writer brings her creation to life by imagining her way into the character's inner self, seeing through his eyes, hearing with his ears, sensing everything he senses. She envisions the character's conflicts, improvises choices and takes moment by moment actions as if the character's fictional life were happening to her. This leap from one consciousness into another requires, as Henry James noted, a certain genius. I call this technique *writing in-character*.

As the in-character writer inhabits a role's inner self, his emotions become hers, her pulse pounds with him, his anger flares inside her; she celebrates his triumphs, she loves his loves. The most powerful inspirations of all strike when the writer experiences what the character experiences. In other words, the character's first actor is the writer.

An author is an improvisationist. She first imagines herself at the pinpoint center of her character's consciousness. Once in-character, her mind, emotions, and energies drive character creation. She paces the floor, arms waving, words flying, acting out her creations—man, woman, child, monster. The writer, like the actor, lives inside her character's senses, seeing and hearing the story's events as if she were the living character herself so that what happens in the character happens in her.

How does a writer get in-character? How does she improvise the character she's creating? How does she use her own emotions to give life to a fictional being? Once again, she calls on Stanislavsky's Magic If.

In an effort to give her character life, the writer could ask, "If I were in this situation, what would I do?" That thought could certainly get juices flowing, but the writer is not the character. So what the writer might say and do in that moment may be nothing like the actions the character would take.

Or the writer could ask, "If my character were in this situation, what would my character do?" But that thought sits the writer in an audience, as it were, picturing the character onstage. Rather than feeling what the character feels, the writer must now guess at his emotions, and guesses are almost always clichés.

To get in-character, therefore, the writer puts the Magic If to work with this thought: "If I were this character in this situation, what would I do?" In other words, the writer acts the scene—not as herself, but as the character. Now the character's emotions flow, not the writer's.

Writing in-character means more than thinking about what goes on inside a character's head. It means living within him, so that your mind occupies his mind, his self-awareness becomes yours, and you two act as one. Mastery of the inside-out technique brings characters to life on page, stage, and screen with a truthfulness and subtlety that cannot be achieved any other way.

Discovering the inspirations that can be found only inside a fictional being calls for sustained, willful and often courageous imaginings. The prerequisite for this feat is insight into your own inner life. The more you understand your true nature, the better you perceive your character's complexities. To know yourself, you must recognize your rock-bottom inner self, compare your dreams to reality and your desires to morality, and from that base explore the social, personal, private, and hidden selves that complete your multifaceted humanity. Your truth will become the truth of every character you create.

So, before you attempt the in-character technique, let's look inside the multilayered complexity of a human being.

THE OBSERVER AND THE OBSERVED

The brain consists of roughly 100 billion neurons laced into 100 trillion interconnections. This immense-beyond-imagining complexity constantly adapts and changes as it interacts with its body, and then through its body with the surrounding physical and social worlds. With every passing day, the brain evolves new thoughts and new feelings, and then stores them in memory as preparation for the future.

Somehow (and science is yet to discover how) consciousness ascends out of this vast conformance, a mind that is not just aware of the things around it but is self-aware—a mind that can step back from itself and see itself as an object.[2]

The nature of the inner self has been debated for centuries. Is it a reality or a fantasy? Does a mind staring at itself see itself or mirror images reflecting into infinity?

Buddha, as we noted, believed that the self is illusionary because what's inside our minds began as sensory impressions of sights and sounds from outside our minds. What we call the self is actually a bundle of external imprints that appear one after the other like an actor coming and going on- and offstage. Therefore, a true self does not exist—it's an anatta (nonself), a sort of mental special effect.

Socrates reversed this. He believed that not only do human beings have a solid inner realm but two selves living within it: the observer and the observed. The *core self* (the observer) is the epicenter of consciousness that watches life go by and tries to understand it. The core self sends the *agent self* (the observed) into the world to take action. The core self then perceives its agent self in action and becomes an audience to its own daily life. This is self-awareness—the performance in your inner theatre that no one attends but you.[3]

Consider this: After doing something foolish, don't you often think the thought, "You idiot!"? When you do, who, exactly, is shaming who? When you manage a success, you often think, "I got that right." Who is patting whose back? How do self-criticism and self-congratulation work? Who talks to whom?

As you read this page, an observing awareness within you follows your every move. You perceive (watch yourself read), and then act (take notes on paper or store them in memory). This pivot from awareness-to-action-to-awareness within the mind separates the core self from the agent self.[4]

Some neuroscientists, however, to this day, still side with Buddhism. They argue that because each region of the brain has a separate function and because no single region, in and of itself, causes self-awareness, a core self does not exist.[5]

Others agree with Socrates: Human beings have motor neurons for movement, sensory neurons for the senses, and interneurons—by far the most numerous—for the heavy lifting of thought. The brain, with its residue of past experiences and imaginings of future happenings, coupled with the body's nervous system and the totality of its moment-by-moment sensory encounters, focuses billions of impulses toward the center of awareness, the core self. Self-awareness, therefore, is the side effect of all the neurons in all these regions working in concert. And that's why damage to any one region of the brain diminishes or extinguishes the sense of self. Peak self-awareness, watching and doing, radiates through the well-nourished brain of a healthy body.[6]

This is nothing new. The Egyptians saw the observing self as a protective spirit and named it the Ba Soul; the Greeks called it the Daemon;[7] the Romans dubbed it the Genius.[8] But if, at the end of the day, science decides that the self is a fiction, as Buddha claimed, fine with me. Then it's our fiction, our nature, what makes us human.[9]

(Try this: Go to a mirror and glance into your eyes. For an instant you'll sense someone else, deep within, looking back. With the next blink, however, you'll realize that what you glimpsed was a split-second image of your core self observing you just before your agent self reacted. These moments happen best when unplanned, but it's worth a test.)

To deepen our understanding of human nature, we must not only accept the idea of the self, but of a cast of selves: the core self (observer); the agent self (observed) plus all the personal and social personae an agent self assumes; all the past selves the core self remembers; and finally, at the deepest level, the hidden self.[10]

FOUR SELVES IN SEARCH OF A CHARACTER

To imagine how each layer of self creates a fully human character, start at the conscious center, the *private realm* in which the core self copes with inner dilemmas, makes decisions, then directs the agent self to take action.

Next, surround that center with two outer strata: the *personal realm* in which the agent self assumes various personae as it deals with intimate relationships, and the *social realm* in which the agent self takes on its public personae as it copes with institutions and individuals.

Finally, underpin these three levels with a substrata: the *subconscious realm* in which the hidden self struggles with contradictory desires.

From story to story, how many of these levels are at play in your characters is up to you, but let's work through them one at a time:

The Private Selves: Variations of Identity

William James gave the core self names such as the "self of selves," the "owner-self," the "proprietor-self." In his analogy, the core self is a sanctuary within a citadel, the epicenter inside our personal and public personae.[11] James's concept of "the stream of thought" inspired fiction writers like Virginia Woolf to create the literary style of "stream of consciousness."

In the William James view of the private realm, the core self maintains a single identity over a lifetime while observing and absorbing its many past selves. We know we are not the same person we used to be, and yet we feel that we are and always have been our core self. Our mind has a permanent, unchanging, stable sense of identity, and yet, simultaneously, its continuously evolving consciousness acts and reacts, learns and forgets, evolves and devolves, keeps some attitudes about values and desires but changes to others about what's worth doing, what's a waste of time, and the like. Day in, day out, we live in a natural state of paradox: We change while we stay the same.[12]

An aside: William James's younger brother was the author Henry James. The two delved into the nature of thought in both science and fiction. Their work inspired Henry to explore the point-of-view techniques that revolutionized the modern psychological novel. The nineteenth century gave America two sets of James brothers: Henry and William (writers and psychologists) and Jesse and Frank (bank robbers and committers of atrocities).

Imprisoned inside our skull, the core self lives essentially alone. Our inner voice is the only inner voice we will ever hear. Because our core self cannot contact another person's private realm telepathically, consciousness becomes a kind of cinema of the mind. Somewhere inside of our head, we sit in a permanent state of isolation—an audience of one in a multisensational, 360-degree movie that crosscuts images from our eyes and our imagination, accompanied by sounds, smells, touches, tastes, feelings, and emotions.[13]

Someone in a deep meditative state may try to face herself within herself. She may turn away from the focal point of her meditation and look back toward her awareness, hoping that her watching self and her acting self will meet. But try as she might, the two never do, never can. For the moment consciousness focuses on the next thing, the core self steps back to observe. This is the Hamlet dilemma.

Hamlet's mind, like two mirrors facing each other, stares at itself throughout the play. As he strives to understand himself, he becomes obsessed with his consciousness of his own consciousness. He tries to step inside self-awareness and study himself from within but cannot. Finally, after the graveyard scene in Act V, "Hamlet discovers that his life has been a quest with no object except his endlessly burgeoning subjectivity."[14] When at last he purges himself of his obsession with himself, he finds peace of mind.

As Hamlet discovers, you cannot face yourself within yourself. You know you're there, but you cannot separate your core self from the rest of your mind and hold it out to look at it. When you turn toward it, it just shifts behind you once again, blocking the gateway to the subconscious. If you could actually squeeze behind your core self, you would fall into a swirling subliminal abyss.

When a character talks about herself in a first-person novel or in soliloquy onstage or in voice-over narration on-screen, the self receiving criticism is usually referred to as "you" as in "You fool," while the self hearing praise is addressed as "I" as in "I got that right." Shakespeare uses "I" in soliloquies because his characters talk to the audience, not themselves. Nonetheless, some actors play soliloquies as if they were duelogues of core self versus agent self, an argument within a split personality.[15]

When the mind decides to take action, the core self sends its agent self into the world and watches what happens. The public performances of the agent self are called by various names: personalities, personae, masks, fronts, poses, and the like. All apt synonyms, but I prefer the term *selves*.

When writing in-character, the writer needs to see her character's behaviors for what they are: impersonations of the core self. So, while staying constantly observing, the writer, as first actor, also becomes an agent self to improvise these performances.

The core self may undergo major variations:

The Extended Self

Henry and William James stretched the core self into the *extended self*. In their view, a person's identity includes all things "mine"—her computer extends her mind, her iPhone extends her reach, her car her legs, her clothes her skin, as do, each in their own way, her friends and ancestors, education and profession, taste in vacations, music, movies, and how she looks in the gym mirror. The sum total of all things she calls her own creates her total sense of self.

As a result, she feels about her things very much the way as she feels about herself. To lose a job, a loved one, or her good looks is to lose a piece of herself. If a friend, lover, or family member does something wrong, she feels ashamed; if they are insulted, she flashes with anger. If they prosper, so does she; if they dwindle, so does she. Although many people feel that coupling one's identity to things, even other people, hints of moral weakness, it is what human beings do.[16]

The Protected Self

The core self, for sanity's sake, must keep its secrets. As Michel de Montaigne put it, "We must reserve a little back-shop all our own, entirely free, wherein we maintain our retreat, liberty and precious solitude."[17] All authors, especially prose writers, look in this "little back-shop" for a voice that's strong enough to narrate a first-person novel or short story. This protected, sane self contains a set of enduring facilities: willpower, rational thought, and moral sensibility.

The Vanished Self

However, when a character comes under extreme stress due to disasters such as physical injury, sudden poverty, drug dependency, insanity, senility, terminal illness, and the like, these derangements attack the core self, causing overpowering emotions, paralyzed thought, seizures, hallucinations, amnesia, lapses of consciousness, or splits or reversals of personality. In a word, a character de-dimensionalizes. Her identity weakens and she becomes unmoored, alone, until her essential self eventually vanishes.

Examples: In Ken Kesey's novel *One Flew over the Cuckoo's Nest*, Chief Bromden, a patient in an insane asylum, tells his tale while plagued with schizophrenic hallucinations; in *Forbidden Planet*, a scientist's research releases a monster from his id; in *Memento*, the protagonist battles anterograde amnesia and short-term memory loss; in Will Self's novel *Phone*, psychiatrist Zachary Busner copes with the onset of Alzheimer's; in Gabriel García Márquez's *One Hundred Years of Solitude*, José Buendia loses his memory, so he marks everything around him with its name: chair, clock, door, and so on; in Eugene Ionesco's play *Exit the King*, the King's mind, horrified by his pending death, splinters like a windshield in a head-on collision.

When a loss of self causes radical change in a character's perception of reality, the writer's talent must rise to the occasion. Now the Magic If becomes, "If I were this character under these extreme circumstances, what would I do?" To take the point of view of a distorted core self, you must imagine its altered reality and invent its coping strategies, as disturbing as they may be.

Because a character's sense of "I" depends on memory and memory is notoriously selective, protective, self-deceptive, and prone to self-justifications, the core self and agent self often have a fallible, illusionary kinship. The core self of certain characters wavers, constantly reinventing itself as it pushes through life. To express that splintering, Joyce Carol Oates, in her novel *Blonde*, fragmented Marilyn Monroe into numerous selves.

Personal Selves: Variations of Intimacy

When we encounter other people, we attune our behavior to the quality of the relationship. We do not treat our mother, for example, the way we treat our sister; we do not treat our current lover the way we treat an ex; we do not treat our best friend the way we treat a coworker. Our agent self adopts timbres of voice, gestures, facial expressions, and emotional energies geared to the relationship's length of acquaintance, balance of power, current history, and many other variables. The changes may be subtle, but they are always in play.

Personal relationships are defined by degrees of intimacy and come in three textures: family, friends, lovers. In the first two, feelings of closeness, belonging, loyalty, and bonding develop through shared experiences, some painful, some pleasureful, that stay secret inside the relationship. Lovers add romantic rituals and sexuality.

We adapt our behaviors, but that doesn't falsify us. Common sense tells us that diverse interactions call for diverse selves. Indeed, the more relationships a character has, the more versions of her the in-character writer must invent and perform. Compared to the core self, personal selves are temporary behaviors, easily dropped as an agent self moves from scene to scene. A character's most important, and hopefully consistent, personal self is the one loved by her loved ones.

Social Selves: Variations of Power

Power is the primary shaper of social interactions, whether it's projected financially, physically, or from inside an institution's hierarchy: boss versus employee, cop versus criminal, server versus served.

From her earliest childhood, your protagonist—while squeezing her mother's hand as she was dragged through shopping malls or coping with other kids on her first day of school—learned the need for social masks, for tactics to avoid friction, and yet get what she wants. All social selves are insincere to a degree, and yet necessary to protect the core self.

So no matter what your character actually thinks or feels about the people around her, her agent self has developed the social persona that she shows her boss, others for her coworkers, yet more masks to wear for duets such as clerk/customer, doctor/patient, lawyer/client, as well as multiple happenstances in classrooms, at political protests, during sporting events, and a very special variation for schmoozing from clique to clique at a party.

So depending on factors such as familiarity and status, her social selves operate with the variety of voices, gestures, attitudes, and aspects of personality that she has invented so she can shift gears from encounter to encounter. She may, for example, play the dominant self with one person, the submissive with another. Lina Wertmüller's film *Swept Away* gave us the wealthy matron Raffaella (Mariangela Melato) as a delightful example of this flip.

A character's selves, both personal and social, are best thought of as sets of performances. Each role has a particular tone of voice, eye expression, body language, and nervosity, depending on the identity of the other person and the quality of power or intimacy between them.

How a writer develops her characters' personal and social selves depends on her theory of psychological cause and effect. Do the social and personal roles her character learns between childhood and adulthood combine to build her core self? Or does her core self design the roles she plays from encounter to encounter? Does a child's role-playing solidify into an adult's core self that then redirects her future role-playing toward more mature performances? Or does she stay forever a child, always at the mercy of her impulsive, reckless self?

The identity a character inherits from her parents—race, religion, culture—gives her common ground with her society. Over time, however, it's what makes her different that evolves and reshapes her identity. Difference is the centrifugal force that throws people into the world, searching for a subculture that fits them and fellow travelers that befriend them. How, for example, does a transgender child, trapped in a zealously orthodox religion, successfully navigate her public life? How can she evolve her social and personal selves so she finally fits in?

The Hidden Self: Variations of Desire

There's someone in my head but it's not me.

—Pink Floyd, paraphrasing Carl Jung

The subconscious self sits in the silent space behind the conscious mind. This realm is complex and structurally sophisticated. Although it stays hidden from the core self, perceptions and feelings flow back and forth between them, each influencing the other. The subconscious is neither a refuge nor a medic for a wounded identity. Anchored in the truth, it never lies, never pretends. Instead, it obeys one imperative: survive.[18]

Although mute, the subconscious "thinks" far faster than the core self realizes. It absorbs millions of sensory stimuli per minute as it sizes up an environment, and then enhances mental efficiency by making immediate decisions and performing countless rote tasks, leaving the core self free to react to the unfamiliar.

The subconscious contains moods and feelings, automatic skills, automatic reactions, unperceived perceptions, habits, phobias, dreams, memories, implicit knowledge, and sudden creative insights. Innate desires arise out of this hidden self—cravings for food, sex, and survival at all cost, as well as for knowledge, love, and peace. Because these drives disrupt the conscious mind, they stay out of view; nonetheless, they sway judgments, feelings, and behavior.[19]

The question, therefore, becomes: Can an author, working in-character, improvise from within the role's subconscious mind? We inherited our subconscious from our tree-dwelling ancestors; like the mind of an animal, it has neither language nor self-awareness, thus making thought, in the usual sense, seemingly impossible. On the other hand, I've often imagined desires and curiosities raging inside my pets. So I don't see why not. If it helps bring your character to life, try it.

MAD MEN: THE FOUR SELVES IN ACTION

To script the longform series *Mad Men*, showrunner Matthew Weiner and his cowriters developed each character at three levels of conflict: their Work Life, Intimate Life, and Secret Life. These levels correspond to the Social Self, Personal Self, and Core Self. I've added a fourth level, the Subconscious Life, so that the interpretations that follow include each character's Hidden Self. Human nature is an unsolved mystery of elegant, glorious confusion. The four-self structure frames character creation, but it's not a set of instructions. The creation of major characters, whether inside out or outside in, should ultimately give you insight into their natures at all four levels of self. Study the following cast members and compare their four-level designs to the roles in your current writings.

Don Draper (Jon Hamm)

Social Self: smooth-talking ad agency creative director with a genius for seducing clients.

Personal Self: His wife and two children seem like a picture-perfect family in a breakfast cereal commercial, but Don's extramarital affairs corrupt and destroy that illusion.

Core Self: Don's real name is Dick Whitman. He stole his Draper identity from a dead officer during the Korean War. As a result, his guilt-ridden conscience renders him incapable of love . . . and he knows it.

Hidden Self: He's haunted by a sense of dread. Despite his great success, he fears his life is meaningless and will come to nothing.

Betty Draper (January Jones)

Social Self: Betty, a college-educated former model, spends her time squabbling with her children, horseback riding, and chain-smoking.

Personal Self: Pregnant with a third child she doesn't want, Betty feels trapped in an empty marriage.

Core Self: She takes revenge on her unfaithful husband by using her sexual charms to torment a neighbor's young son and indulge in one-night stands with anonymous men.

Hidden Self: Gnawing self-doubt tells her she's lucky she was born beautiful because otherwise she'd be ordinary.

Roger Sterling (John Slattery)

Social Self: Roger, partner and rainmaker for the firm, suffers two heart attacks.

Personal Self: He wants to divorce his wife but can't decide which of his mistresses, if any, he actually loves.

Core Self: Roger pines for the voluptuous Joan but can't admit it.

Hidden Self: His greatest fear is being alone.

Peggy Olson (Elisabeth Moss)

Social Self: By dint of IQ and willpower, Peggy works her way up from secretary to copywriter, landing her own office and secretary.

Personal Self: Peggy, a devout Catholic, pursues her career against pressure from her marriage-minded family.

Core Self: Peggy hides her secret pregnancy by letting others think she's just gaining weight.

Hidden Self: She's the smartest person in the room and tempted by strange sexual impulses she can't admit to herself.

Pete Campbell (Vincent Kartheiser)

Social Self: Pete, a young executive, engineers power games as he climbs the corporate pyramid.

Personal Self: Because his wife desperately wants a child but cannot conceive, Pete can never find balance in his marriage.

Core Self: On his wedding eve, Pete slept with Peggy Olson, and she later gave birth to his son. He longs for the child he'll never know.

Hidden Self: He's talentless but never lets that truth get in his way.

Joan Holloway (Christina Hendricks)

Social Self: Joan's stunning looks camouflage her brainy insights into people.

Personal Self: Her loveless marriage to an incompetent doctor leads to an illegitimate child and divorce.

Core Self: She deceives herself into thinking that marriage gives a woman's life meaning, thus denying her business prowess.

Hidden Self: She's a loner who doesn't want to work for anyone but herself.

Sal Romano (Bryan Batt)

Social Self: Sal, the agency's art director, illustrates Don's snappy slogans.

Personal Self: He's married but without children.

Core Self: Sal desperately hides his homosexuality from his homophobic colleagues.

Hidden Self: He hates being gay.

OUTSIDE IN / INSIDE OUT

The technique of writing in-character links the artist's creative self to the character's inner life, but few writers work exclusively from the inside out. Rather, they take a double path, alternating between perspectives. First, they gather clues to the character's identity from the outer shells of her setting and society, as well as from her age, IQ, and genetic givens. Then they peer down through the various levels of behavior to her core, instinctive self. The Magic If puts them in-character, and from there, they improvise. But even while in-character, they often alternate points of view from character to character.

For example: If a writer were sketching a scene between Characters A and B, she would find a true-to-character choice and action by asking, "If I were Character A in this moment, what would I do?" Then, in the next beat, she would switch point of view and ask, "If I were Character B in this situation, how would I react to what Character A just said and did?"

Each time the writer steps out of character, she reflects on the actions and reactions just created and the effects they caused on both roles. Her thoughts and feelings shift from inside to out, then outside to in, subjective to objective, objective to subjective, repeating these cycles until the scene is perfected.

E. L. Doctorow, a superb practitioner of this alternating technique, worked both ends against the middle. In his historical fictions, such as *Ragtime* and *The Waterworks*, he researched his subject until he was a world-class authority on it, but then, as he acted out his characters, he gave them guises. Doctorow's fictional characters often seem as if they were historical personages, while his historical figures seem as if they had been improvised in his ingenious brain.[20]

6

ROLES VERSUS CHARACTERS

A role is not a character. A role simply assumes a generic position in a story's social order (Mother, Boss, Artist, Loner) and then carries out that role's tasks (feeding children, managing employees, painting canvases, avoiding people). Like a picture frame around an empty canvas, a role offers an artist a blank space that needs a character.

When a fully realized character enters a story, he first assumes a basic role but then fills it with his singular personality and executes the role's tasks in a unique manner, striking a one-of-a-kind relationship with each member of the cast. A cast's design strategically arranges its roles and relationships so that no two take the same position nor perform the same tasks in the same way.

CAST FORMATION

Characters come in casts, complete with complex networks of relationships. To sort these interconnections, picture a cast as a solar system of planets, moons, comets, and asteroids surrounding the star blazing at the center. Three concentric rings of supporting roles orbit the sun at various distances, affecting him and each other to greater or lesser degrees. The most influential characters cycle closest to the protagonist; less impactful minor roles rotate further out; and at the farthest reaches, one-scene-only bit parts, nonspeaking walk-ons and crowds-on-streets complete the social universe. A third-person narrator, like an unseen god, views this cosmos from a distance.

To design your cast, begin with the star role and expand to the outermost reaches.

Protagonist

It takes guts to place a character front and center before readers and audiences and imply that this guy is so interesting, so involving, he deserves a major chunk of their precious time. So before you take that step, let's examine the essential qualities of a protagonist:

(1) Willpower

The mind, fearing extinction above all else, yearns for security, so when a story's inciting incident throws life out of kilter, the protagonist's instincts react as if his survival were at stake. He then conceives an object of desire—a physical, personal, or social objective that he feels would restore life's equilibrium. As he pursues this goal, antagonistic forces block his efforts. At the final crisis, he faces the story's most powerful, most focused oppositions. A true protagonist has the willpower to take on this ultimate dilemma, make the ultimate decision, and take the ultimate action as a last attempt to achieve his purpose and restore life's balance. His final action may fail, but not until he has exhausted his willpower.

(2) Multiple capabilities

The protagonist's mental, emotional, and physical capacities combine to propel his life's pursuit to or beyond his personal limits. In every story these capabilities are different. In one telling he must be young enough, in another old enough, rich enough, or poor enough, educated or ignorant, and so on down the list of qualities that allow the reader/audience to believe that the choices the protagonist makes and the actions he takes are his alone, true to his nature, and credible.

The effect of his actions must go wide enough and/or deep enough to bring the story to an ending beyond which the reader/audience cannot imagine another. Once again, he may or may not get what he wants, but his efforts will ultimately reveal his full humanity.

To expand events out wide into a story's social and physical settings, writers often find their protagonists among the elites: doctors, lawyers, warriors, politicians, scientists, detectives, executives, crime lords, celebrities, and the like. An elite's elevated status gives his actions broad consequence in the social hierarchy, driving the telling into more and more lives.

When a story confounds events inward into the hidden realm, protagonists can be found in any walk of life, so long as they are complex enough to reward explorations of their depths and flexible enough to undergo change.

And, of course, a story can take its protagonist both wide and deep at once. Consider, for example, Jimmy McGill in the longform series *Breaking Bad* and its prequel *Better Call Saul*. When Jimmy's story opens, he's a charming, gregarious street hustler and wannabe lawyer. But when he hides behind the persona of Saul Goodman, he buries his true self deeper and deeper inside. At the same time, his storefront legal career expands wider and wider until he's embroiled in a billion-dollar meth empire.

(3) An underdog status

Do this: Put your protagonist in the palm of one hand and weigh his mental, emotional, and physical capacities. Then in the other hand, add up the power of all antagonistic forces he will confront over the course of the story: negative thoughts and feelings from his inner life; personal conflicts with friends, family, and lovers; all obstructing institutions and the people in them; and finally the physical world from foul weather to lethal diseases to never enough time.

When you test the strength of your protagonist against the concentrated force of all negative powers, you should see that the forces of antagonism virtually overwhelm him, and he is clearly an underdog. He has a chance of achieving his object of desire, but just that, a chance.

(4) An empathic nature

The moment a reader or an audience member enters a fictional world, he quickly inspects the story's value-charged universe, sorting positives from negatives, rights from wrongs, goods from evils, things of interest from things of no interest, searching for a Center of Good, a secure place to attach his empathy.

Definition: The Center of Good is a positive charge of value (e.g., justice, goodness, love, etc.) glowing deep within a story that contrasts with a dark, negative charge (e.g., tyranny, evil, hate, etc.) surrounding it. This positive light attracts empathy because human beings, in their heart of hearts, feel they are overall good or right, and so they naturally identify with their perception of the positive. With a few exceptions, most stories locate their Center of Good in the protagonist.

Two examples:

Mario Puzo's *Godfather* trilogy creates a criminal universe of mafia families surrounded by corrupt cops and for-hire judges. But the Corleone family has one positive quality: loyalty. The other crime families betray one another and stab each other in the back. That makes them the bad bad guys. The Godfather's family sticks together and defends each other, making them the good bad guys. When an audience finds this positive center in the Corleones, they instinctively identify with gangsters.

In *The Silence of the Lambs*, novelist Thomas Harris splits the reader's focus toward two centers of good: The heroism of FBI agent Clarice Starling draws immediate empathy, but as the story unfolds, a second hub of affinity forms in Dr. Hannibal Lecter.

First, Harris places Lecter in a dark, dishonorable world: The FBI attempts to bribe him with the false offer of a prison cell with an ocean view; his jailer is a sadist and publicity hound; the cops Lecter kills are dullards.

Second, bright lights glow within Lecter: He has a massive IQ, a keen sense of humor, and a remarkably calm, polite manner while living in hell. Lecter's positive qualities inside a negative society cause the reader to shrug, "So he eats people. There are worse things. Offhand I can't think what, but there must be." The reader identifies, thinking, "If I were a psychopathic, cannibalistic serial killer, I'd want to be just like Lecter. He's cool."

(5) Intrigue

A story's protagonist is its most complex and therefore most intriguing character. When two qualities within a character contradict each other, the reader/audience naturally wonders, "Who is this guy?" Pursuing the answer to that question glues them to the telling.

(6) Length and depth

The protagonist stands in the story's foreground and occupies the reader's/audience's mind for the greater part of the telling. As a result, his subconscious motivations and hidden desires are ultimately revealed with each pressure-filled choice he makes. By climax, this exposure makes him the character known in greatest depth.

(7) Capacity for change

Human beings gather knowledge over time, discover new beliefs, adapt to new conditions, and adjust to an aging body, but their inner natures tend to stay fixed and their core selves, with few exceptions, do not change. They may daydream about change, especially for the better, but that's more wish fulfillment than likelihood. Because most human beings keep their essential selves intact over a lifetime, characters who do not change seem the most true-to-life, the most realistic.

For those characters who do change, the more they arc, the more they lean away from the realistic and toward the symbolic. A character progressing to the positive evolves toward the ideal; one descending to the negative devolves toward a dark archetype. And of all cast members, the one most likely to undergo change is the protagonist.

Protagonists may reform like Scrooge (*A Christmas Carol*) or Jesse Pinkman (*Breaking Bad*), or learn their lesson like Theo Decker (*The Goldfinch*) or Fleabag (*Fleabag*), or degenerate like Jackie Peyton (*Nurse Jackie*) or Truman Capote (*Capote*), or become disillusioned like Tony Webster (*The Sense of an Ending*) or David Lurie (*Disgrace*), or grow into their author like Davy Copperfield (*David Copperfield*) or Stephen Dedalus (*A Portrait of the Artist as a Young Man*).

(8) Insight

When conflict throws a character's life out of balance, his mind seeks insight into how and why things happen, how and why people do the things they do. The most powerful conflicts fester in the protagonist, making this character the one most likely to experience an epiphany.

In ancient times, the word "epiphany" named the moment a deity suddenly appeared before its awestruck worshippers. In the modern usage, the term means a flash of insight into reality—an intuitive perception of an essential cause or force hidden beneath the surface of things. When a protagonist undergoes an epiphany, a startling realization spins him from ignorance to knowledge, from unawareness to a mind-blazing truth. With this flash of acuity, his life pivots, and the consequences make or break him.

Tragedies often climax on an epiphany of identity, a startling flash of self-recognition as the protagonist suddenly discovers the truth of who he really is. When Sophocles's Oedipus realizes that he is his wife's son and his father's murderer, he gouges out his eyes. Shakespeare's Othello drives a knife into his heart when he realizes that he was duped into murdering his innocent wife. In Anton Chekhov's *The Seagull*, Konstantin kills himself when he realizes Nina will never love him. In *The Empire Strikes Back*, when Luke Skywalker discovers that Darth Vader is his father, he attempts suicide.

In a classical comedy, a humble servant learns that he has an identical twin with an identifying mole. Their mother gave birth on a storm-tossed sea and they were swept apart. What's more, their mother is queen of a distant land, making them heirs to a fortune. Two thousand four hundred years of comedy writing later, Larry David, in an episode of *Curb Your Enthusiasm*, learns that he is not Jewish but was in fact adopted from a very Christian, very Scandinavian family in Minnesota. After visiting his birth family, Larry realizes he'd rather be a Jew.

Beyond discoveries of identity, epiphanies often expose a disquieting insight. In his last soliloquy, Macbeth laments that life has no more meaning than "a tale told by an idiot."

Four hundred years later, in Samuel Beckett's *Waiting for Godot*, Pozzo bemoans the brevity of life. He imagines a woman in labor straddling a pit, her baby's life lived in the time it takes to fall out of her womb and into a tomb. As he puts it, "They give birth astride a grave, the light gleams an instant, then it's night once more."

In *Nurse Jackie*, Jackie Peyton's epiphany forces her to admit that she turned to drugs because she couldn't cope with her firstborn's endless crying. Her addiction, therefore, is her own fault. This truth, however, fails to save her life because she hasn't the willpower to quit.

Epiphanies are all-or-nothing events and, for that reason, dangerous.

They may create a story's most magnificent, memorable moment...or its most embarrassingly overwritten moment.

Onstage or on-screen, an epiphany demands excellent writing before, during, and after the character's burst of insight and an excellent actor to pull it off. At the Act Three climax of *Casablanca*, for example, when Rick Blaine gazes into his future and says, "It seems that destiny has taken a hand," the audience enjoys a plunge into the ocean of subtext beneath his words.

Prose epiphanies, however, pose an even greater risk. A rush of illumination igniting a character's mind tests not only an author's gift for language but the reader's imagination and the character's credibility. That's why prose descriptions of meaning-packed, life-changing, all-at-once insights often turn purple.

Protagonist Variations

In most stories, the protagonist is a single human being—man, woman, child. This central role, however, can be filled in a variety of ways:

Co-protagonists

Rather than creating one multidimensional protagonist, you can achieve complexity by uniting two characters with sharply contrasting qualities into a duet of co-protagonists:

On the page, Rudyard Kipling's "The Man Who Would Be King" melds Daniel Dravot and Peachey Carnehan into a multifaceted team. Crime series such as Janet Evanovich and Lee Goldberg's Fox and O'Hare novels also employ co-protagonists.

On-screen, William Goldman joined the Sundance Kid with Butch Cassidy; Callie Khouri did the same for Louise and Thelma. Dick Wolf cast co-protagonists in his long-running series *Law and Order* as teams of police and prosecutors.

Onstage, modernist works such as Tom Stoppard's *Rosencrantz and Guildenstern Are Dead*, Beckett's *Waiting for Godot*, and Ionesco's *The Chairs* use dual protagonists but not to create complexity. Rather, for the opposite reason: to stress sameness. Each duet is dimensionless, nonrealistic, and virtually indistinguishable.

Group Protagonists

A collection of characters becomes a story's protagonist under two conditions: (1) despite superficial differences, at heart they all share the same desire; (2) as they struggle to reach their goals, they suffer and benefit mutually—what happens to one affects them all. If one individual has a success, they all share in it and move forward together. If one has a loss, they all fall back together.

Film examples: *Seven Samurai*, *The Dirty Dozen*, *Inglorious Basterds*.

How large can a group protagonist become? In *Battleship Potemkin*, Sergei Eisenstein cast thousands of sailors and citizens in a revolt against tyranny. In *October: Ten Days That Shook the World*, Russia's entire working-class population became Eisenstein's massive plural protagonist.

Multi-protagonists

Multiplot tellings have no central plot. Instead, they unite a number of story lines around a theme, and then either crosscut them (*Crash*) or string them end to end (*Wild Tales*). Each has its own protagonist.

Split Protagonists

In novels such as Robert Louis Stevenson's *The Strange Case of Dr. Jekyll and Mr. Hyde* and Chuck Palahniuk's *Fight Club*, two sides of a split personality struggle for control of a protagonist's moral self.

On-screen, Woody Allen's *Crimes and Misdemeanors* two crosscut stories mirror each other until their protagonists merge in the audience's mind as one weak-willed, immoral, self-deceived loser. Charlie Kaufman's *Adaptation* and every film that ever featured a werewolf do much the same.

Passive Protagonists

When a storyteller shifts to an inner battlefield and engages in psychological warfare over a protagonist's morality, mentality, or humanity, the character may seem passive to those around him. Because his unexpressed thoughts rarely convert to action, outwardly he floats through his days, a philosophical tourist with a paralyzed persona, while inwardly he wages a desperate but invisible struggle not to make the same mistake again and again, or to calm a mind flooded with too many choices, or to force a choice between the lesser of two evils.

Examples: In Anna Burn's *Milkman*, an unnamed protagonist reads novels while walking, doing her best to avoid life and a creepy stalker. In *About Schmidt*, Schmidt (Jack Nicholson) spends his retirement years writing letters to an orphan in Africa, filled with regrets about his life—past, present, and future.

Switching Protagonists

When a character misleads the reader/audience into believing that he's the story's protagonist, and then dies, exits or turns into an antagonist, the story jolts in a radically new direction.

For the first half of *The Killing Fields* Sydney Schanberg, an American journalist, plays the protagonist, but as he flees the Cambodian genocide, the story-torch passes to his cameraman, Dith Pran, who takes over the film and carries it to climax.

Psycho kills its protagonist halfway through the film, making her death all the more shocking and the villain far more frightening. The victim's sister and boyfriend then step in as co-protagonists.

Metaphorical Protagonists

Metaphors for humanity—cartoons (Bugs Bunny), animals (*Babe*), inanimate objects (*Wall-E*)—can become protagonists if, in the face of conflict, they make free will choices to pursue their desires.

First Circle Characters

The first circle contains major characters who help or hinder, focus or defocus, support or service the protagonist. A support role changes the course of events; a service role does not. In a classic crime story, for example, the cop who discovers a murder victim's body is a service character; the coroner who deduces a clue to the killer's identity is a support character; the detective who apprehends and punishes the killer is the protagonist.

A role, whether supporting or servicing, becomes major when multiple traits and dimensions round out his character, while at the same time, his unique actions and single-minded purpose invites readers and audiences to picture his life outside the enacted events. In other words, a major character has the potential for a story of his own.

These roles have many possible uses:

Subplot Protagonists

The protagonist of a subplot that intersects the central plot and affects its course of action is a major support character. The protagonist of a subplot that runs parallel to the central plot but does not affect its course is a major service character. In *The Godfather*, for example, Michael's ascension to godfather arcs the central plot. The Tessio betrayal subplot turns and supports this arc, while the love story subplot deepens and services his character.

The Focal Character

A cast's focal character is the role that draws the most interest from the reader/audience, and is, therefore, almost always the protagonist. In rare tellings, however, a character who adds exceptional energy or excitement to the story becomes the focus of attention and decenters the telling away from the protagonist. Antonio is the title character of Shakespeare's *The Merchant of Venice*, but Shylock steals the spotlight. Clarice Starling plays protagonist in *The Silence of the Lambs*, but Hannibal Lecter draws focus. Christine is the protagonist of Gaston Leroux's novel *The Phantom of the Opera*, but the focal character is the Phantom.

The Foil Character

In the eighteenth century, jewelers found that by backing a diamond with a thin sheet of reflective foil they could double a gem's intensity. Writers put this same principle to work when they use a foil role to enhance a protagonist.[1]

Foils service protagonists in numerous ways:

1. They illuminate the protagonist.

When a thing is compared to its opposite, understanding sharpens. A black chair sitting against a white wall seems all the more dark. To hone your protagonist's image, stand him next to a counterpointing foil.

Examples: Sancho Panza, Doctor Watson, and Arnold Rothstein are three chubby foils who comically contrast with their rail-thin protagonists: Don Quixote, Sherlock Holmes, and Nucky Thompson. The duo of Mr. Spock and Captain Kirk pit solemn seriousness against fun-loving daring. *Casablanca* juxtaposes Captain Renault's sexual adventures to Rick's romantic anguish; Victor Lazlo's anti-Fascist heroism to Rick's political indifference. Dual protagonists such as Thelma/Louise and Butch Cassidy / Sundance Kid act as each other's foil.

2. They see what the protagonist cannot.

The protagonist's struggle to reach his object of desire often blinds him as the spine of action sweeps him from one impulsive judgment to another. A calm foil may serve as the voice of reason.

Example: In the longform series *Ozark*, husband and wife Marty and Wendy Byrde (Jason Bateman and Laura Linney) take turns playing each other's foil. When one loses sight of their goal and acts impulsively, the other calms him or her down and refocuses the couple's spine of action.

3. They contradict the protagonist's morality.

A foil could define the protagonist by striking either a morally superior or an inferior counterpoint.

Examples: In *Mean Streets*, the criminally crazed Johnny Boy (Robert De Niro) is the childhood pal of the deeply religious Charlie (Harvey Keitel). In *Nurse Jackie*, the steady-handed Dr. Eleanor O'Hara (Eve Best) balances the wild gyrations of Jackie Peyton (Edie Falco). In *Platoon*, the good Sergeant Elias (Willem Dafoe) and the evil Sergeant Barnes (Tom Berenger) fight for the soul of Private Chris Taylor (Charlie Sheen). In *A Tale of Two Cities*, Charles Dickens creates two characters who look as alike as twins, but then polarizes them into the noble Charles Darney versus the corrupt Sydney Carton. Bury an immoral foil in the subconscious of a morally pure mind and he becomes *The Strange Case of Dr. Jekyll and Mr. Hyde*.

4. They guide us to the protagonist.

To create story-long suspense, an author may wrap his protagonist in mystery—no backstory, no friends, no confessions. This arouses intense curiosity about the character's unspoken thoughts and desires, his true feelings and plans. Having provoked questions about the inner life, the writer then withholds the answers to create tension. The reader/audience, with nowhere else to turn, looks to other characters, especially a foil, for clues and insights.

The foil may only partially understand the protagonist, or, for that matter, may completely misunderstand him, but in either case, every time the foil interacts with the protagonist the reader/audience learns a little something about the central character—what could be true, what is not true, what more they need to know.

A wise foil may funnel deep perspectives into the protagonist's hidden truths. If, for example, the central character's nature is more than mysterious, if he undergoes experiences of a unique intensity beyond even the most worldly-wise reader/audience, if the protagonist is a saint, genius, or madman like Captain Ahab, then the reader/audience may need an Ishmael to pilot them through the churning depths of obsession, or, more recently, a Dr. Melfi to make sense of the chaos raging inside Tony Soprano.

5. They interpret a protagonist's epiphany.

When a protagonist undergoes a sudden, massive epiphany, he may respond to it quietly, inwardly, secretly. The change this causes may never reveal itself overtly, but a foil who knows him well can read his enigmatic behaviors and interpret his flashes of insight. The foil then becomes a Jesse Pinkman to the protagonist's Walter White.

6. They interpret the protagonist's complexities.

Epiphanies aside, multidimensional characters often need more than one foil to guide the reader/audience to a full understanding of the protagonist's inner machinations.

Consider the longform series *Succession*. The clear-thinking Kendall Roy, plus his three scheming siblings Connor, Siobhan, and Roman, as well as Karolina, Frank, and other corporate survivors, all give us slivers of insight into the ruthless Logan Roy.

7. They ground the protagonist in his setting.

A complex protagonist often strikes us as an extraordinary human being—so extraordinary, in fact, that he may project archetypal overtones such as warrior, healer, trickster, goddess, magician, etc. The more a protagonist's qualities inflate toward the symbolic, the more he risks losing credibility in the eyes of the reader/audience. The protagonists of Shakespeare's tragedies, Hemingway's novels, and the DC Universe all take this high-speed risk.

The safety belt is a down-to-earth foil—a Horatio for Hamlet, an Anselmo for Robert Jordan, a Lois Lane for Clark Kent. Because foils seem typical of their society, they ground the protagonist in reality and yet at the same time make him seem unique. In fact, a story's entire cast can be seen as a massive foil that gives the protagonist weight and credibility. (More of this in Chapter 17.)

The POV Character

Point of view is normally funneled through the protagonist. But not always. Dr. Watson, a first-person narrator, is the POV character in Arthur Conan Doyle's Sherlock Holmes stories, but Holmes is both protagonist and focal character. Nick Carraway and Jay Gatsby strike the same relationships in F. Scott Fitzgerald's *The Great Gatsby*.

Major Support Roles

From the protagonist's point of view, major support characters either help him or hinder him. Some influence events to the positive, others to the negative. They further or block his efforts, bending him either toward or away from his object of desire. Chief among these are antagonistic characters who directly oppose the protagonist's struggle to rebalance life.

In action genres from High Adventure to Crime to Horror, we call these characters villains. They range from purely evil monsters to complex antiheroes. In the six character-driven genres (see Chapter 14), the protagonist often discovers that he is his own worst enemy.

Major Service Roles

A major service role seems to have a life of his own going on outside the reader's/audience's view. He doesn't turn the story's events and they don't change him. He has a fixed personality combined with a kind of freedom, so that regardless of the story's outcome, he is an end in himself who can't be otherwise. Any function he serves seems to happen as he passes through the story.

For example: In Charles Dickens's *Bleak House*, Miss Flite is a sweet, elderly, delusional woman obsessed with lawsuits. Her family was destroyed by a long-running case, and so she sits in court every day watching trials, some comic, others tragic. She says things people think crazy, but they turn out to have symbolic meaning. She owns a bevy of caged birds that she plans to set free on Judgment Day.

A character can fulfill any one or all of these major functions. However, if such creatures become overly interesting and out of proportion to their cast functions, they may mutiny, take over the telling and sink it.

In *The Fighter*, for example, the protagonist, Micky Ward (Mark Wahlberg), seems rather bland compared to Dicky Eklund (Christian Bale), who nearly steals the film.

Second Circle Characters

By limiting a character's dimensions to just one (sad/cheerful), or, even less, a single trait (always cheerful), and then reducing his appearance time, you can compress an entire human being inside a role from the middle circle. Nonetheless, all levels of conflict operate in all human beings. Therefore, no character, not even the lowliest bit part, should be imagined on only one plane. Which level you emphasize must fit your purpose. For reasons of exposition you may choose to make a coffee shop cook a gossip, but giving thought to his inner, private, and personal selves may enrich his banter with an amusing style.

Second Circle Support Roles

Middle-ground support characters help or hinder a story's course but do not have a personal magnetism to interest us beyond the scenes they are in. No one cares what Claudius and Laertes do when Hamlet's not around, or how Milo Minderbinder spends his day without John Yossarian in *Catch-22*, or what Ida Sessions feels when she's not on the phone to J. J. Gittes in *Chinatown*.

Second Circle Service Roles

The chief asset of a second circle service role is predictability of behavior. Archetypes (earth mother), types (the klutz), or stocks (gym trainer) ground the story's setting. Their single external trait may vary from scene to scene: A loudmouth, for example, is loud in different ways on a phone or in a restaurant, but he is always loud. If that changes, he's either not the same character or he's added a dimension.

Third Circle Characters

Minor characters move at the greatest distance from the protagonist, usually appearing only once in a telling and almost always playing a service role. On rare occasions a bit part may be given a moment of intensity (a terrified face in a Horror film), but generally they are kept dimensionless and anonymous (bus driver). Like a newscaster on a television playing in the background, minor roles may pour exposition into the telling, but like dead bodies on a battlefield, they're props that service the plot.

These nether reaches include the background masses, the social component of a story's setting. Like a crowd screaming in a stadium, they represent the density of people through which principal characters must move.

Narrators

Narrators provide readers and audiences with exposition about the story's physical and social settings, past lives of the cast, as well as the traits and qualities of observable behaviors in the characters. Narrators come in multiple varieties depending on person, medium, and reliability.

First, three possible persons:

1. A first-person narrator is a character who tells his story from the page, stage, or voice-over, speaking directly to the eavesdropping reader/audience.
2. A second-person narrator speaks as if he were the reader/audience personally experiencing the story's events. Instead of the pronouns "I"/"me" or "she"/"he"/"they," the author calls on the pronoun

"you," as in, "You fool, look what you've done now." "You" turns the reader into a protagonist, musing and straining within himself.

3. A third-person narrator is not a character, but rather the voice of knowledge and awareness an author adapts to convey exposition. This mind exists outside events, and therefore the reader/audience has no interest in either its well-being or its future.

These three storytellers may inhabit any of the three media. They may or may not know all relevant facts, may or may not be honest about them even if they do, and, therefore, from the reader's/audience's POV, they may or may not be 100 percent reliable. But in either case, their relative reliability must serve the author's purpose.

Reliable Narrators

Onstage: First-person narrators, such as Tom Wingfield in Tennessee Williams's *The Glass Menagerie*, tell us facts, although his emotional memories often cloud his recollections. Second-person narration calls the audience up onstage and invites them to participate and improvise. Third-person narrators, such as the Stage Manager in Thornton Wilder's *Our Town*, or the Narrator in Erwin Piscator's stage adaptation of *War and Peace*, are wise and reliable.

On the Page: First-person novels are often narrated by quiet, empathetic characters who observe adventurous, duplicitous characters: *The Great Gatsby*, *Brideshead Revisited*, and *All the King's Men* and their like. Full-length second-person narration is difficult to pull off (Jay McInerney's *Bright Lights, Big City* is a famous exception) and for that reason, rare. Trustworthy, all-knowing third-person narrators have told novels since their invention—Jonathan Franzen's *The Corrections* is a twenty-first-century example.

On-screen: The first-person narrators of *Annie Hall* and *Memento* tell the truth as they understand it. In a second-person experiment, the camera in *Lady of the Lake* becomes the protagonist (and with that the audience's eyes), and then stays locked in that subjective POV as it moves throughout the film. In *Y Tu Mama Tambien*, the third-person narrator is worldly and reliable.

The Unreliable Narrator

When one character lies to another and we see the deception for what it is, this insight enriches our experience. But if a narrator, such as Roger "Verbal" Kint (Kevin Spacey) in *The Usual Suspects*, deliberately deceives us, what purpose does unreliable exposition serve? Why would a writer mislead us about fictional facts? Two reasons: enhanced credibility and enhanced curiosity.

Enhanced Credibility

Dimensionless roles that symbolize pure ideas such as Wisdom, Innocence, Good, Evil, and the like only feel at home in fantasies and allegories. Flawless characters seem unreal; real people are scarred with imperfections. They misperceive the world around them and self-deceive the truth within themselves for at least two reasons: First, the natural human tendency to distort or misinterpret facts, to rationalize and excuse failures, to gain advantage with feints and lies. Second, in an insane mind, memory disconnects from reality itself, but even in the most rational mind, memory is notoriously unreliable. In realistic tellings, therefore, imperfect narrators reflect our human reality and gain a greater credibility.

But beyond their flaws, the foremost reason for unreliability in first-person narrators is that sooner or later they talk about themselves, and when they do, truth becomes difficult. As noted previously, whenever a line of dialogue begins with the pronoun "I," what follows is, to some degree, a lie. The mind finds unvarnished honesty about itself next to impossible; a self-protective shield softens the blow. As a result, all statements of self are self-serving, while at the same time ironically deepening the reader's/audience's belief in the character.

Greater Curiosity

When a first-person narrator lies, a character lies. For example, throughout Iain Banks's novel *The Wasp Factory*, Frank, the narrator, tells us that as an infant he was attacked by a vicious dog and castrated. At the novel's climax, however, Frank reveals that in fact his father fed him lies about the dog attack as well as experimental hormones ever since he was too little to remember. Now in his teens, Frank confesses that he is and always has been a girl. With that, the reader's curiosity leaps from surprise to shock.

When a third-person narrator lies, an author lies. Unreliability in a third-person narrator seems self-defeating. The very reason an author assumes a third-person voice is to build the reader's trust in fictional facts. So when third-person narrators distort exposition, the reader/audience either tosses the story aside in annoyance or grows ever more interested. Some authors simply tell us on page one that they are no more trustworthy than a character. In *Slaughterhouse-Five*, for example, Kurt Vonnegut delights in calling attention to his fallibility, making us wonder what's true, what's false, and if those terms even matter. For those who go along with these authors, curiosity about trustworthiness multiplies tension.

Faulty interpretations and biased beliefs are easily expressed in images and language. With just a slight warp in point of view, each mode becomes unreliable. For this reason, the two most subjective media for storytelling are the screen and the page.

On-screen

Unreliable first-person: Protagonists may become unreliable due to faulty memories (*How I Met Your Mother*), faulty knowledge (*Forrest Gump*), or outright deceit (*The Usual Suspects*). In the longform series *The Affair*, the co-protagonists see the same event from two very personal POVs. In *Rashomon*, four characters recall the same fateful event in four radically different ways. In *The Man Who Lies*, the same character tells his wartime story seven different ways, depending on who he's talking to and what he wants out of them.

Unreliable second-person: This is yet to be attempted on-screen but may await us in the future of virtual reality.

Unreliable third-person: A film's writer/director/editor can distort a story's past in various ways: a false flashback (*The Cabinet of Dr. Caligari*), a false reality (*A Beautiful Mind*), or a falsified history (*Inglorious Basterds*).

On the Page

Unreliable first-person: Authors often call on unreliability to express an unstable mind. For example, the unnamed narrator of Edgar Allan Poe's "The Tell-Tale Heart" and Chief Bromden in Ken Kesey's *One Flew over the*

Cuckoo's Nest. The same is true for protagonists burdened with ignorance or immaturity, such as Holden Caulfield in *The Catcher in the Rye*. When the narrator purposefully deceives the reader, unreliability is the MO, as in Agatha Christie's *The Murder of Roger Ackroyd*. In Caroline Kepnes's *You*, Joe, the first-person narrator, recounts his romance with Guinevere, the love of his life...until he murders her. In Iain Pears's *An Instance of the Fingerpost*, four characters, one of whom is insane, tell the same story from their biased points of view until the reader has no clear idea of what actually happened.

Unreliable second-person: In *A Prayer for the Dying* by Stewart O'Nan, the "you-as-protagonist" slowly goes mad.

Unreliable third-person: In *Home* by Toni Morrison, narration splits between the protagonist in the first person and the author as a seemingly omniscient third person. These alternating voices, however, often contradict one another. Because war and racial violence have poisoned the protagonist's memory, the facts fail him, but then the same becomes true for the narrator as she realizes that no one can know anything for certain.

Onstage

The theatre is storytelling's most objective medium. For twenty-five centuries, audiences have treated the stage as a viewing platform to display characters who do not see us so we can see them for who they are. This rigorously reliable third-person form demands imaginative writing and staging to orient a theatre audience to see things through an unreliable first-, second-, or third-person sensibility.

Unreliable first-person: In *Dancing at Lughnasa*, contradictions between the onstage narrator's memories of his childhood and the lives of his five older sisters make us realize that there are as many pasts as there are minds to remember it.

Unreliable second-person: In Florian Zeller's *The Father*, the stage itself becomes the mind of a man with dementia. The audience, as if living inside the protagonist's head, senses his desperate struggle to control reality. A character introduced as his daughter in one scene reappears in the next played by a different actor, suddenly becoming a stranger to him and us. Two seemingly sequential moments, we slowly realize, in fact happened ten years apart. As his confusion grows, so does ours, until finally, his inner chaos evokes a direct and personal experience of what it must be like when your mind falls apart.

Unreliable third-person: In Mark Haddon's novel *The Curious Incident of the Dog in the Night-Time*, Christopher, an autistic first-person narrator, tells a uniquely eccentric story. To translate his mind's distortions, the London stage used literal smoke, mirrors, and ear-pounding sound to express the terrifying unreliability of autism.

7

THE OUTER CHARACTER

Human beings, as social animals, need to manage the impressions they make on others. They do so by playing a great variety of roles. The evolutionary purpose of these recitals is to get along, get ahead, and get laid. Because their survival depended on stellar performances, our ingenious ancestors evolved consummate skills for imitation and expression. In short, humans are now, and always have been, actors.

This doesn't mean we're insincere. It's simply the commonsense realization that as we move from situation to situation, we subtly shift from self to self, depending on the relationship of the moment: priest/confessor, boss/employee, wife/husband, stranger/stranger. A human being can swing from acting like a child to acting like a lover to acting like a New Yorker, or all three at once.

So once you have circled the orbits of your cast galaxy, you will need to bring each character to life. In this chapter we explore the composite of vivid social and personal selves that make first and ongoing impressions on readers and audiences. This collection of outer-facing behaviors, mannerisms, and personality traits becomes the role's *Characterization*.

CHARACTERIZATION

To organize your creative work, divide complex characters into two aspects: characterization and true character.

The term *true character* names the crew of inner selves—core, agent, hidden—that live out of sight inside the mind and will be the subject of the next chapter.

Characterization names the composite of social and personal selves—the sum total of all observable and inferable traits. Discovery of the many traits expressed through these selves is hard, imaginative work. So try following your character around 24/7. As you do, you will come to know all her explicit traits, such as name, age, sexuality, her home and how she furnishes it, her occupation and the living it gives her. You will learn the grammar of her body language—gestures, facial expressions, tones of voice, moods, and vibes.

By listening carefully to what she says and closely observing how she treats people, you can also sense her implicit traits, such as her talents and intelligence, beliefs and attitudes, moods and hopes—all that she appears to be, all that the world sees.

THE THREE FUNCTIONS OF CHARACTERIZATION

Characterization supports your story with three primary functions: credibility, originality, intrigue.

Credibility

What's a writer's worst fear? That the reader or audience will find her work boring? Dislike her characters? Disagree with her ideas? Possibly. But the greatest dread, it seems to me, is disbelief.

When a reader or audience does not believe in the actions characters take, when they sour on the telling, thinking thoughts like, "I don't believe that kind of woman would do things like that," they toss the book aside or click the remote or head for an exit.

Credibility begins with characterization. Readers and audiences involve themselves when they sense an honest connection between the cast's mental, emotional, and physical traits and what they say, feel, and do. Honest characterizations induce readers and audiences to surrender to a telling, even the most fantastic, as if it were actual—Harry Potter and Luke Skywalker are two famous examples.

Originality

We do not go to a storyteller to learn what we already know. We go with a prayer: "Please let me gain insights into life I've never had before; let the characters be originals I've never met before."

Originality begins with specificity. The more generalized the characterization, the more imitative, predictable, and inflexible the role; but the more specific the characterization, the more original, surprising, and changeable the character.

Suppose you felt that your character, in general, would be fashion conscious. If you then followed that up with exhaustive research into the state of fashion today, plus firsthand observations of trends you see on the street, plus hours spend faux shopping in the hippest of shops, filling notebooks full of details, taking photos with your phone, then you could come away with a one-of-a-kind characterization, a look no one has ever quite seen before—a credible original.

Intrigue

A unique characterization captures our curiosity, making us want to know the true, inner character who lives behind the mask of outer traits.

Suppose we were shown a drunken, abusive, angry, out-of-work husband, sitting in a darkened living room in his underwear, swilling a can of beer, sweating away, running his grease-stained fingers through his beard, watching an NFL rerun. Would that image make us wonder, "But who is he really?" Doubtful. Clichés destroy intrigue.

A clichéd characterization raises a question that answers itself: Who is this character? Exactly who she seems to be. Like a block of cement, she's the same on the inside as the outside. To create creditable characters that spike the reader's/audience's curiosity and reward their intrigue, build a fascinating world and populate this setting with equally fascinating originals.

SETTING: WORLD BUILDING

Characterization begins in the genes with traits like gender and hair color, but once a character is born, an array of physical and social settings buffet and mold her outer selves. Time and space frame all such events, greatly influencing outer appearances and behaviors.

Time comes in two dimensions: location and duration. An author could locate a story in a contemporary setting, historical period, hypothetical future, or timeless fantasy. Within each period, the storyteller also sets the duration of the telling in relationship to the lives of her characters. Storytelling time and lifetime could be equal: *My Dinner with Andre* is a two-hour film about a two-hour dinner. Or the telling could span days, months, years, even a lifetime: Terrance Winter's longform series *Boardwalk Empire* and Jonathan Franzen's novel *The Corrections*.

Storied space is also two-dimensional: physical location plus level of conflict. A story could be found anywhere—a mountain peak, a farm, a space station, a certain street in a certain city, a certain building on that street, and a certain room in that building. Once set, the physical location houses a cast of characters, and so the writer must determine its level(s) of conflict: physical (woman against nature), social (woman against the law), personal (woman against her in-laws), inner (self against self), or any combination.

Patterns of behavior, usually routine, sometimes ritualized, begin at birth and develop through infancy. Daily needs generate activities such as eating and playing, greetings and goodbyes. Humdrum as these customs may be, they embed themselves in a role's characterization.[1]

MORAL IMAGINATION

An author with a strong moral imagination sees meaning in every aspect of a story's setting; nothing and no one is neutral—not cop, prop, or raindrop. This writer marshals a constellation of charged values so that everything in her story rings either positively, negatively, or with an ironic fusion of both. Nothing is without value. All things neutral are kept off-page, offstage, offscreen.

In the same sense that the writer is the character's first actor, she's also the story's first production designer, intent on making every element in a setting reveal, reflect, counterpoint, or change at least one character, perhaps the whole cast. When an automobile enters, a writer without moral imagination sees it as no more than a vehicle, but to a production designer it comes charged with a value. As a bright pink Maserati pulls up to an opera house, the writer's choices not only characterize its absurdly wealthy owner but the parking attendant who takes her key with a sarcastic smile.

A moral imagination also ranks values by importance from most to least. Life/Death is a possibility that shadows all stories, but a psychothriller may foreground it as its core value, while a Romantic Comedy backgrounds it as irrelevant. The core value of a War Story is Victory/Defeat, but Life/Death haunts every action. Without a moral imagination, a setting amounts to little more than furniture.[2]

CULTURAL RESTRAINTS

Time, place, and people not only restrain what a character can do but stipulate what she must not do. As a character enters a scene, webs of restraint curtail her relationship with every person and object: how to walk safely down a dark alley, how to respond to someone's touch, what to say in a courtroom. In principle, the more positive the relationships that surround a character's life, the more restricted, more civilized her behavior. The reverse is also true: When a character has nothing to lose, she's capable of anything.

PHYSICAL SETTINGS

Like all things in life, the world's physical and temporal forces—lethal diseases, the car that won't start, not enough time to get something done, too far to go to get what you need—cut both ways: Sunshine tans you or burns you. Farms and cities provide food and shelter, then pollute rivers with fertilizers and fill the air with noxious pollutants.

Environments shape the people who live in them. Scandinavia and the Mediterranean produce people with distinctively different dispositions. Why? The weather. Objects can prompt the conscious mind in one direction and the subconscious in another: Putting a briefcase on a church pew makes people feel competitive; Japan reduced suicides by installing streetlights that gave off a blue glow; the smell of a cleaning liquid makes coal miners want to tidy up.[3]

When creating a story's physical setting, ask questions in two directions: (1) How does my story's time, space, and objects affect the personalities of my characters? (2) How do the setting's antagonistic forces thwart my characters' desires?

SOCIAL SETTINGS

A character and her society constantly interact. Social settings provide various groups—nationalities, religions, neighborhoods, schools, professions—to which an individual aspires or rebels. Either way, they anchor her identity.

For example, the two cultures known as scientists and artists tend to inspire two very contrasted personalities. The same can be said about the citizens of small southern towns versus big northern cities, or kindergarten teachers versus porn stars. Yet within the shared traits of any community, the variety of personalities seems limitless.

The most striking feature of massive social systems is the price they extract for membership. After successfully climbing a corporate pyramid, an executive may become a superbly efficient employee but a woefully deficient human being. Make no mistake, however, institutions couldn't dehumanize without help. Many persons secretly welcome their loss of soul and live comfortably inside a shell of self-deception. Cracking it open would demand blunt force honesty, but they put that away long ago.[4]

As the story-driven documentaries of Frederick Wiseman (*High School, Basic Training, Hospital, Ballet*) make clear, people working inside institutions unknowingly dehumanize one another. For a lucky few, however, they sometimes rehumanize.

When creating a setting, think deeply about the effects of its total culture on your characters, then map out your cast's specific interactions (see Chapter Fifteen), and finally, whenever complex characters meet, refine them with subtle but distinctive social personae.

PERSONAL SETTINGS

The inescapable intimacies of families, friends, and lovers create conflicts like none other in life: Friends embrace in joy until they betray each other; a mother's love shines like the sun until she's disrespected; nothing explodes into optimism or crumples into pessimism faster than romance. For reasons no family member can understand, one sibling joins a religious cult while another edits *American Atheist* magazine. Their quarrels never end.

When setting up your story, give extended thought to the relationships of intimacy within your cast. This level of conflict offers the greatest opportunity for originality and nuance of characterization.

SETTING VERSUS CHARACTERIZATION

A character's collisions with her physical, social, and personal worlds etch her characterization, trait by trait. To trace the influence of these settings on your cast, consider these eight possible relationships:

1. The setting submerges a character in things such as home, car, job, and poker club, until her belongings become extensions of her core self. In Henry James's *The Portrait of a Lady*, Madame Merle explains the principle of character extension to her young admirer, Isabel Archer:

> *"When you've lived as long as I you'll see that every human being has his shell and that you must take the shell into account. By the shell I mean the whole envelope of circumstances. There's no such thing as an isolated man or woman; we're each of us made up of some cluster of appurtenances. What shall we call our 'self'? Where does it begin? Where does it end? It overflows into everything that belongs to us—and then it flows back again. I know a large part of myself is in the clothes I choose to wear. I've a great respect for things! One's self—for other people—is one's expression of one's self; and one's house, one's furniture, one's garments, the books one reads, the company one keeps—these things are all expressive."*

This principle guided writings such as Michael Ondaatje's *The English Patient* and Jonathan Franzen's *The Corrections*.

2. The setting releases forces of antagonism that block the characters' desires.

In *All Is Lost*, the Indian Ocean overwhelms a lone sailor; in *Three Billboards Outside Ebbing, Missouri*, injustice drives the mother of a murdered daughter to murder; in *Girls Trip*, friends, lovers, and ex-lovers sabotage a bachelorette weekend.

When unexpected reactions suddenly open gaps between what a character thinks will happen and what actually does, these fractures on the surface of life send quakes downward to disrupt the subconscious. Then, as if from the floor of a volcano, unwanted desires surge upward into improvised, usually unwanted, and often regretted behavior. This movement radiating down from the setting to the deepest self gives a character depth; the energy rebounding up from the depths of self to the setting gives a story power.

3. The setting and its cast form one grand metaphor for reality. Like pieces of a puzzle, setting and cast fit together; like mirror opposites, they define each other. The characters give meaning to their setting; the setting reflects back on its characters; and together they stand for life.

In Lewis Carroll's *Alice's Adventures in Wonderland*, Wonderland is ruled by magic, not physics, and its events obey lunacy, not logic. As a result, its cast members, including Alice, reflect their setting by undergoing nonsensical transformations—all working together to create a multidimensional metaphor for the real world, real people, and human absurdity.

This pattern of a setting mirroring its cast and a cast mirroring its society is clearly seen in works such as *Succession* and *Parasite*. Each of these tellings merges Domestic Drama with the Thriller Genre so that the characters, their families, and their society mutually infect each other. The stories in turn reflect the politics of the real world in which corruption acts as the secret cement that holds society together.[5]

4. The setting floods a character's mind and sends an onrush of objects, people, and memories streaming through her thoughts: Toni Morrison's *Beloved* and David Means's short story "The Knocking."

5. The setting recedes into the background as the foreground overflows with characters. In Larry David's *Curb Your Enthusiasm* and Matthew Weiner's *Mad Men*, homes, offices, and restaurants serve as picture frames for character portraits.

6. The setting leads an existence so indifferent, so separate from its characters that they seem isolated on an island: Tom Stoppard's *Rosencrantz and Guildenstern Are Dead* and Samuel Beckett's *Waiting for Godot*.

7. The setting's objects seem to have a will of their own: Edgar Allan Poe's "The Fall of the House of Usher" and Brian Evenson's "A Collapse of Horses."

8. The setting's objects turn into characters. In Lewis Carroll's *Alice Through the Looking Glass*, King, Queen, and Knight, three chess pieces,

join Humpty Dumpty, an anthropomorphic egg, to fill out the cast. *Guardians of the Galaxy* features Groot, a humanoid tree, and Rocket, a genetically engineered raccoon.[6]

CHARACTERIZATION CHANGE

When your characters confront physical, social, and personal settings, they put on various outer selves. But none of these encounters are static, and all can dramatically and believably cause changes in a role's characterization. I can think of four commonplace ways:

1. Rebellion: A character may change her setting in hope of sending her personality in the direction she wants it to go. Rural artists head for the big city; scholars drop out of school and enlist in the military.
2. Travel: Adventures abroad encourage a hybrid global identity. Youth culture is one example. Jeans and tennis shoes invented in the USA and made in Asia are the uniform worn by young people everywhere on the seven continents.
3. Time Travel: A character can hide in a pocket of time. Nostalgics live in the past; rat racers live in the future; hedonists live in a perverse present.[7]
4. The internet: Borderless travel to electronic geographies inhabited by citizens with placeless addresses can radically alter an identity. Online culture is instantaneous, anonymous, depthless, and yet real because within it, actual things happen to actual people, changing them for better or worse.

EXPLICIT TRAITS

Once you apply your broad strokes, you need to sharpen the explicit traits that express your characters as individuals. No one is simply "born that way." All complex characterizations display both genetically given and actively acquired traits. Genetic traits (e.g., vocal timbre) tend to last, while acquired traits (e.g., vocabulary) evolve. To create any one trait, hundreds of genes must interact, while at the same time they absorb random impacts from countless external forces. When you work your imagination through both sources, traits coalesce into unique, fascinating characterizations.[8]

Every observable trait sits on a spectrum that ranges from positive to negative. First are those traits acted out in public—such as sophisticated/ unsophisticated, social/antisocial, and charismatic/boring—that define a character's relationships to acquaintances and strangers. Then come behaviors acted out in private—such as generous/selfish, encouraging/ fault-finding, and concerned/unconcerned—that mark her personal relationships with family, lovers, and friends.

How many traits or how few? In the visual arts, if an empty canvas is 1 and a completely filled canvas is 2, the optimal density that the eye enjoys is 1.3, or three-tenths full. The same, I believe, applies to character. Leave seven-tenths of a protagonist unknown and mysterious. Based on the three-tenths you express, the reader/audience will fill in the rest as needed from their own imagination. For if a writer were to dramatize every possible trait a character might display, the telling would take forever, the role would become incomprehensible, and the reader/audience would be overwhelmed. On the other hand, one lone trait—a foreign accent, for example—shrinks a character to a bit part.

Only the writer can discover the ideal number of traits for any particular character. A trait's necessity depends on how much is changed by its removal. If you want to cut or add a trait, ask, "What, if anything, is lost or gained?"

What follows is a short list of topics that generate traits of characterization. Your particular story will add or subtract from them.

NAMES AND NICKNAMES

Like the roles they identify, names express more meaning in fiction than real life. The deliberate plainness of "John" and "Mary," for instance, gives a character a particular quality of ordinariness that someone actually named "Mary" or "John" would not have.

But be careful. Unless you're hoping for laughs, avoid blatantly symbolic names, such as branding a corporate executive "Mr. Biggman." On the other hand, in *Death of a Salesman*, Arthur Miller called his impoverished salesman Willy Loman, a name that, for some reason, never raises an eyebrow.

Allegorical genres, such as Fantasy and Horror, create boldly symbolic settings and add fun by giving their characters emblematic names. For example, in C. S. Lewis's religious allegory *The Lion, the Witch, and the Wardrobe*, the founder of a new kingdom is named Peter, echoing St. Peter, founder of the Christian church; the betrayer of the story's Christ figure is a witch named Jadis, as in Judas; an autocratic housekeeper is called Mrs. Macready, as in the imperative "Get ready!"

NAKED AND CLOTHED

Strip your character naked and run a checklist of biographical items: age and eye appeal, height and weight, texture of muscle and fat, head and body hair, shade and grain of skin, posture and walk. Use your imagination to take her shopping and see what she would like to wear, then look in her closet and find out what she actually owns.

GENDER AND SEX LIFE

What does your character find irresistibly erotic? What is her gender? What, if anything, does she do about it?

VOCAL TONE AND LANGUAGE

Now close your eyes and listen. Like music, a character's voice touches unconscious feelings in readers and audiences. Give each of your characters a speech style with a unique vocabulary, sentence structure, pitch, diction, and imagery.[9] The total effect becomes a concert of form and content—not only what she has to say, but how she says it.

FACIAL EXPRESSIONS AND GESTURES

Audiences read the flitting expressions on a character's face at one-twenty-fifth of a second. So study what's in your character's eyes, and then pull back to witness her mannerisms, ticks, and energy.

Gestures create a language of their own in three varieties: (1) hand waves, head tilts, and shoulder shrugs that enrich speech; (2) symbolic gestures like an erect middle finger; (3) imitative gestures like the thumb dance that means "Text me."

PROFESSION AND RECREATION

People often take their identity from what they do for a living. Some take a second identity from what they do for play: golfer, hunter, body builder, and the like. Determine what your character does in both cases and then how much it means to who she is.

HOME AND TRANSPORTATION

Honore de Balzac said, "Show me what a man owns and I'll tell you who he is." The extended self puts its arms around all it owns. For most characters, their two biggest extra-identities are their house and car. Picture them both, then look inside.

KNOWLEDGE AND IGNORANCE

What does my character know and not know? The amount and quality of her formal education set the ground for this question, but beyond that, life lessons passed and flunked will also matter.

RELIGION AND BELIEFS

A character's core beliefs, ranging from whether or not God exists to whether or not people can be trusted, determine her choices in the face of conflict. So start a conversation about values. Ask your character if human beings are good or evil, listen to her answer, and keep her talking.

CONVERSATION

If you spend enough time with your character, patterns of talk will recur—money, politics, death, her husband, her children, her health, the latest tech, or ancient history. What she talks about is what she thinks about.

MANNERS

Edmund Burke believed that politeness and manners give birth to all other virtues and are ultimately more important than laws. To put it in twenty-first-century terms, Burke knew that the quality of respect human beings show one another sets the tone for every relationship inside a civilization. How does your character treat people?[10]

IMPLICIT TRAITS

All characters begin in mystery. Their outer traits offer clues to possibilities that lie beneath. As scenes unfold, the reader/audience treats the outer traits of each role as clues to their inner traits. So these must be thoroughly explored and mined as well. Here are some ways to think about personalities, intelligence, attitudes, emotions, and more.

VARIETIES OF PERSONALITY

Personalities come in a seemingly infinite array. In 319 BC, Theophrastus, a student of Aristotle, tried to catalogue every ill-behaved character-type he could imagine from "Flatterer" to "Slanderer" but stopped at just thirty.[11] In recent centuries, sharp-eyed humorists, such as Mark Twain, have noted modern versions of the pain in the neck, and some listed noble types as well, but still, no one sees an end.

To make sense of this anarchy, psychologists have clustered the universe of personalities inside five grand galaxies. As outlined below, each presents a spectrum that runs from positive to negative. The personality of any character you create should fit somewhere inside each of these binaries of behavior.

1. Openness/Closedness

Openness reflects independence, curiosity, love of the arts, and all things new. A highly open character enjoys euphoric experiences such as skydiving and gambling but may seem unpredictable or unfocused. Conversely, closedness suggests pragmaticism, perseverance, and, occasionally, dogmatic single-mindedness.

2. Conscientiousness/Capriciousness

Conscientiousness leads to a sense of honor, self-discipline, and planned rather than impulsive behavior. Extreme conscientiousness is often perceived as stubbornness and obsession. Capriciousness may be spontaneous, but it can also seem unreliable and sloppy.

3. Extraversion/Introversion

The extravert leans toward sociability, talkativeness, and assertiveness, often becoming attention-seeking and overbearing. The introvert may be a shy, reflective personality and yet perceived as aloof or self-absorbed.

4. Agreeableness/Argumentativeness

Agreeableness tends to reflect compassion and generosity. All-smiles agreeableness is often seen as naïve or foolish. Argumentativeness can make one antagonistic, competitive, suspicious, and untrustworthy.

5. Rationality/Neuroticism

Rationality encourages a calm, constant personality which, when pushed to its limits, may turn coldhearted and indifferent. Neuroticism, on the other hand, experiences negative emotions such as anger and anxiety, sadness and fear quickly and extremely. Fragile and insecure, a neurotic hungers for stability.[12]

These five spectra, mixed and merged, create endless possibilities. But beyond these types, I think the reason personalities are so various is simple. Coincidence. Every human being is a combination of determinism and chance. The trillions of daily collisions between human genomes and countless aspects of their environments are so random, so unpredictable, so riddled with luck, good and bad, that they generate an infinite variety of selves.

What's more, personalities bend and flex depending on the nature of relationships such as boss-employee, parent-child, lover-friend. This pattern holds, not only for her voice but her gestures, facial expression, posture, word choices, temperament, and the like. In other words, her personality sets certain limits, but as she engages in her social and personal relationships, she shifts expression from one quality to the next.

VARIETIES OF INTELLIGENCE

Have you given your character a mind fit to do what you want her to do? If you want her to do dumb things, is she convincingly dumb in all ways? Dumb dialogue? Dumb haircut? Or the reverse—smart to do smart? Above all, is she credible?

Give thought to more than your character's IQ, but to her EQ and various CIs as well. IQ measures analytical thinking, spatial recognition, and problem solving. EQ measures emotional intelligence—the ability to perceive a subtle variety of feelings and emotions in yourself and others. CIs measure creative intelligence (the power of imagination), intellectual curiosity (the drive to know), and cultural intelligence (the ability to thrive in foreign settings).

Starting with your character's particular mix of intelligences, what are her habits of thought? Every human being, for example, develops a personal strategy for relationships. If her method has worked in the past, it doesn't easily bend when circumstances demand change. How flexible is your character's mind?

ATTITUDES, BELIEFS, VALUES

What are your character's attitudes? Her likes and dislikes? Loves and hates? Fears and dreads? Is she optimistic? Pessimistic?

To get answers, interrogate your character. What she thinks about herself shapes her beliefs, so ask the key psychological question first: "Who are you?" Does her answer describe her inner nature or name her profession? How much of an identity has she carved out for herself and how much is wrapped up in her career?

Ask big questions such as "What do you wish to achieve in the future? What must you do for yourself? For others? What must you never do to yourself? To others? How do you judge the essential nature of mankind? Good? Evil? Some of both?"

EMOTION, MOOD, TEMPERAMENT

Emotion is the side effect of change. As the dominant value in a character's life changes charge from positive (e.g., wealth) to negative (e.g., poverty), the character suffers a negative emotion; as the value charge moves from negative (e.g., pain) to positive (e.g., pleasure), the character's mood changes to delight.[13] These experiences, however, are relative to what the character sees as meaningful in her life—what's negative, what's positive.

If you were to put your character in a romantic relationship, and then have her lover walk out on her, how would change in the key values of Love/Hate, Happiness/Sadness, and Companionship/Loneliness change her mood? It may not be what you expect.

Mood is a character trait that tends to draw the same reaction from different experiences. Sober-minded people, for example, often find fun-loving hobbies, such as folk dancing and drone flying, boring and annoying.

Children have temperaments; adults have personalities. Temperament is the by-product of a character's brain chemistry, whereas personality is the by-product of socialization. As a child interacts with her world, her temperament evolves from juvenile to adolescent to adult. But no matter how mature she may become, her childhood temperament will follow like her shadow. Is she overall cheery or grouchy? Focused or daydreamy? Thrill-seeking or reclusive? Her fifth-grade teacher could tell you.

One spectrum of temperament, for example, runs from authoritarianism to antiauthoritarianism. Does your character back in-groups or defend out-groups? Authoritarians favor militarism and religious fundamentalism; antiauthoritarians reject both. Authoritarians look on artists with suspicion; artists, especially comic artists, ridicule authority. Authoritarians champion family unity and the self-discipline of being on time for a job they don't like very much and then putting in eight productive hours without attitude; antiauthoritarians often flit from job to job, dragging their children with them, forever in search of personal fulfillment.

MIRROR, WORLD, AUTHOR

The person a character sees in her makeup mirror today depends in great part on her past. Her memories, however, tend to be interpretations of what happened rather than actual events. The moment an event hits a character's life, her mind begins to reshape its details, cut much of it, reorder some of it, and often invent things that never happened. From her reconstruction, she construes the meaning of the event and how it affects who she is.

Others who witnessed the event will have a second, rather different, interpretation; you, as author, know the facts and have a third point of view; the reader/audience adds a fourth.

As you write, alternate from all points of view, until every trait, explicit and implicit, serves one purpose: characterization.

EXPRESSING CHARACTERIZATION

A characterization can be expressed by what it is, what it is not, and what it is like. These three general categories offer the writer at least nine distinctive techniques:

1. Simile: an analogy that compares a characterization to other people or things. James Thurber, for example, said his boss at the *New Yorker* "looked like a dishonest Abe Lincoln."
2. Metaphor: a direct link that connects a characterization to other people or things. Like the above, you may draw on figures from history, mythology, literature, or pop culture: "She's the Tony Soprano of self-control."

3. Correlations: characterization as an extension of personal habits or possessions. "She found her hair color in the same place she found her courage . . . a bottle."

4. Contrasts: Differences compare generally: "She's unlike the typical college grad."

5. Oppositions: Contradictions compare more sharply: "She's an anti-intellectual PhD."

6. Telling: Sometimes readers may need telling language to picture a characterization: "She stood six feet, two inches tall," but onstage or on-screen, the audience sees the actor and instinctively judges her height.

7. Showing: actions for the eye: "At six-two, she had to duck into my car," or for the ear: "When she got in my car, I heard Crack! as her skull smacked the door frame, followed by 'God damn it!'" Both activate the imagination.

8. Self-assessments: What the character says about herself may or may not be true, given the gift people have for self-deception, but that she says it and to whom can be a clue to characterization. "I'm a people person."

9. Other-assessments: What one person says about another may or may not be true, given the axes people have to grind, but that it is said and by whom can be an important clue to characterization. "She says she's a people person, but . . ."

In "The Short Happy Life of Francis Macomber," Hemingway introduces Margot Macomber with an inventory of her traits, then seals her true character with a past choice:

> *She was an extremely handsome and well-kept woman of the beauty and social position which had, five years before, commanded five thousand dollars as the price of endorsing, with photographs, a beauty product which she had never used.*

The phrases "woman of the beauty" and "with photographs" flash the image of a face you might glimpse while paging a fashion magazine (explicit trait), while "well-kept" and "social position" give her an aura of privilege (implicit trait). That she took money to endorse a product she never used suggests an elastic morality (true character) and the dark events to come.

YES, BUT WHO IS SHE, REALLY?

The ancient adage "Nothing is what it seems" applies directly and deeply to character creation. Explicit and implicit traits form surfaces, and these surfaces hide a truth. Characterization, therefore, expresses only who a character appears to be and not, in fact, who she is.

When readers or audiences find a characterization credible and intriguing, their thoughts run something like this: "Interesting, but who is she really? Is she honest or dishonest? Loving or cruel? Strong or weak? Generous or selfish? Good or evil? What is her essential, true character?" The next chapter looks at the inner aspects of true character that live out of sight and inside the mind.

8

THE INNER CHARACTER

A character's public and personal personae combine to form his characterization, the outer facade of who he seems to be. His private and hidden selves generate his true character, the inner person he is in fact. When we first encounter a character, we instinctively peer past the surface of characterization into his depths, seeking an answer to the question we always ask whenever we meet someone new: Who this person... really? As the character takes action in the face of conflict, answers arrive.

What a character chooses to do in his lightest moments expresses little because they cost him little, but at his darkest, when he's up against powerful, negative forces, when risks are greatest, his actions reveal the truth. Who is he? Honest or a liar? Loving or cruel? Generous or selfish? Strong or weak? Compulsive or cool? Good or evil? Will he help or hinder? Will he comfort or punish? Will he give his life or take a life? What is his true character?

The character, of course, never asks these questions of himself. He may speculate about what other people think of him; he may wonder about what goes on in his subconscious; but only his author knows all. He created him. He knows his social and personal personae, plus every tactic of self-deception the character uses to hide from what he can't face in himself.

To answer the question "Who is he?" the writer merges his character's inner world of conscious thought with his hidden subconscious drives. Eventually, after much trial, error and improvisation, the two selves fuse into an irreducible true character.

Let's look at the motivational forces that drive these complex characters:

MOTIVATION: PUTTING CHARACTER INTO ACTION

Why do people do the things they do?
—Every psychologist's dying thought

Motivation is the least understood term in the writer's vocabulary and a conundrum for psychologists as well. When researchers ask their subjects why they do what they do, back come rationalizations, not insights. The whys of character action run much deeper than alibis, so let's first trace their sources.

Do the forces that drive human beings press from behind in the past or pull from ahead in the future?[1] In my view, motives and desires form two very different energies. Motivations plant their footings in a character's past and push from behind, while desires anchor the future and entice a character toward what's yet to come.[2]

Scientific theories about what pushes from the past divide into two groups: drives rooted in genes versus pressures wrought by social forces.

INSIDE-OUT MOTIVATIONS

Every human being is born with a collection of drives for survival, love, meaning, and more. These hungers are subconscious and unfocused. Like winds billowing a ship's sails, they push from behind and urge a character forward. A motivation, therefore, is an unsated appetite.

When there's nothing to eat, man does indeed live by bread alone. But once fed, his higher internal motivations emerge, and when these are satisfied, newer, still higher drives arise, and so on in a never-ending hunger for something greater. A human being is a perpetually wanting animal.

Below are a dozen inner motivations in human nature, ranked from primal to elevated. Review this checklist to see if, when, and how they drive your character.

1. Immortality

Death, according to Ernest Becker, is life's most powerful motivator.[3] Knowing we must die inspires the wish to leave behind something of value to symbolize, like a gravestone, that we were here. Indeed, the dread of death motivates humanity to build monuments to itself: cities and their skyscrapers, religions and their sanctuaries, universities and their libraries, and, most immortally, works of art. The most lasting expression of our Ice Age ancestors is the paintings they left on the walls of the caves. Ever since the first burial rites over one hundred thousand years ago, everything human beings have put on this earth is simply one vast immortality project.

2. Survival

The imperative to survive compels all living things toward what they perceive as positive. This is why mousetraps work. The human sense of what's positive, however, hinges on complex subjectivities. If a human being views an action as necessary for survival but at the same time immoral, he will, after some hesitation, ultimately act to survive. Moral/ Immoral, Good/Evil, Right/Wrong, and Survival/Extinction are four very different sets of values. The first three pairs express the ideal; the last reflects the real. From a character's point of view, any action that preserves his genes—in himself, his family, his tribe—is positive. This is why wars work.

3. Balance

A tiny scale in the brain weighs the positive versus negative charges around it, seeking balance. Radical imbalance threatens survival and takes sanity for a ride, so the mind naturally craves a sovereignty over its existence. When, for example, a crime tilts Justice/Injustice to the negative, society demands revenge as a positive charge that restores balance. When the three brothers in *Ray Donovan* murder the priest who molested them, all breathe a sigh of relief. Justice done, their lives finally rest in balance.

4. Pleasure

The craving for pleasure can be irresistible, even if it causes pain in the future. Victims of abuse, haunted by cruel memories, drown their nightmares in fathoms of opiate-induced amnesia, knowing full well that pleasure is temporary and even greater pain lies ahead.

5. Sex

At the turn of the twentieth century, many psychologists based their theories of human behavior on a single cause. The most famous was Sigmund Freud's contention that sexual instincts drive all of life's objectives.

6. Power

Alfred Adler, originator of the "inferiority complex," said that desire for power focuses all strivings. No matter where people perch on the social pyramid, they constantly survey those above and below, trying to measure their relative power.

7. Empathy

The hunger to belong creates tribes. With belonging comes the feeling that if one member suffers, all others ache in empathetic harmony, and somehow that makes people feel better.[4]

8. More

Enough is never enough. Avarice progresses in three steps:

A. Greed: the craving for more. Human beings are insatiable and eternally disappointed. When a character wants more than he can reasonably expect, he lives in a state of emptiness. "I pay more and more for greater and greater dissatisfactions," complained Antonia Wolff to Carl Jung in Morris West's novel *The World Is Made of Glass*.

B. Envy: the tortured feeling that someone has something you don't. When a desired thing seems forever out of reach, the urge to gain the thing reverses into an urge to destroy it. If destructiveness fails, the envious character wallows in self-pity.

In Shakespeare's *The Tragedy of Othello*, Iago envies Othello's prowess and prestige, so he destroys him; in Herman Melville's *Billy Budd*, Claggart envies Billy's beauty and goodness, so he destroys him.

C. Jealousy: Envy escalates into jealousy when a rival enters. Jealousy reaches fever pitch when it fears that a beloved prefers a rival.

In *Amadeus*, Salieri seethes with envy of Mozart's talent. He pleads with God, "Why Mozart? Why not me?" In a rage, he rips a crucifix off the wall and burns it in the fireplace. Risking damnation, greedy for esteem, riven by jealousy, and desperate for the adoration of Vienna's music patrons, Salieri destroys his young rival, Mozart.

9. Interest

The difference between "want to" and "have to" is all the difference in the world. That's why a repetitious job is a shit job, no matter the paycheck, and its only cure is curiosity. The mind prefers doing things for their own sake. It likes tasks that demand skill, jobs done right, problems that need solutions simply because they're problems. This is why the creative process satisfies more than the finished work. Means is its end.

10. Meaning

Victor Frankl believed that a meaningless life is a life of vertigo, dizzily out of control.[5] When people get what they thought they wanted—money, fame, a C-suite job—they often fall into depression. Achievement ends the struggle that gave their lives purpose. The obvious solution would be to search for a new, even deeper purpose, but for many people, one life purpose per lifetime is all they'll ever know.

11. Fulfillment

A self-knowing mind senses its untapped humanity, its mental and emotional potential. The thoughtful character longs to plumb those depths and fulfill his inner promise.

12. Transcendence

Carl Jung believed that the ultimate motivation is a subconscious longing for Faustian supremacy, for godlike knowledge beyond the mind's reach—a metaphysical perfection.

These internal drives, in various combinations, often unawares and beyond control, push us toward the future. Like prehistoric man, we are still kind to friends and fierce to enemies. Progress gives us hospitals instead of magicians, nuclear missiles instead of bows and arrows. Science has made us more efficient at either helping people or killing them, but motivation never changes.[6]

OUTSIDE-IN MOTIVATIONS

Now let's take the reverse point of view and look at motivation from the outside in.

A storyteller studies his setting's social institutions—economic, political, religious—to measure their impact on his cast. Although cultural systems influence trends (consider the vast effect of social media), if a writer imposes a theory of mass motivation on a specific character, he risks mistaking conditions for causes. Poverty and wealth, for example, are conditions, not causes. The physical and psychological pains caused by poverty may influence a character to become a spiritual leader to relieve suffering, or they may influence a violent criminal to add to it. Or he may simply grit his teeth and persevere. Neither poverty nor wealth cause crime directly. Felons inhabit both extremes in more or less equal percentages.

So for an external social force (e.g., a TV commercial) to motivate a character to act, it must first strike the character's senses (he sees an ad), and then work its way through his subconscious motivators (arousing an appetite) before he finally chooses an action (buying something). Massive social forces certainly influence a cast, but they must work their way through each unique personality, and who knows what will come out the other side?

Because a character is educated doesn't mean he's sophisticated; because he's ignorant doesn't mean he's crude; because he's a servant doesn't mean he's servile. The same painful events that destroy one character may inspire another, while a third sleeps it off.[7] When a specific character acts in a specific scene, the effects of the surrounding culture become one of a kind and unpredictable.

THE OBJECT OF DESIRE

A classically told story opens with its protagonist's life in overall balance, his ups and downs more or less routine. But then something happens: An inciting incident caused either by random chance or someone's decision throws the protagonist's life radically out of balance.

An inciting incident could pivot a protagonist's life sharply to the positive (Romeo falls for Juliet) or darkly to the negative (Hamlet discovers his father's murder). In either case, when life goes out of kilter, a subconscious desire for a stable life stirs into consciousness. This drive for equilibrium becomes a character's super-objective.

Sensing that life has swung out of control, the protagonist imagines a solution in the form of a life change that's expressed either situationally (committed love) or physically (dead villain). That which would bring about a positive change we call the object of desire. The protagonist feels that if he could secure this, his life would swing back on an even keel. Now that he knows what he wants, he's able to act. His super-objective to restore life's balance and his pursuit of his object of desire points him toward his story's final crisis and climax.

In every story, the protagonist's super-objective directs his action toward a unique object of desire. The Action Genre, for example, often aims at something you could hold in your hands. In *Jaws*, a dead shark. The Education Plot's object of desire is usually something you could hold in your mind. In Ralph Ellison's novel *Invisible Man*, the protagonist searches for an identity, an answer to the question "Who am I?"

Therefore, a motivation (e.g., the lust for power) is an unfocused subconscious latency until an inciting incident spurs it to life and focuses it on a desire. By causing the need for a balanced future, the inciting incident puts motivation into action and forms the object of desire that pulls the protagonist through his story-long trek.

Examples:

In tragic plots, such as *The Tragedy of Romeo and Juliet*, Romeo's aroused libido (motivation #5) fixates on a stimulus (the exquisite Juliet) that inspires action (climbing a balcony) in pursuit of the protagonist's ultimate object of desire (Juliet-as-wife).

In Action Plots, such as *Vikings*, a young warrior tastes victory for the first time and this inciting incident unites motivations #7 and #8, arousing his appetite to rule. The throne, his glittering object of desire, draws him toward the future.

In Degeneration Plots, such as *A Confederacy of Dunces* by John Kennedy Toole, *The Tin Drum* by Gunter Grass, *Perfume* by Patrick Suskind, and *The Beauty Queen of Leenane* by Martin McDonagh, protagonists suffer psychic traumas that ignite subconscious motivations #1, #2, and #3. Their objects of desire call for bizarre, even murderous, deeds until they end either suicidal or insane, or both.

TRUE CHARACTER THROUGH CHOICES

How does a writer express a character's inner nature?

Not by characterization. In fact, the more fascinating a character's outer behavior, the more the reader/audience wants to discover his true inner counterpoints: Jack seems tough, but where's his soft spot?

Not by what others say about him. What one character believes about another may or may not be true, but what's said and by whom may set up future revelations.

Not by what a character says about himself. Audiences and readers listen to a character's confessions or braggings with high skepticism. They know that people are as self-deceived as self-aware.

Instead, they look for events to build pressure and expose true character in the only way they trust: choices. A human being is the choices he makes over a lifetime.

From amoebas to apes, all earthly critters obey nature's First Law: Choose Life. Nature compels every living thing to preserve its genes by acting toward the positive as it sees the positive. What is a violent death to a gazelle is lunch to a lion.

Nature's bias of life over death channels all human choice toward the positive (anything that enhances life) and away from the negative (anything that hints of death). As Socrates taught, no one willingly does what he believes to be wrong; instead, everyone acts toward a perceived positive. In such matters, subjectivity is all. When survival demands it, the mind simply redefines immorality into virtue.[8]

If the reader/audience understands a character's point of view and sees him confront a simple positive/negative choice (happiness/misery, right/wrong), they know in advance (probably before the character himself knows) how he will choose. He will reject the negative and choose what he perceives is the positive. The core self always does. It's the First Law. Therefore, clear choices between negative and positive charges of the same thing (poverty versus wealth, ignorance versus wisdom, ugliness versus beauty) are trivial.

TRUE CHARACTER THROUGH DILEMMA

The only dramatically compelling and character-revealing decision is a choice between two things of more or less equal value. These dilemmas come in two varieties: positive and negative.

A positive dilemma confronts a character with two equally desirable but irreconcilable possibilities. He wants both but circumstances force him to choose only one. For example, in the classic dilemma of Romantic Comedy, a woman finds herself caught between a man who is loving, devoted, and generous but boring versus another who is passionate, brilliant, and fascinating but certain to break her heart.

A negative dilemma confronts a character with two equally undesirable possibilities. He wants neither, but circumstances force him to choose one of two evils. For example, the classic marriage drama: If a woman doesn't marry the man her family favors, they will disown her, but if she does marry her family's pick, she will suffer a lifetime of boredom.

Clear choices are easily made and without jeopardy, but dilemma puts a character under pressure and at risk. A clear choice reveals little or nothing the reader/audience doesn't already know; a decision in dilemma sends alternative choices running through a character's imagination. As he struggles to make his choice, the push and pull of possibilities propels the reader's/audience's curiosity toward the story's climax: What will he finally do?

Either way he chooses, his action under pressure will reveal his true character.

Three examples: In *No Country for Old Men*, the Coen brothers' film adaptation of Cormac McCarthy's novel, Llewelyn Moss risks his life for $2.4 million in stolen drug money. He chooses the money and pays for it with the lives of both himself and his wife. In *Sweat*, a play by Lynn Nottage, Cynthia must choose between going on strike with her life-long working-class pals versus her new job in low-level management. She chooses her job and sacrifices her friendships. In *Less*, a novel by Andrew Sean Greer, Arthur Less faces this dilemma: struggling for full creative achievement and the painful sacrifices that demands versus accepting less and gaining the pleasures of an easier life. He chooses the latter.

TRUE CHARACTER THROUGH ANTAGONISM

When a character takes action in a high-risk dilemma, he inevitably provokes forces of antagonism in his world. To overcome these obstacles, he must continuously improvise anew. His choices are sometimes instinctive, sometimes deliberate, but always under pressure: He stands to lose in order to gain. The greater this risk-filled pressure, the deeper and truer his choice to who, at heart, he is.

As further events impact his life, his evolving nature chooses to conform or rebel, accept or reject his previous beliefs and values. No deeply felt experience is neutral; no choice is impartial; no action is impersonal. Thus, by choice and action he either civilizes or decivilizes himself, he either grows as a human being or shrivels.

Degrees of pressure, therefore, measure the depth and quality of true character. How, for example, do we know for certain whether a character is honest or dishonest? When nothing is at risk, pressure is light and therefore telling the truth painless. But when everything, even life itself, is at stake, when consequences stretch to the limits of human endurance, then excruciating pressure builds around the choice to tell the truth or lie. Whichever way the character acts, his choice delivers a profound insight into his core self.

Once a character chooses a tactic, he hands the doing of the deed to his agent self, who then takes on one of his personal or social personae. When not directing the show, the core self spends the day like a documentary film crew, watching, listening, and recording every interesting thing his outer selves do. Afterward, the core self usually wishes he had done things a bit better.

When creating a complex character, imagine his values along spectra that run from extreme positives (e.g., love, courage, hope) to extreme negatives (e.g., hate, cowardice, despair). For example, if his life is in danger, where does he stand on the courage/cowardice spectrum? Complex characters feel some of both. If his life has lost meaning, how does he see his future along the hope/despair spectrum? If he's in an intimate relationship, is he capable of love? Where along the love/hate spectrum would you place him?

Consider the value of honesty/dishonesty. A character may appear truthful, others may say he is, he may insist he is, but how will a reader/

audience know for certain whether he's an honest man, a liar, or morally flexible? If he has nothing to lose and chooses to tell the truth, his honesty seems trivial because it's risk free. But if he's under grave threat and he chooses to tell the truth when a lie would save his life, his depth of honesty seems profound. If, on the other hand, the character is a priest who, under threat, refuses to deny his faith, his honesty may seem less impressive because his sacred vows make his choice less free.

The interplay between choice and self gives the writer three grand principles to guide the work:

1. When a character at risk and under pressure pursues desire, his choices of action express his true character.
2. The greater the risk and pressure, the deeper and truer the choice.
3. The freer the choice, the even deeper and truer the choice to a character's identity.

Consider four tragic roles: Othello, Lear, Macbeth, and Hamlet. Brilliant characters all, but Hamlet is the most complex. Why? Choices. Othello's jealousy blinds him, Lear's daughters make his decisions for him, and the witches' prophecies funnel Macbeth to his destiny. Hamlet's choices are freer and more numerous. He might kill himself or not, revenge himself or not, love Ophelia or not, kill Polonius or not, find life meaningless or meaningful, stay sane or go crazy...all because of his unlimited freedom to choose.

Therefore, choice and character development relate this way: If a character makes only a few risk-free choices around a single value, he stays shallow and monodimensional. But if the character makes numerous risk-taking choices in the face of various values, he becomes complex and thus involves the reader/audience deeply in his inner life.

For example: In the opening episodes of *Succession*, the autocratic Logan Roy (Brian Cox) dominates his coke-abusing son, Kendall (Jeremy Strong), giving him few if any choices. Kendall's reactions make him seem weak, shallow, petty. But once he breaks free from his father and follows his own dangerous choices, his character gains heft and complexity, and wins our empathy.

TRUE CHARACTER AND EMOTION

When a character takes an action and his world reacts with antagonism, the charge of value at stake in the scene undergoes change. If a value charge moves from negative to positive, the character experiences an overall positive emotion. And the reverse: If a value's charge swings from positive to negative, his experience turns overall negative. Emotion, as noted in Chapter Seven, is the side effect of change.

A stimulus, such as good or bad news, causes glands to open and flood the bloodstream with a chemical cocktail that instills a particular emotion. A beautiful sight floods the brain with dopamine and serotonin, triggering a rush of pleasure; a grotesque image sends chemicals that affect the amygdala and insula cortex, causing woozy pangs of disgust. Soon, however, the limbic system produces counter chemicals to quiet and dispel emotions, returning the mind and body to a state of equilibrium. The intense experiences of pleasure and pain peak, then recede.

Pleasure and pain can be subdivided into various tones or qualities, although there's no scientific agreement on how many. Traditional psychology names just six: joy, fear, anger, sadness, disgust, and surprise. (Notice that the only clearly positive emotion here is joy.) To turn these states into tools for the writer, I've expanded the list by pairing them into six oppositions that give the writer a pallet of twelve emotions: Love/Hate, Amity/Anger, Joy/Grief, Surprise/Shock, Pleasure/Disgust, Courage/Fear.

The words *emotion* and *feeling* are often used interchangeably, but in my thinking, they differ greatly by the quality of their impact. Emotion hits with an intense suddenness, peaks in power, then in time fades away. A feeling comes over you more slowly, sits in the background of experience and lasts for long periods of time. Joy is an emotion; happiness is a feeling; grief is an emotion; sadness is a feeling.

You know how it goes. One morning you wake up feeling great and spend the whole day behind a smile. No particular reason for this; you're just at the optimistic pitch of your inner teeter-totter. Or you spend a day with a cloud over your head, again for no good reason; you've just hit your cynical bottom.

Feelings—pride of achievement versus shame of failure, hope for a bright future versus a premonition of disaster, a light heart versus a grumpy soul, trust of a loved one versus suspicions of infidelity—often color a personality long after the original stimulus is forgotten, shaping a role's characterization over a lifetime.

From turning point to turning point, change in the dynamic charge of a life value puts a character through one of the twelve emotions listed above. In a Romantic Comedy, for example, falling in love could fill a grieving character with joy, while losing love could inflict a joyful character with grief.

But when writing a scene, knowing the underlying emotion is only a starting point. An emotion in its pure state strikes a character like a blunt instrument. In life, the twelve prime passions range across an infinite variety of qualities and subtle intensities. What, therefore, determines which particular shade of emotion a character expresses in any particular scene? Answer: characterization. The mood, feeling, tone, and texture that emanates from a distinctive personality shapes a primal emotion into a genuinely original performance. Joy in one character might be expressed with a high-stepping song and dance routine, while another only smiles around the edges of his eyes.

TRUE CHARACTER AND REACTIONS

Reality limits the number of basic actions a human being can take. A person could choose to educate himself or live in ignorance, marry or live alone, work or laze, eat smart or pig out, face life or hide from it, and so on down a rather short list. On the other hand, the variety of moment-to-moment reactions a person may have to any action seems infinite.

When a character struggles to educate himself, for instance, his possible reactions to the trials of learning are as different and as many as they are for all students in all schools everywhere. The same is true of romance, work, health, and every other major aspect of life. The choices a character makes when negative forces block his path express his core identity, but the ways he reacts make him one of a kind.

In *Casablanca*, Rick Blaine (Humphrey Bogart) asks Victor Lazlo (Paul Henreid) why he keeps risking his life for the anti-Fascist cause:

> **LAZLO:** We might as well question why we breathe. We stop breathing, we'll die. We stop fighting our enemies, the world will die.
>
> **RICK:** What of it? Then it'll be out of its misery.

Lazlo's elegant declaration is an answer any idealist might give, but Rick's reaction, his belief that the death of civilization would be an act of mercy, is character-specific. Rick's choices, unique to him alone, set him apart from every version of the American antihero before and since.

Let this principle guide your character work: Choices of action under pressure express true character, but detailed, never-seen-before reactions make a characterization distinctive and intriguing.

TRUE CHARACTER AND FREE WILL

A writer's imagination is the sole source for every decision a character makes and every action he takes; a character's choices are in fact his author's choices. But from the point of view of audiences and readers, the opposite seems true. In a fictional world, independent characters lead independent lives, acting of their own free will. So in both realms, the *as is* and the *as if*, how free is human choice?

The Matrix explores this question as its protagonist, Neo (Keanu Reeves), discovers that what he experiences as reality is in fact an induced delusion known as the Matrix. This false world was created by an all-powerful AI to deceive enslaved human beings into thinking they are free while the AI uses their bodies as biological batteries to run its machines. Neo fights to gain the willpower he needs to defeat the AI's agents and break free from the Matrix.

The free will / determinism debate is eons old, but with the recent rise of neuroscience and quantum theory, ancient arguments have found new intensity. One side insists that free will is a delusion and that all choice is caused by forces outside human control;[9] others believe the will operates free of any cause, external or internal.[10] This dispute has influenced writers of both speculative and realistic fiction. The side you favor shapes the stories you tell and the casts that populate them.

Against Free Will

Free will deniers argue that for the will to be free, choice must be uncaused. An uncaused decision has no connection to anything in the past and is, therefore, utterly spontaneous. But, of course, as we know, in the physical universe, all actions, human or cosmic, are caused. Even the Big Bang had its cause (albeit as yet unknown). Denier logic argues that because an uncaused cause is a non sequitur, the human choice cannot be free.

For Free Will

In *Fawlty Towers*, Basil's car breaks down. After making dire threats to it, he counts to three, gives his car one last chance, then shouts:

> **BASIL:** I've warned you! I've laid it on the line to you time and time again! Right! I'm going to give you a damn good thrashing!

He rips a branch from a nearby tree and beats the paint off the fenders. Basil blames the car; we blame Basil.

Suppose, however, that like the car, Basil had no choice. Suppose the fault is a schizophrenic flaw in his brain chemistry? Or a defect in his upbringing? If so, do we blame his parents? But if his parents have no free will, how can we condemn them? We don't. Fault finding chases blame after blame into an infinite regress, so we choose to believe that Basil abused his car of his own free will.

Believing we don't have free will is not the same as believing we don't make choices.[11] No matter how our genes and personal history combine to influence our mind, our choices seem real. We sense that deep inside us our neural processes select actions based on a sense of probable consequences, what we think will happen when we take an action. We merge our sum total of living experience with an immediate situation, imagine an outcome, then make a choice. Without belief in choice, we could not hold ourselves responsible for anything we did. Law would evaporate, personal binds unravel, and *The Purge* would become a 24/365 reality.

If we have no free will, how can we change, cut, add, merge, or rework ourselves into someone we've never been before? If the human will is not free, at least to some degree, how are creativity and change possible? If all choice is determined by the past, how does anything new ever find its way into the world? If free will didn't exist, nothing unnecessary would exist, yet history is littered with things human beings made just for the fun of it. Like a child making up a game out of things he finds around the house, an artist creates by inventing something that never existed out of what already exists. Childhood play is the essence of free choice, and mature art is its fullest expression.[12]

As we noted earlier, any story you create argues both for and against free will. When a story begins and we look into its unknown future, virtually everything and anything seems possible. But at climax, now that we know the protagonist's psychology in depth, and now that we see the full array of social, personal, and physical forces that surrounded him, we realize that the choices he made were the only choices he could and would have made; the reactions he got from his world were the only reactions his world could and would have given him. The path he took was the only path he could have taken. Character choices seem free and unpredictable when seen from the inciting incident and looking toward the story's climax, but inevitable and fated when looking back from the climax to the inciting incident. Free will in one direction; retroactive determinism in the other.

Our sense of free will may be a delusion that arises out of ignorance of its causes, but if so, then it's our delusion and we have no choice but to embrace it. When your characters make choices, they face four possible pathways to a decision, two beyond their control and two within their free will choices:

1. Circumstances push a character's life one way or another and determine the choice, for better or worse, whether he likes it or not.
2. The subconscious self makes choices the core self never realizes or rationalizes away.
3. The character quickly considers what to do. As choices come to mind, one takes hold, and he makes an instinctive decision.

4. The character slowly considers his choices, makes lists of pros and cons, followed by a concatenation of all possible consequences and a judicious weighing of their effects. He finally makes his choice. This rational mode usually precedes a character's greatest mistakes in life.

Ultimately, as author, all choices are yours.

9

THE DIMENSIONAL CHARACTER

A UNITY OF OPPOSITES

To review: A role's characterization conceals her true character, and together they float atop her subconscious, that ocean of drives and desires, unthinking habits and sea tides of temperament. These three aspects—outer, inner, hidden—gather to complete a character, but what keeps them from flying apart? What pulls surface personae, inner selves, and subconscious drives together into one unified character?

Answer: the power of contradiction.

In the fifth century BCE, the philosopher Heraclitus argued that reality holds itself together through a system of contradictions: "Cold things warm up, the hot cool off; wet becomes dry, dry becomes wet." Hot/cold merge to create temperature, dry/wet unite into humidity, birth/death forge life. Thus runs the dynamic of all physical existence, creating *A Unity of Opposites*.

This principle applies to humankind as well. The moment a person is born, she begins to die. At every point in her life, she is evolved yet evolving, dreaming while awake, awake while dreaming. No matter her age, she's both young and old—younger than anyone older, older than anyone younger. No matter her sexual orientation, she's both female and male.

Within the harmony of every well-designed role, a set of living contradictions intersect. The unity of opposites, therefore, is the founding principle of character complexity. Stories populated by complex characters preserve, in an aesthetically purified form, the essential contradictions that unite ugliness with beauty, tyranny with freedom, good with evil, truth with lie, and the like.

CHARACTER DIMENSION

Human nature's emotional instrument was strung in a violent past, hundreds of thousands of years before Socrates, Buddha, or Jesus could retune it. Virtues such as honesty, generosity, and courage constantly revert to treachery, selfishness, and cowardice in the same society, the same person. As a result, paradox rules humanity: People love their families yet hate their families, save time yet waste time, seek the truth yet deny the obvious, prize nature yet pollute nature, hunger for peace yet rush to war. Complex characters first display a specific self, then change into its opposite and then back again.

These dynamics have a pattern. They swing back and forth from pole to pole depending on the relationships a character has with other characters and within herself—some positive, some negative. The in-vogue client of a professional dominant is a high-powered but highly stressed executive who distains those she subordinates and deifies those who subordinate her. To balance the pleasures of power with the pangs of humiliation, she submits to the whip. Psychologists coined *sadomasochist* as the perfect oxymoron to name this contradiction in a Dior suit.

When a character's inner and outer natures fuse into a single function, the role congeals into a type: Nurse, Cop, Teacher, Superhero, Villain, Sidekick, and the like. But when contradictions underpin a role, they activate a more complete, complex, and fascinating character. These oppositions form *Dimensions*.

Dimensional characters arouse our curiosity by making us wonder how two sides of a contradiction can live within one person. That, in turn, makes them unpredictable and all the more fascinating. From moment to moment, who knows which side will show up?

COMPLEXITY IN SIX DIMENSIONS

Dimensions span between aspects of a role's outer characterization, between various inner selves and between facets of the hidden self. What's more, these three levels often contradict one another. As a result, a complex character may contain six distinct kinds of dimensions.

1. A Contradiction Between Two Aspects of Characterization

Picture a woman who spends an hour each morning getting her makeup just right but doesn't bother to brush her teeth. Suppose this woman abuses her partner but coddles her children; kisses up to her boss but tyrannizes her staff. These three dimensions fuse qualities of characterization—her physical, personal, and social selves—into intriguing behaviors, giving the reader/audience insight into what's important and unimportant to her.

At the level of characterization, characters are often aware of their traits, although they rarely perceive them as contradictory. Instead, they rationalize them as necessary. These behaviors are also visible to the rest of the cast who think whatever they choose to think about them.

2. A Contradiction Between Characterization and True Character

Envision an elderly woman dozing in a wheelchair. As she awakes, she gazes at the men in her retirement home and suddenly a glint flashes in her eye, lit by her ever-young dream of romantic love.

3. A Contradiction Between Characterization and Subconscious Desire

Imagine a hyperactive woman who never stops doing things, and yet her hidden self always stays deeply calm. This serene self comes out only when she faces danger. Under threat, she goes still, strong and focused.

To discover a character's subconscious, the key, once again, is contradiction. When a character says one thing and does another, what are the possibilities? One, she's lying. She knows what she really wants but outwardly pretends to want the opposite. Or two, she's honest. She really believes what she says, really wants what she wants, but when she tries to get it, something undercuts her efforts. She doesn't know why, but every once in a while, she turns a rather dark face to the world. A contradictory force lives in her subconscious.

4. A Contradiction Between Two Conscious Desires

The adulterer's dilemma: a woman caught between devotion to her husband and passion for her lover.

At the level of true character, a conscious, self-aware mind analyzes her inner contradiction, worries about it, and struggles to make a choice. If she talks about her dilemma with others, it becomes an aspect of characterization. If she keeps a subtextual conflict to herself, the reader/audience can perceive it only by implication. Once she makes a choice of action, however, the reader/audience reads her mind clearly and senses her inner dimension.

To symbolize dimensions between two conscious desires, playwrights such as Samuel Beckett (*Waiting for Godot*), Jean Genet (*The Maids*), and Suzan-Lori Parks (*Topdog/Underdog*) resort to splitting the mind in two and symbolizing an inner contradiction as a pair of bickering characters.

5. A Contradiction Between a Conscious Desire and a Subconscious Desire

The lover's dilemma: fervent passion for a fiancée versus fear of commitment.

To symbolize dimensions of this fifth type, novels such as Robert Louis Stevenson's *The Strange Case of Dr. Jekyll and Mr. Hyde* and two novels titled *The Double*, one by Fyodor Dostoevsky and the other by Jose Saramago, cast conscious/subconscious contradiction as a duet of characters with contradictory drives (one toward good, the other toward evil) that mirror each other.

In *Breaking Bad*, showrunner Vince Gilligan gives his protagonist, Walter White, a secret second self known as Heisenberg. This doppelgänger comes vividly to the surface in Season 5, Episode 14: Jack, leader of a Nazi biker gang, has Walter's brother-in-law, Hank, at his mercy. As

Jack raises his gun, Walt pleads for Hank's life. While he's begging, he is Walter, a man capable of conscious caring.

But immediately after Nazi Jack murders Hank, Walt betrays Jesse, his dearest friend and partner. In that act, Heisenberg, the manifestation of Walter's savage subconscious, takes charge.

6. A Contradiction Between Two Subconscious Motivations

The family dilemma: the need to sacrifice your desires for the people you love versus the need to sacrifice other people to fulfill your personal ambitions.

Subconscious dimensions live below the level of awareness, unthought, and unexpressed. Once again, the reader/audience can perceive an inner contradiction only through the character's choices of action under pressure.

Children, for example, often harbor contradictory subconscious attitudes toward their parents: fear and awe, love and hate. In *The Tragedy of Hamlet*, Shakespeare projected a son's contradictory feelings onto two characters: the noble father versus the dastardly uncle. *The Lion King* (*Hamlet* with a happy ending) repeated this duality onstage and on-screen. The fairy godmother versus wicked stepmother in "Cinderella" does the same for daughters.

In *Persona*, Ingmar Bergman expressed the split soul by merging a nurse and patient into one woman, then separated them back into two, then one again, two again...

In *Black Swan*, Nina Sayers (Natalie Portman), a ballet dancer rehearsing Tchaikovsky's *Swan Lake*, suffers a conflict between split selves. Because the ballet calls for the same dancer to perform two opposed protagonists, White Swan and Black Swan, the film uses this setup to dramatize her dual self.

The White Swan role calls for symmetry, grace, cool antisexuality, and, above all, precise skills that define Nina's longing for poised perfection. The Black Swan demands the opposite talents: creativity, spontaneity, sexual abandon—powerful, animalistic energies alive within Nina that she fiercely suppresses. The war between her uptight White Swan and her voluptuous but stifled Black Swan surfaces in paranoid hallucinations. At the climax, Nina's two selves finally join forces in a glorious, life-fulfilling performance, then consume each other as she dies, whispering, "It was perfect."

For a real-life example of the unity of opposites, consider the novelist, playwright, screenwriter, and multidimensional celebrity Graham Greene. Greene was self-hating versus self-glorifying, meticulously disciplined versus self-destructive, deliriously romantic versus bitterly cynical, devout Catholic versus lifelong adulterer, Nobel Prize–nominated novelist versus pulp hack, strict theologian versus moral relativist, salon communist versus closet monarchist, anti-imperialist crusader versus postcolonial parasite, civilized to a fault versus drugged to distraction. Greene was an exceptional artist but no exception to human nature.[1]

To unify characters over time, dimensions must be consistent. If a man rescues a kitten up a tree once, that's not a dimension; it's a gratuitous kindness to gain cheap sympathy from the reader/audience. If a woman rescues cats throughout a story but then suddenly kicks a dog, that's not a dimension, either; it's a snit.

Dimensions must be variable. A character who loves cats but hates dogs and so rescues kittens but abandons puppies wages war within herself. A reader/audience would be amused and curious to discover the roots of this neurotic contradiction, so long as the pattern doesn't become repetitive. A dimension needs a certain unpredictability and progression—not the same cat and same dog rescued and abandoned in the same backyard.

What's more, to keep its tension, a dimension must seem unresolvable: an atheist who argues that nothing is permanent but subconsciously yearns for the eternal; a neuroscientist who chooses of her own free will to believe that free will is an illusion; a Las Vegas oddsmaker who secretly delights in unpredictable outcomes.

THE DEFINING DIMENSION

A protagonist may house many more than three dimensions, while first circle supporting roles generally feature only one or two, but no matter how many dimensions elaborate a role, they do not have equal weight and focus. One tends to stand in the foreground, defining a character's essential spirit, while the others complete the portrait.

Of the nine dimensions I ascribed to Graham Greene, which one is so crucial to his identity that if it were removed, he would vanish with it? I would suggest Artist/Hack. The other eight dimensions could inhabit someone else, but the creative battle Greene waged within himself was his alone. It defined him.

To repeat for clarity: A dimension is a consistent contradiction within or between the planes of a character's nature. In a complex, multidimensional character, one of these steps forward to define her unique identity.

CASE STUDY: ODYSSEUS

In a recent survey of "The 100 Stories that Shaped the World," international experts ranked the *Odyssey*, Homer's three-thousand-year-old epic, number one, with his *Iliad* close behind.[2] As Homer's human characters strive against vindictive, hypersexed gods and demonic, nightmarish monsters, many scenes in both stories seem like fever dreams, and yet, for all their lust and gore, the *Iliad* and *Odyssey* are the foundational stories of European culture, and their pivotal character, Odysseus, King of Ithaca, is history's first multidimensional character.

The battered hero of these tales spends ten years at war against the city of Troy (*Iliad*), then another decade struggling to sail home (*Odyssey*). Odysseus duels enemy warriors, wrathful gods, covetous goddesses, and bloodthirsty beasts, ultimately prevailing through grit, luck, and ingenious improvisations.

The *Iliad* gives Odysseus his first two dimensions—Pragmatic/Idealistic and Obedient/Defiant. But after the *Odyssey*'s opening line introduces him as "a complicated man," he gains six more: Truthful/Deceitful, Brilliant/Blundering, Protecting/Jeopardizing, Honorable/Thieving, Cool/Raging, and Faithful/Unfaithful.[3]

Pragmatic/Idealistic

Odysseus is a battlefield pragmatist. To him, idealistic codes of honor end when war begins. In ancient heroic tradition, for example, poison was an ignoble, deceitful weapon no true champion would use. Even so, Odysseus coats his arrowheads with arsenic.

When a captured Trojan spy begs Odysseus for mercy, he manipulates the man into thinking he'll spare his life in exchange for a military secret. But the moment the spy reveals what he knows, he's beheaded. Then using the spy's information, Odysseus and his comrade slaughter an enemy force in their sleep.

In the tenth year of the war, the Trojans back the Greek army against the sea. Facing massacre, the Greek foot soldiers rise up against their incompetent leaders. In the face of mutiny and certain defeat, a pragmatist might hoist sail for home, but Odysseus stays true to the ideals of victory. Using his powerfully persuasive voice, he reverses the revolt with a fiery prophecy that turns mutineers into warriors and sends them roaring back into the teeth of battle.

Obedient/Defiant

Odysseus dutifully obeys his commanding general, King Agamemnon, but when he feels that the king's tactics are ruinous, he defies his leader, telling him, "Your words are wind and have no meaning."

Truthful/Deceitful

As an advisor to Agamemnon's war council, Odysseus always speaks with truthfulness, insight, and wisdom. No comrade ever doubts his word. But once he sets sail for home, he lies from one end of the Mediterranean to the other.

Again and again, his gift for storytelling charms his way out of trouble. He tricks people by disguising himself as an old man or a beggar or an immigrant from Crete, an island famous for its liars. Odysseus even tries to con his sacred protectress, the goddess Athena, but she sees through him and scolds him with: "You perverse man, how you love your artful, deceitful words."

Brilliant/Blundering

When the war with Troy seems all but lost, Odysseus wins victory for the Greeks by improvising history's most brilliant military tactic—the Wooden Horse. On the voyage home, however, Odysseus, greedy for loot, sneaks into the cave of Polyphemus, the cannibalistic cyclops. The giant traps Odysseus inside and devours half of his crew.

That night Odysseus lulls Polyphemus into a drunken stupor, then drives a stake into his one and only eye. Once safely back on ship, however, Odysseus unleashes yet another arrogant impulse. He taunts the now-blind Polyphemus, enraging not only the giant but the giant's father, Poseidon, Lord of the Seas. The furious sea god batters Odysseus's ship with massive storms and blows him wildly off course.

Protecting/Jeopardizing

Odysseus protected his warriors throughout the Trojan War, making certain they were well fed and well doctored. But while sailing home, his men discover a tribe addicted to the lotus plant—a narcotic that erases painful memories. These war-damaged, PTSD-suffering veterans, longing to forget, rush to devour the drug. To save his men from themselves, Odysseus drags them back to the ships.

Later, however, as Odysseus's fleet sails toward a foreign shore, he again senses danger, but this time he jeopardizes his men's lives by anchoring their ships in the open, while concealing his behind rocks. Suddenly, gargantuan cannibals attack and capsize the ships, spearing and eating his men as if they were fish. Only Odysseus and his crew escape.

Honorable/Thieving

Throughout the war, Odysseus fought courageously, dividing spoils honorably and treating his fellow warriors with respect. But on the voyage home, he turns pirate, plundering peaceful towns, killing their defenders, and taking women as slaves.

Cool/Raging

In war and at sea, in the face of armies and monsters, Odysseus always keeps his cool, solving problems with calm, clear, balanced decisions.

Meanwhile, back in Ithaca, a group of boisterous young men known as the Suitors invade his palace and revel in his wealth. For ten years, each of them tries repeatedly to seduce Odysseus's wife, Penelope. Once home, Odysseus, roiled with Achilles-like rage, takes revenge. He slaughters all 108 suitors, then all the servants who served the suitors and the female slaves who slept with them.

Faithful/Unfaithful

Away from home, Odysseus is repeatedly adulterous, bedding nymphs such as Circe. But when Calypso, a goddess of divine beauty, offers Odysseus an eternity of pleasure, he stays faithful to his beloved Penelope.

Odysseus's Eight Dimensions

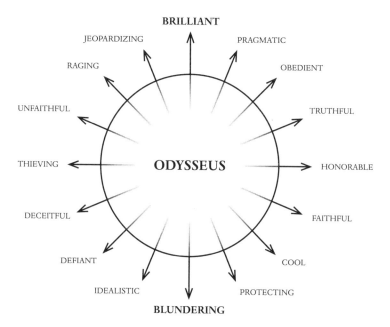

What makes Odysseus an enduring creation is the dark side of his dimensions. Any clichéd hero can act out positive charges such as bravery, intelligence, and calm under pressure, but it's his impulsive, hardhearted, raging, thieving, self-serving, and deceitful traits that expand Odysseus's character, giving him a multidimensional nature, the power of unpredictability, and a depth of character that makes his surprising choices satisfyingly creditable.

Of his eight dynamic contradictions, the one that serves as his defining dimension is his dazzling brilliance versus his erratic impulses. Odysseus, after all, devised the Trojan Horse ploy that ended a decade of war, but then he blundered his way into Polyphemus's cave. His impulsive adventures risk his life repeatedly, but his hypnotic storytelling saves it just as often. He's both brilliant and foolish. There's no one quite like him in the three thousand years of fiction that followed Homer.

Odysseus remains perpetually modern—conflicted yet willful, death damaged yet life embracing. He set the stage for psychologically and morally complex characters of future generations: Anonymous's Beowulf, Shakespeare's Macbeth, Stendhal's Julien Sorel, F. Scott Fitzgerald's Jay Gatsby, Raymond Chandler's Philip Marlowe, Vladimir Nabokov's Humbert Humbert, Mario Puzo's Michael Corleone, Philip Roth's Alexander Portnoy, Hilary Mantel's Thomas Cromwell.

CASE STUDY: TONY SOPRANO

How dimensional can a character become? Consider David Chase's creation, the New Jersey mafia don, Tony Soprano. *The Sopranos* ran for eighty-six episodes, and Tony was the only character to appear in every episode.

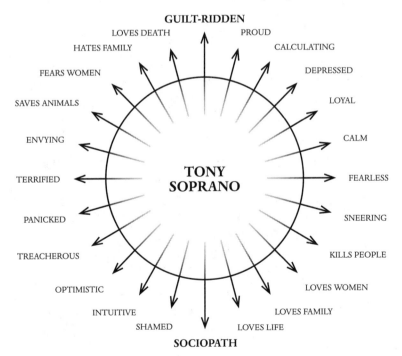

The Twelve Dimensions of Tony Soprano

To portray a man's life enmeshed in this huge number of interconnected relationships, dramatized over eighty-six hours, with dozens of backstory events waiting for revelation, reaching back decades to Tony's infancy—all this time and content called for one of the most complex characters ever conceived for any storytelling medium.

Moving counterclockwise:

#1. Guilt-ridden/Sociopath. A sociopath is someone without a conscience, an antisocial, self-centered personality who's incapable of feeling shame or remorse. At times, Tony is clearly a sociopath.

Except at other times, Tony is as guilt-ridden as Macbeth. His remorseful heart pursues him relentlessly, nagging and tormenting him into panic attacks.

This Macbeth-like core contradiction of outer cruelty versus inner conscience makes Tony Soprano one of the most fascinating characters ever written for page, stage, or screen.

When it's time to kill, Tony acts without hesitation. Nothing can restrain his raging impulses. Over the years he commits eight murders on-screen, and who can count how many hits he orders or commits off-screen? He is a sociopath, no doubt, but a genuinely sociopathic personality would never join any collective organization, even the mafia.

Professional assassins, like Javier Bardem's Anton Chigurh and Woody Harrelson's Carson Wells from *No Country for Old Men*, would happily fill contracts to kill for the mafia, but they rarely join it. The mafia is an illegal society within our legal society, but it demands all those qualities of good citizenship conventional society demands: loyalty, honesty, hard work, a stable family life, sobriety, obedience to the tribe's laws, respectful manners and etiquette, and, most important, submission to the authorities who stand above you in the hierarchy of power.

If you belong to this society, breaking its commandments inflicts the pain of guilt as you accuse and belittle yourself with that nagging voice of self-disgust known as a conscience.

If you have a conscience, that is, and Tony certainly does. His conscience works overtime to fill his dreams with horrifying images and drive him to a psychiatrist for help. This profound dimension of sociopathic callousness contradicted by guilty self-punishment is the axle of Tony's inner nature, and all his other many dimensions extend like spokes off that hub.

#2. Proud/Shamed. He's proud of his son's loving gentleness yet shamed by the boy's weak-willed, suicidal nature.

#3. Calculating/Intuitive. For months, Tony plays Sherlock Holmes as he gathers evidence in his search for the informant who's ratting him out to the FBI. Then in a dream while suffering food poisoning, a fish comes to Tony, speaking in the voice of his longtime friend and family strong arm, Sal "Big Pussy" Bonpensiero. The fish tells him that his suspicions about Big Pussy are correct. Big Pussy is the FBI rat. So based on a dream, Tony murders his friend.

#4. Depressed/Optimistic. Despair versus hope war within him.

#5. Loyal/Treacherous. He's devoted to his wife yet betrays her with his many mistresses.

#6. Calm/Panicked. He's logical and emotional; he's cool under pressure but a victim of panic attacks.

#7. Fearless/Terrified. When threatened by gangsters, he's fearless, but the chance of a terrorist attack terrifies him.

#8. Sneering/Envying. Tony sneers at the lives of normal people, yet he envies the lives of normal people.

#9. Kills/Saves. He hates human beings and kills them, but he loves animals and protects them.

#10. Loves women / Fears women. Tony is a macho sex addict, yet he is tortured by nightmares of castration.

#11. Loves family / Hates family. He hates his mother / loves his mother, hates his uncle Junior / loves his uncle Junior, and above all he loves himself / hates himself.

#12. Loves life / Loves death. He enjoys life's beauty but finds death more and more intoxicating with each murder he commits.

Tony Soprano is far more dimensional than Hamlet. Shakespeare surrounded Hamlet with a cast of just ten over only four hours of dramatization. David Chase set Tony in a cast of many dozens through eighty-six hours of choices, actions, and reactions socially, personally, privately, consciously, and subconsciously. Tony is a modern model of character complexity because his dimensions crisscross all levels of his being.

Yet try as he may, unlike Hamlet, Tony cannot change. The series' narrative drive raises the major dramatic question: Will Tony change into a morally better human being? Answer: No. The Tonys of this world cannot and do not change their core selves.

10

THE COMPLEX CHARACTER

COMPLEXITY THROUGH ANTAGONISM

Stoic philosophers, beginning around 300 BC, taught that the gods predetermine life. Olympians know all of mankind's future events but hide them until they happen. Stoics called this force Fate, and this belief lives on today. When, for example, a tragic accident takes a child's life, his parents often tell the TV cameras that they bow to "God's will."

Epicurean philosophers took the opposite view. They held that what we mistake for a power outside of ourselves is the work of a free will hidden within ourselves. Random events beyond human control may disrupt us, but our will-driven reactions determine the path life takes. The choices we make under these pressures shape our future. As Heraclitus put it, "Character is destiny."

The latter belief seems the more likely. An invisible force, as it were, does shape a character's life, but it emanates from within himself. As Carl Jung taught, the conscious mind lives on the edge of a volcano, and unless a character becomes aware of his subconscious impulses, life will always seem beyond control, and surprising things will always happen to him as if by fate.

Picture two ships in a raging storm: One stays afloat; the other goes under. The same seas batter both; the difference is not luck but who captains. As Cassius puts it in *The Tragedy of Julius Caesar*: "The fault, dear Brutus, is not in our stars, but in ourselves, that we are underlings."

As a young character comes of age, a perfect storm of external forces affects his sense of values: What is worth pursuing? What's foolish to pursue? When his subconscious reinforces his inclinations, they become beliefs. These convictions, rooted in his true character, guide him through this pattern:

1. Based on his beliefs, his core self determines the choices and actions he makes and takes; conversely, his choices express his true character.
2. His choices under pressure shape his future, not only revealing who he is but how he changes into who he becomes.
3. The more various the antagonisms in his life, the more diverse his choices.
4. The more diverse his choices, the more complex his nature, and thus the more dimensional, unpredictable, surprising, and ultimately revealing his reactions and actions.
5. His character, therefore, becomes only as multidimensional as the story's complex of antagonistic forces that conflict within him.

Levels and qualities of conflict range from the physical (nature's powers spanning from the massive forces of the universe to microscopic diseases) to the social (demands of employment and citizenship) and personal (demands of intimate relationships) to the internal (the mind's conflicting desires).

Let's work from outermost to the innermost to see how levels of antagonism multiply dimensionality into a complex character.

PHYSICAL CONFLICTS

A story's outermost level of conflict embraces the four grand components of the physical world:

1. Natural environments and the powers they contain. From the human point of view, nature is as random as a tornado, as fierce as a wolf pack, and as morally indifferent as evolution.

2. Man-made environments and the systems they control. Civilizations were conceived with a moral as well as a practical purpose. We human beings, therefore, share responsibility for both the beauty of our creations and the ill effects of pollution, global warming, war, and all other man-made disasters.

3. Our bodily environment and its many maladies. The brain lives inside a trouble-prone beast. This body inflicts aggravations on the mind that range from illnesses to aging to an unfortunately shaped nose. These conflicts are partly random, partly predictable, partly indifferent, partly self-inflicted.

4. Our temporal environment and its brevity. Time contains all that exists, and over time it will erase all.

Let's sketch out a characterization based on behaviors at the physical level only: A young man is a daredevil who ski-jumps from frightening heights. If he buys trendy outfits he really can't afford, he enjoys provoking envy in the ski-lodge spotlight. If he arrives for jump practice hours before sunup, then nervously glances at his watch until his coach arrives, he suffers from time anxiety. If he constantly calls his mother for advice, he lacks maturity. Put these traits together and he becomes an athletic, hyperimpatient, self-absorbed, immature thrill seeker.

At this point, his multifaceted characterization prepares him only for a supporting role. To evolve him into a complex protagonist, we need to transform his traits into dimensions. As noted above, when one trait consistently contradicts another, the tension between them fuses into a dimension. So, let's take each of his traits, imagine its opposite, and see where that leads.

If his vanity hides self-doubt, if PEDs fuel his athleticism, if the adrenaline rush that propels his death-defying stunts masks a mama's boy longing for a dead father, if his every leap off a ski jump is a minisuicide, if his anxiousness only calms when he's in midair, he might earn a story of his own.

SOCIAL CONFLICTS

Now let's look at social structures and a character's struggles at this level of life.

Massive institutions harden over time into hierarchies on a scale so great that the people in them feel little or no personal responsibility. These hierarchies shape human beings into the roles to be played, then organize them inside a pyramidal system in which the people at the bottom have no power, the people at the top have great power, and the people in the middle grab for power as they jostle up and down the chain of command. Stressful as these massive systems are, they couldn't exist unless the people in them welcomed their roles. Indeed, institutions raise us, educate us, support us, and mold the roles we play.

As the documentarian Frederick Wiseman exposed in more than forty film studies of institutions, those who reach an organization's pinnacle tend to be efficient but callous. As a result, from governments, corporations, and militaries to hospitals, monasteries, and families, institutions, to some degree, narrow their members into someone less than the ideal human being. The grand irony of civilization is that although social structures protect us from one kind of suffering (death by starvation), they inflict misery of another (begrudging obedience).[1] And humanity has no alternative. We need institutions to progress us on an outer level while we pay a price on an inner level.

The ideologies that govern institutions span a spectrum that runs from "I am my brother's keeper" to "Every man for himself." At the "Every man for himself" end of the spectrum sits predatory capitalism. This system exploits our innate drives for self-importance, wealth, and power. Sociopaths thrive in this environment. In the population as a whole, sociopaths constitute 1 percent; on Wall Street, 10 percent.[2] At the "I am my brother's keeper" pole sit absolute governments and dictators claiming to care for their citizens but giving them no choice in what they get. Sociopaths feel equally at home here.

In between these two extremes are meritocracies that promote people up the ladder of power based on hard work, intelligence, and achievement. Once in power, however, these elites pull the ladder up after them, turning their meritocracy into an oligarchy. In the United States, for example, wealthy white Protestant men wrote the Constitution, then created industries and universities—but at the same time, they built their power on slavery, Jim Crow, anti-Catholicism, anti-Semitism, anti-Hispanicism, and anti-feminism.[3]

Because institutions deindividualize, they cause people to do things they normally wouldn't. Would a normal person taunt a stranger into killing himself? No, but a study of suicides committed in public found that once onlookers gather, they often become a mob, a momentary institution working in unison to bait the guy on the ledge into jumping. Every year during religious ceremonies and sporting events, panicking out-of-control crowds of passionate, like-minded people trample each other to death.[4]

To cope with institutions, a character, beginning in childhood, straps on various social selves to guide his public interactions. Each social self has a set of traits designed to deal with the various institutions he faces. He does not chat with his professor in the same manner he talks to his rabbi or the clerk at the DMV or his boss at work or his cohorts at QAnon or his commanding officer in the National Guard.

So let's give a character a half-dozen traits based on the roles he plays when coping with stress and conflict within these institutions: (1) humble when meeting with his professor, (2) shamed when confessing to his rabbi, (3) obsequious while taking his DMV license renewal test, (4) generous when helping his boss solve a problem, (5) skeptical while conspiring about politics online, and (6) frightened when yelled at by his commanding officer.

These traits add up to a kind, shy, easily intimidated man—someone in need of the friends he finds in a chat room. This monochrome characterization may create a supporting role on the edge of events, but once again, to take him center stage, contradictions are needed to turn his traits into dimensions.

Suppose the humble excuses he uses in his professor's office become bragging recitations that bore his classmates; suppose his shame in his rabbi's office feeds a secret, perverse sex life; suppose he fawns at the DMV, then drives off like a maniac; suppose his generosity toward his boss reverses into stinginess with coworkers; suppose his conspiracy theory cynicism stems from the gullible belief that people in power actually know what they're doing; suppose his fear of military authority unleashes a murderous fury on the battlefield. If we were to wrap a story around him that expresses these dimensions, he might carry a telling to a staggering climax.

PERSONAL CONFLICTS

Public relationships value consequences; personal relationships value intentions. When a person with social power chooses a course of action, outcome matters more than sincerity. When someone in a personal relationship takes action, sincerity matters more than outcome. We condemn an investor's financial mistakes no matter his personal intentions; we forgive a lover's insult in the hope he didn't mean it.

Human beings suffer in social alienation but thrive in close company. The difference between social and personal relationships is intimacy. What bonds family to family, friend to friend, lover to lover are shared thoughts and feelings normally never revealed in public. The chemistry of intimacy takes two people beyond their social roles (coworkers, for example) to friendship and rapport. Depending on the personalities involved, of course, intimacy can be either joyful or painful.

As the core self moves from childhood to adulthood, it develops its identity along a spectrum of experiences that runs from approving, intense, and multiple loving intimacies at one end to insulting, cold, and singularly cruel intimacies at the other. It is possible, as we often observe, for two people to go through life in a personal relationship—father and son, for example—and never share intimacy, only shifting balances of power. The same is true for business partners who never become pals and strangers who never become lovers.

Feelings run deepest at the personal level. This is why dramas of personal catastrophe have greater impact than tales of social conflict: Compare *Macbeth* to *Coriolanus*, *Othello* to *The Winter's Tale*, *King Lear* to *Julius Caesar*.

With each close friend, relative, or lover, a character evolves a version of himself that he could not bring out all on his own. If intimacy ends, he not only loses a loved one, he loses the version of himself that she inspired.

To extend the method of character enrichment I used at the physical and social levels, I'll add complexity to three characters by contradicting a trait of characterization with a pattern of intimate behavior.

GENEROUS/SELFISH

Imagine a waiter working for tips who sends thoughtfully inscribed cards to everyone in his family on every birthday and holiday; who bakes far more cookies than necessary so he can share them by the dozen with neighborhood friends; who drifts from heart-breaking love affair to heart-breaking love affair in search of his dream lover. To everyone who knows him, he's an idealistic, people-loving saint. Then he wins the lottery.

A saint would donate his megamillions to charity, but this character gives nothing to anyone. He banks it all, moves to a warmer clime, and lives like royalty. When he baked cookies, sent cards, and slept around, he was greedy for love. Now that he is rich, this ex-waiter finally gets what he's always wanted: people sucking up to him.

SUPPORTIVE/SUBVERSIVE

Picture a husband who does everything for his wife—shop and cook, fold the laundry, and record her favorite shows. He listens patiently to her complaints and never complains in return. His characterization convinces his wife that he loves her and so she naturally loves him in return.

At parties, however, after a couple of drinks, he tells amusing tales about his wife that implicitly belittle her. He then ends each sly insult with a cheery "Isn't that right, sweetheart?" Everyone who hears his anecdotes knows that he thinks his wife is a fool. She, however, only nods and smiles. He wounds her, and then forces her to show love in return by tagging his attacks with "sweetheart."

GUILT/FORGIVENESS

Imagine a hardworking careerist who takes his frustrations out on his children, abuse after abuse. Then one day he tells them that his doctor diagnosed him at risk for a stress-induced heart attack. Nonetheless, he continues to work day and night, so the kids have to forgive his malice and admire his courage. Better still, if he does not tell anyone about his pending coronary and eventually collapses on the job, his kids are forced to love his stoic sacrifice. Either way, his suffering vindicates his cruelty and his children forgive his past abuse.[5]

As you labor over a character in the making, any pair of positive/negative adjectives that comes to mind could inspire a dimension. Hard/soft, sweet/sour, calm/hyper are three quick examples.

INNER DIMENSIONS

The mind is its own place and in itself can make a heaven of hell, a hell of heaven.

—John Milton, *Paradise Lost*

All outer dimensions—physical, social, personal—trace their roots back to the mind that gave them birth. As a result, complex characters tend to pull the storytelling inside themselves until their inner conflicts become more important, more fascinating than their outer struggles. This is true even when a character's inner conflicts finally burst into violence. Two examples: Raskolnikov in Dostoevsky's *Crime and Punishment* and Katherine (Florence Pugh) in Alice Birch's screenplay for *Lady Macbeth*.

As a writer works to fit a complex character to events and events to a complex character, the turning points that matter most take place below the surface. The author peers beneath the character's words and gestures, searching behind his eyes, drawn to his churning psychology, trying to puzzle out the inner effects of what outwardly happens.

He may discover that his story's external events cause internal reactions that send his character on an arc of change that alters his nature for better or worse: He becomes stronger or weaker, more childish or mature, more fulfilled or emptied out. Interest in the hows and whys of this inner evolution leads the writer's imagination to enter the character's core self, and from this subjective point of view invent new events that will enhance and express the character's evolving nature. Changes in event design lead to further exploration of inner character; changes in inner character lead to a reinvention of events... and on the process goes.

Pensive minds like Shakespeare's Hamlet and Virginia Woolf's Clarissa Dalloway suffer what today we term *cognitive dissonance*. They flail in the chasm between thought and action. Their minds rage with an inner turmoil of memories, longings, night and day fantasies, streaming conscious and semiconscious anxieties over acting or not acting, sorting the real from the unreal, the true from the false, until their final choice is carried out in a single action.

More often than not the spark of contradiction that ignites a dimension comes from the negative side of human nature, the side people hide but writers excavate. These primal sources of character complexity flow from two inner levels: thought-driven contradictions vying in the conscious mind and wordless conflicts warring in the subconscious.

CONSCIOUS CONFLICTS

Depending on his depth of self-awareness, a complex character thinks about, or to some degree senses, his inner incongruities and the disruptions they cause. In his private realm, he knows that sometimes he sees the truth of things, at other times he's blind to the obvious; sometimes he's kind, at other times cruel. In most cases, he tries to resolve these contradictions or at least get them under control.

Some private dimensions operate at the thinking level and connect two opposed qualities such as Intelligent/Unintelligent, Curious/Incurious, or Imaginative/Unimaginative. Other paradoxes come from the more sentient dimensions of Impulsive/Reflective, Angry/Calm, and Courageous/Timid that give a role emotional complexity.

Many social institutions were invented specifically to address one of these inner conflicts: Alcoholics Anonymous copes with the Craving/Spurning mind of the addicted. Buddhism calms the chronic worrier's Past/Future frets, what Buddhists call the Monkey Mind—frantic images and words screeching and swinging from idea to idea, flinging thought feces at mental walls.

Let's sketch a couple examples of inner contradiction in the private realm. We'll start once again with a trait and contradict it into a dimension.

LESS VERSUS MORE

Imagine a character who asks for nothing and lives a quiet life of less. Because he wants nothing, he lacks the focused desire of a protagonist. Now suppose an experience were to inspire in him a desire to expand outwardly into the noisy life of more. An inner contradiction could take hold between his wish to be celebrated and his need to stay hidden, between his impulse to express himself and his fear of exposure. With these dimensions, he could now star in his own story, as does Arthur Less in *Less*, a novel by Andrew Sean Greer.

This contradiction between the need for less and the need for more, between inner and outer lives anchors Shakespeare's most complex character: Hamlet. When Hamlet looks outward, trying to change the public world for the better, the corruption he finds disgusts him. When he looks inward, trying to change his inner world for the better, the paralysis he finds also disgusts him. He is withdrawn yet theatrical, consumed with grief yet flamboyant with wit, hyperaware of his inner self yet blind to his effect on others, an intellect without a strategy, an unstable self in search of an identity. Because both his inner and outer worlds seem meaningless, he verges on madness.

BELIEF VERSUS SKEPTICISM

Beliefs treat illusions as truths. Commonly held ideas such as "Human beings are more good than evil," "The Constitution embodies the perfect political system," "God rules the universe," and "My people are superior to your people" unify a society. When reality finally drags an illusion into the light, public belief withers, unity fractures, and people revolt. In the aftermath of revolution, however, society regroups around a more credible illusion and builds institutions to replace an old belief with a new fallacy.

Understanding this cycle, novelist Joseph Conrad divided his characters into two types: Idiots and Convicts. Idiots believe in illusions and enslave themselves to these ideas. Conradian idiots become heroes and nemeses, superpatriots and supervillains.

Convicts see illusions for what they are—comforting deceptions that protect us from an indifferent, hostile, chaotic universe. To a Conradian convict, action seems pointless. They often become the passive/reactive characters of pensive films, plays, and novels.

The writer's problem becomes this: A belief inspires something worth doing; stories put beliefs into action. A character void of belief can only pose like a statue.

Imagine, for example, a chronic skeptic who thinks beliefs are for fools. He trusts no one and nothing. He never acts, he only scoffs; sardonic wit is his sole trait. This convict might make an amusing sidekick or subject for a short story, but he hasn't the heft to carry a full-length telling. A story's spine of action needs a lightning charge of belief to animate action.

So, to prepare a skeptic for his story, give him a belief; to add complexity, contradict it. You could, for example, test his views about the supernatural. Does he believe in the existence of a supreme being or not? As a cynic, he's probably an agnostic who believes that the only logical position on the question of God's existence is to doubt both theism and atheism. On that point he's unshakable... until he falls in love with a believer and begins to doubt his doubt. What will he finally believe or not believe? Whichever way it turns, he's now an interesting man with story potential.

Each of these examples explored just one dominant dimension, but multiple inner contradictions can easily coexist in the same character, as they did in Odysseus and Tony Soprano. Indeed, the modern writer's ambition for the longform hundred-hour screen series demands characters of seemingly inexhaustible dimensionality, so that five years after their debut they still amaze audiences with hitherto unrevealed dynamics.

The list of conflicting contradictions in human consciousness seems endless. Think of any adjective, imagine its opposite, and you have the beginning of a character dimension: Independent/Dependent, Neuroticism/Stability, Extraversion/Introversion, Agreeableness/Disagreeableness, Open-to-experience/Closed-to-experience, Conscientiousness/Carelessness, and on it goes. The only limit is your imagination.[6]

CONSCIOUS VERSUS SUBCONSCIOUS CONFLICT

When talking about the innermost self, I prefer the term *subconscious* to *unconscious*. To me, the *un-* in *unconscious* suggests an inert, coma-like state, mindless as a rock. In fact, this deepest realm is an active, cognitive subconscious. *Sub-* simply means *"below* consciousness."[7]

During the night, the subconscious rises into mindfulness, disguised inside the symbolic objects and irrational story lines of dreams. Throughout the day, however, the hidden self stays unknown and unheard, busily driving the desires that consciousness puts into action.

Because the core self is unaware of this process, a character believes he guides his own life. In fact, he is not in command. An alien, hidden self also occupies him. As Freud said, "The manifestations I notice in myself but do not know how to link up with the rest of my mental life seem to belong to another person."

The conscious and subconscious aspects of the mind are Janus-faced, inseparable, conflicted, and overlapping. Where does the subconscious end and the conscious begin? When does a character become aware of his subconscious desires? When does a conscious habit sink into the unthinking and instinctive? No clear line separates the two. In the sections that follow, I hold these inner realms apart to illustrate the principles of character design. In your work to create multidimensional roles, however, you will have to draw the line specifically, character by character.

Confronting antisocial, often violent subconscious impulses is the primary moral struggle for almost every complex character you create. Embracing the hidden self's dark heart as well as its halo of light is essential to self-knowledge. Light, of course, is easy to see; making darkness visible takes courage.

When a story's inciting incident throws the life of a complex character out of balance, two desires appear simultaneously: (1) a conscious object of desire, a specific thing or situation that he feels would restore balance. (2) a subconscious, nascent desire that has lain undisturbed for years stirs to life.

THE CONSCIOUS OBJECT OF DESIRE

Everyone wants reasonable control over their existence and the events that impact it. When an inciting incident throws life out of kilter, the desire to restore equilibrium naturally arises within a protagonist. What he must do to achieve this rebalance may be unclear at first, but sooner or later he will conceive of his object of desire, something he believes has the power to put his life back on its feet.

Depending on the genre, his object of desire could be a physical thing such as a dead monster in the Horror film like *Splinter*; a situation such as a family reunion in a Domestic Drama like *The Corrections* by Jonathan Franzen; or an experience such as a spiritual transformation in an Evolution Plot like *The Razor's Edge* by W. Somerset Maugham.

In the vast majority of stories, the protagonist's conscious pursuit of an object of desire is sufficient to carry the telling.

THE SUBCONSCIOUS OBJECT OF DESIRE

When a deeply conflicted, complex protagonist begins pursuit of his object of desire, his subconscious often comes into play as well and adds a counterdesire. The subconscious has its own wants and knows what steps to take.

As a result, the inciting incident also provokes a subconscious drive, a hidden hunger that seeks its own object of desire, one that will satisfy a long dormant and unrecognized wish or grievance. This subconscious desire contradicts the protagonist's conscious desire, making the character, in many ways, his own worst enemy. A nascent counterdesire rarely, if ever, focuses on a physical object alone. Once again, depending on genre, his counterdesire could be either a situation such as the domination of an older sibling in a Domestic Drama, like the Skyler/Marie subplot in *Breaking Bad*, or an experience such as a transcendent, life-fulfilling romance in a Love Story, like *The Bridges of Madison County*.

If a character's conscious and subconscious desires are the same (hungry, he opens his refrigerator; horny, he masturbates; depressed, he calls a friend) they add neither complexity nor depth. Why give a character a subconscious desire if it just happens to be the same thing he wants consciously? Who would notice?

But if these two desires contradict each other, if his subconscious desire blocks and reverses his conscious will, then things get interesting. Psychologists from William James to Jacques Lacan have argued that the subconscious is a contra-mirror of its conscious cousin. For writers, reverse reflection has been common knowledge for centuries.

For a subconscious desire to draw the interest of a reader/audience, it must directly contradict or sharply contrast with the character's conscious hopes and longings. Then people notice . . . with interest.

The exact balance of power between a character's conscious and subconscious selves is up to the writer to strike: Neither dismiss it cynically as animal instinct, nor smugly treat it with a mechanical calculation.

LOVE VERSUS HATE

Consider the dimension that contradicts love with hate:

Jules Feiffer's screenplay for *Carnal Knowledge* spans the life of Jonathan Fuerst (Jack Nicholson) from his college days to middle age. If we were to ask Jonathan what he wants out of life, his conscious answer would be: "I'm a good-looking, fun-loving financial success. My life would be paradise if I could just find the perfect woman to share it." Over the decades he meets woman after woman, all attractive, all intelligent, all loving, but every affair falls into the same pattern: a beautifully amorous beginning, a bitter, boring middle, an ugly, humiliating break-up. In the wreckage of romance, each woman finds herself abandoned.

Jonathan's dominant dimension follows the tradition set by Don Juan and Vicomte de Valmont: the woman-hating romantic. Consciously, he tells himself that he gave a lifetime of love to women, and yet they, for various reasons, always broke his heart. Subconsciously, he loathed each and every one. Every year, he seduced a woman into adoration, then once he trapped her in that vulnerable place, he systematically crushed the heart out of her. The conscious desire to love and subconscious urge to hate have coexisted since monogamy.

FEAR VERSUS COURAGE

Action writers work along a spectrum that runs from life-risking action to paralyzed terror. When a dimension connects these two extremes, the result is genuine heroism.

Fear is an instinctive reaction to the threat of death, followed by an impulse to flee; courage is a deliberate choice to risk death, followed by action against the threat. Absolute fear begins in the subconscious and ultimately takes full control of a coward; absolute courage begins in a conscious choice and drives an Action Hero.

Superheroes, such as Spider-Man and Wolverine, build a character around one fantastic dimension, often fusing the human with the mythical, animal, magical, or pseudoscientific. Crime fighters, such as John McClane or Dirty Harry Callahan, cluster a characterization of true-to-life yet cool traits into a romanticized tough guy. Both types exhibit superlative, self-sacrificial, courageous altruism on behalf of the victimized, but nothing from their interior ever contradicts anything on their exterior.

Complex heroes such as Henry Fleming in Stephen Crane's novel *The Red Badge of Courage* or Richard Phillips (Tom Hanks) in *Captain Phillips* pit their conscious moral strength against a fear-soaked subconscious. In other words, unlike the idealized calm of an action hero, the mind of a realistic hero does not disconnect the conscious from the subconscious. Rather, the character makes decisions to take life-risking actions while simultaneously gripped by fear.

CONFLICTS WITHIN THE SUBCONSCIOUS

Readers and audiences perceive subconscious dimensions by implication. They compare what a character says with what he does; they match the reasons and rationalizations he gives others against the actual choices and actions he takes in the world. When they spot an inconsistency, they sense a clash of forces at work behind his eyes, fears skulking in the darkness versus angers aimed at the world. These deepest of all wars pit two irreconcilable hungers against each other. Ineffable subconscious conflicts, invisible to the character but glimpsed by the reader/audience, then push and pull through the story.

Portraying these hidden, primal conflicts may be the most difficult work that ever confronts an author. Novelists and short story writers often use an omniscient third-person narrator to describe a character's psychic tensions directly to the reader. Screenwriters and playwrights also use this device but rarely. Of the two kinds of storytellers—those who explain and those who imply—I prefer the latter.

SELF VERSUS OTHER

The lower brain obeys two imperatives: Protect yourself and protect your gene pool. In the balance, the life force feels that the second duty is more important than the first. For this reason, parents sacrifice themselves for their children, soldiers die for their country, and believers strap on dynamite vests to kill nonbelievers. The choice between self and genes may seem irrational at times, but it drove the evolution of life on our planet. Consequently, the most persistent, virtually daily conflict waged within the subconscious mind is self-love versus other-love.[8]

As a famous example, consider Robert Benton's screenplay for *Kramer vs. Kramer*. Ted Kramer (Dustin Hoffman) begins the story as a self-absorbed, immature workaholic whose wife labors as a stay-at-home mom for his son while playing surrogate mother to him. Her sudden abandonment of both throws Kramer's self-content life radically out of balance. This negative turning point arouses within Kramer a previously suppressed, never-acted-on need: the subconscious longing to be a mensch, a loving human being. His son's well-being becomes far more important than his own. At the climax, he acts to forfeit his needs for his son's.

ILLUSION VERSUS DELUSION

Another conflict that could arise in the subconscious concerns a character's processing of reality—the difference between illusion and delusion. An illusion is belief in a false perception, such as a mirage, a phantom limb, or faith in the impossible; a delusion is a rigid belief in a false reality, a symptom typical of mental disorder.

In the backstory of *A Streetcar Named Desire*, Tennessee Williams's protagonist, Blanche DuBois, pursued girlhood illusions of romantic love into a ruinous marriage, loss of her family estate, and secret years as a prostitute. Despite it all, she held on to her princess illusions and fantasized an ideal life to come. Finally, under extremes of alcohol, humiliation, and sexual violence, her self-deceptions collapse into total delusion and an asylum for the insane.

Absurdist farces, such as Edward Albee's *A Delicate Balance*, aside, characters beset with dimensions of subconscious contradiction often end in death or madness.

CASE STUDY: ANTONY AND CLEOPATRA

For two examples of how dimensions on multiple levels crisscross in a complex character, consider Shakespeare's magnificent lovers, Antony and Cleopatra.

Antony's prime dimension pits his social self against his hidden self: his command of the Roman Empire versus his lust for the queen of Egypt. Or put another way, a conflict between conscious reason and subconscious drive. Antony's political self pushes his reputation to its furthest reaches, while his inner self craves carnality at its most intense.

This clever, articulate, pragmatic, proud general is not confused about the politics of Rome. Antony knows what he ought to do. But he's also a pleasure-loving, beauty-obsessed, lovesick fool. His hunger for Cleopatra drives what he wants to do. And, as noted, the difference between ought and want is all the difference in the world.

To further enrich Antony's nature, Shakespeare added numerous contradictions over a wide range of behaviors. When he is on the world's stage, he roars in the rugged, heedless voice of a warrior-general. When he lounges with Cleopatra, he speaks with the kiss-soaked, caressing voice of a poet. He commands legions yet enslaves himself to a woman. He's an adult at the head of his armies, an adolescent at the feet of his beloved. He is willful on the battlefield, will-less in Cleopatra's bed.

If we look into the heart of Antony, we may see that for him war and love are just two versions of passion and pleasure. As people who love war will tell you, killing is a passion and victory a deep pleasure. In the film *Patton*, for example, when General George Patton surveys the carnage of dead and bleeding soldiers on a smoldering battlefield, he whispers, "God help me, but I love it so." The same words he might whisper in a midnight passion.

Cleopatra is one of Shakespeare's most complex characters. She's a royal decadent and an innocent enchantress. She's courageous in the face of her enemies yet panic-driven in war. She is a nonstop actress who fills her performances with such truth of feeling, no one doubts her.

In fact, men find her so alluring, that what in other women would be defects and vices, in her become perfections and virtues: Her vicious anger becomes aristocratic command; her wild wailings become the tears of sorrow; her immature clowning becomes charming humor; her drunkenness becomes queenly celebration; her nagging becomes concern for Antony; her begging and bargaining become humility and reasonableness; her bad jokes become wit; her wanton sexuality becomes charisma; her limitless ego and vanity get reinterpreted into patriotism and love of country.

Cleopatra's genius is this: When forces of rage, greed, and lust arise from her subconscious, her perceptive mind captures them before they can reach the world and converts them into entrancing, persuasive performances. What her lover, her enemies, and subjects see is not darkness but greatness. As a result, her core dimension mirrors Antony's: shrewd, willful, calculating ambition versus foolish, weak-willed, surrender to passion.

Some define tragedy as never getting what you want; others suggest that true tragedy gives you exactly what you want at its full price.

CHARACTER CONFLICT IN DEPTH

We often think of characters as if they were containers. We package their qualities inside spatial modifiers such as "round" and "flat." We label the incurious as "square," bores as "shallow," and bigots as "narrow," while a mind open to new ideas seems "broad." And perhaps the most common person-as-a-vessel allusion: "deep."

These adjectives serve as conversational shorthand, but to invent an intriguing, multidimensional role, an author takes the measure of a soul. By what gauge does someone seem full or empty? How can a writer sound the depths of character?

Human beings have an inborn echo device that pings into play the moment they meet someone. This instantaneous instinct needs no thought; it knows it when it sees it. Our subconscious sonar quickly tracks signs in the face, hears tremors in the voice, senses tensions in gestures, then looks behind the eyes to plumb the inner energies of a human vessel. This sounding of depth has a name: First Impression.

The first-impression instinct evolved to answer the question, "Can I trust this person?" The answer was (and still is) a key to survival. Characters that readers and audiences instinctively trust and admire over time tend to have inner dimensions reaching into their private and hidden selves. This sense of depth encourages empathy and trust.

Below are ten traits associated with depth of character, followed by examples taken from stage, screen, and page. If your storytelling ambitions call for characters of complexity and depth, this list should spur your imagination.

1. Ironic Self-Awareness

He is always on guard against self-deception and rarely fooled by what goes on inside his own mind. Example: Claire Underwood (Robin Wright) in Beau Willimon's longform series *House of Cards*.

2. Insight into Others

He is always aware of public pretensions and never fooled by what goes on inside society. Example: Madame Merle in Henry James's *The Portrait of a Lady*.

3. Intelligence

He can think. He gathers knowledge from all disciplines and commands the logic that puts it to work. Example: Miss Marple in twelve novels and twenty short stories by Agatha Christie.

4. A History of Suffering

As Aeschylus wrote in *The Oresteia*:

> *Even in our sleep, pain which cannot forget falls drop by drop upon the heart until, in our despair, against our will, through the terrible grace of God, comes wisdom.*

Although a character wishes for happiness, he finds depth through suffering. The happy mind thinks about life's benefits; the suffering mind sinks deeper into itself. Suffering takes a character beneath his routines to discover he is not who he thought he was. Losing a loved one smashes through the floor of the core self, revealing a deeper level. Grief then smashes through that floor, revealing yet greater depth.[9]

Try as people may, they cannot tell themselves to stop feeling pain. Suffering gives them a more accurate sense of their limitations, what they can and cannot control. Pain propels a callow mind into maturity. The wise response places anguished experiences in a moral context and redeems something bad by turning it into something precious. In short, a deep soul has witnessed pain, caused pain, and lived with the guilt. Example: Mike Ehrmantraut (Jonathan Banks) in *Breaking Bad* and *Better Call Saul* risks his life in crime after crime to provide a future for his granddaughter.

5. Broad Experience over Time

A young character may seem wise beyond his years, but in truth, depth needs wide-ranging experience and, above all, time. Example: Claudia Hampton in Penelope Lively's novel *Moon Tiger*.

6. Focused Attention

Face-to-face, he listens intently, makes eye contact and reads subtext. Example: Don Vito Corleone (Marlon Brando / Robert De Niro) in *The Godfather* and *The Godfather Part II*.

7. Love of Beauty

Depth sharpens his sensitivity until beauty is almost painful. Example: Aaliya Sohbi in *An Unnecessary Woman* by Rabih Alameddine.

8. Calm

No matter the threat or stress, he keeps his passions under control. Example: Captain Augustus "Gus" McCrae (Robert Duvall) in Larry McMurtry's miniseries, *Lonesome Dove*, which was based on his novel.

9. Cynic and Skeptic

Hope, he believes, is the denial of reality. He doesn't trust anything anyone says until he tests it against his own mind. Example: Mama Nadi in *Ruined* by playwright Lynn Nottage.

10. A Searcher for Meaning

He gets God's joke. He knows life has no intrinsic meaning. So he searches for one somewhere in the gap between living for yourself and living for others. Example: Benna Carpenter in Lorrie Moore's novel *Anagrams*.

Roll these traits into one role and they often create an antihero—a loner hardened by bad luck but vulnerable to the suffering of others; a stoic bemused by his own suffering; sharp-witted in public, self-mocking when alone; cynical about society's rules, committed to a personal code; a romantic wary of romance.

All ten traits embedded themselves in Sam Spade (*The Maltese Falcon*), Rick Blaine (*Casablanca*), and Philip Marlowe (*The Big Sleep*), who were portrayed to perfection three times over by Humphrey Bogart. Few actors since have been tested to that depth; Denzel Washington first among the best.

LIFE IN THE SUBTEXT

Text: a character's outer behavior in word and action. These verbal and physical expressions stimulate images in a reader's imagination or strike the eye and ear of an audience. Together, they create his characterization.

Subtext: a character's thoughts and feelings that are conscious but unexpressed as well as subconscious and thus inexpressible. The core self plies these ideas and attitudes within himself and to no one else; while at a deepest level of subtext, his ineffable moods and desires pulse below his awareness.[10]

Minor characters are text only. These roles serve a story by acting out exactly who they seem to be. The writer deliberately denies them depth and an inner life worth knowing.

A major character, on the other hand, is not who he seems. His text of characterization masks the mystery of his core self, alive in the subtext. His implicit inner life intrigues readers and audiences, sparking the question, "Who is this character...really?" The scent of subtext invites them to explore and unearth the truth of this unknown self. In short, a beautifully conceived and executed multidimensional character turns readers and audiences into psychics.

Think about your own story-going hours. When you follow a character's life, turning pages of prose or sitting in a dark theatre, don't you have the distinct impression that you're reading minds, reading emotions? Your perceptions seem to travel beneath their behaviors, and you think to yourself, "I know what's going on inside that character better than he knows. I can see from the surface to the substance of what he's really thinking, really feeling, and really wanting, consciously and subconsciously."

You gain these insights on your own, as you must, because as in life, depth can only be intuited. This is why two people experiencing the same character often come away with very different interpretations. The subtextural someone living inside a complex role can never be fully explained in words, no matter who writes them. No one can tell you what to think about a character, not even the character himself in his most heartfelt confessions. The godlike omniscient narrators of the greatest of novels imply more than they tell, leave far more unsaid than said. This is why the archives of libraries stack thousands of works of literary criticism, all asking who questions: Who is Hamlet? Who is Anna Karenina? Who is Walter White?

The partition of text and subtext—what the world sees in the outer self versus the truth concealed behind the eyes—is essential to sanity. If the invasive world cannot be kept safely outside the mind, the inner life becomes unlivable.

Like readers and audiences, characters themselves peer into the subtextural depths of each other, trying to discover a hidden truth: Can I believe him? What does he really mean? Really want? Who does he care about? Himself or others? And on it goes as each character reads the subtext of the others: Othello must discover if his wife is virtuous; Lear must discover which daughter, if any, loves him; Hamlet must discover if his uncle murdered his father and finally does so by reading Claudio's guilty reaction to a murder scene played out onstage.

Introspective characters rerun personal experiences as if they were TV episodes, searching through their subtexts, analyzing their actions, trying to figure out who they really are and how they got that way. Sometimes the self-reflective mind uncovers hidden insights, learns from mistakes, and increases self-awareness; at other times, it obsesses over its failures, doubts its worth, and blinds itself to the truth.

Three examples: the self-absorbed, self-narrating protagonists of the novels *A Fan's Notes* by Frederick Exley; *The Sea, The Sea* by Iris Murdoch; and *The Woman Upstairs* by Claire Messud.

11

THE COMPLETED CHARACTER

The golden ideal of character creation:

First, conceive of a compelling, complex nature, rich in human promise but, like anyone with life left to live, incomplete. Then, as she makes and takes pressure-filled decisions and actions over the course of the story, progressively realize her unfulfilled potential. Finally, at the story's climax, send her through an experience, both emotionally and mentally, that propels her to the absolute limits of her humanity: nothing left undiscovered, nothing left unexplored, nothing left unused, nothing left unfelt, nothing left unexpressed. Everything latent fulfilled, everything actable performed, everything knowable revealed, everything latent expressed, every emotion lived in full. The character is complete.

To achieve this ideal, role design takes four major steps: Preparation, Revelation, Change, Completion.

FOUR MAJOR STEPS OF CHARACTER DESIGN

1. Preparation

Principle: At the inciting incident, major characters are incomplete.

As a story begins, its major characters, like most people, have never experienced their mental, emotional, and moral possibilities to their absolute limits. Their feelings and thoughts have known a certain depth but never the fullest range of passion and insight because life has never asked it of them. They are incomplete but unaware of it. The story that lies ahead will bring them experiences they've never known before and affect them in ways they cannot see coming. Only the author knows what's nascent within them and what their true range of experience may be.

In my definition, *character need* is a void in a role's humanity: unthought intelligence, underfelt emotion, unused talent, underlived life. Need is something half done that needs to be finished; something missing that yearns to be found.

Therefore, as a complex character enters your story, she is a work in progress. To reach the golden ideal, you must put your character through encounters that will take her mentally and emotionally into the deepest depths and farthest stretches of her humanity.

But what is her potential? Before your protagonist enters your story, take her measure. What is her IQ and EQ? Her willpower? Her imagination? The depth of her empathy? The height of her courage? Give thought to how far life has taken her and how much deeper the future might carry her.

Next, ask this key question: What event would send my protagonist along a spine of action that ends in a climax of such emotional power and mind-expanding insight that she experiences her humanity at its supreme limit and thus, for better or worse, completes herself? The answer, once you find it, will become your story's inciting incident. The choice of an inciting incident perfectly tuned to the protagonist's need makes fine writing possible.

Four examples:

At the inciting incident of *The Leftovers*, the longform series by Damon Lindelof and Tom Perrotta, 2 percent of the world's population instantly disappears. With that, co-protagonists Kevin Garvey (Justin Theroux) and Nora Durst (Carrie Coon) suddenly find life meaningless.

At the inciting incident of *Machinal*, a play by Sophie Treadwell, Helen, submitting to parental and social pressure, marries a man who disgusts her, thinking that this will give her a secure life.

At the inciting incident of *Fight Club*, a novel by Chuck Palahniuk, the protagonist, known only in the first-person voice of the narrator, moves in with Tyler Durden, and together they build a fight club.

At the inciting incident of *Mrs. Soffel*, a film written by Ron Nyswaner, Kate Soffel (Diane Keaton), a prison warden's wife, decides to save the soul of a condemned prisoner.

2. Revelation

Principle: A story's dynamic of events reveals true character in contrast with or contradiction to characterization.

The vast majority of all genres reveal an inner truth of their characters but do not arc them. As Samuel Butler put it, "It is one against legion when a creature tries to differ from his own past selves." Deep character change is difficult and exceptional. Six genres, however, do arc their protagonists over the course of a telling, and these will be laid out in Chapter Fourteen.

The genres of Action/Adventure, War, Horror, Fantasy, and Crime, as well as most dramas and comedies about physical, political, domestic, and romantic struggles, submerge a core self beneath layers of believable yet intriguing characterization. They then reveal this inner nature, exposing but never changing the character's psychology and morality. What changes is the reader's/audience's insight.

The most powerful revelations occur when events put a character at maximum risk. The choice, for example, between life and death is easily made and any insight that follows relatively shallow. But a choice between two deaths—one by a long, painful disease, the other by quick suicide—strips away a character's public and personal personae, revealing the core self. By the same token, if she stands to lose a thing of great value in order to gain another thing of equal value, her choice expresses who she is.

In Martin McDonagh's play *The Beauty Queen of Leenane*, Maureen Folan, a forty-year-old former inmate of an insane asylum, seems like a submissive, intimidated overgrown child until she murders her mother, puts on her mother's clothes, and takes her mother's place in the living room rocking chair. In Maureen's schizophrenic mind, she has always been her mother; playing her daughter was just a temporary guise.

In J. D. Salinger's novel *The Catcher in the Rye,* the cynical, lonely Holden Caulfield suffers confusion about his sexuality and longing for an idealized romance. He feels alienated from people and alienates others in return. His attitudes vary, but his core self never fundamentally alters from first page to last.

In Woody Allen's *Annie Hall*, Alvy Singer's boyhood insecurities poisoned his adulthood. He so hates the truth, he chooses fantasy over reality. Happiness so sours him, he chooses misery over joy. His obsession with himself renders him incapable of love. Over time, his choices expose a twisted, unchanging neurotic lurking under his wit and charm.

To sum up: As the outer circumstances in a protagonist's life undergo change, her choices and actions slowly uncover her core self. With each word and gesture, her characterization peels away, leaving her true self standing naked, as it were, at the climax. Although the true character, once revealed, did not evolve, the reader's or audience's perceptions did, growing deeper and deeper in understanding. Once again, this archetypal pattern of a revealed but unchanged character underlies the vast majority of major characters in the vast majority of all stories ever told.

Test this principle in your own work by asking two simple questions of primary characters: Who do we *think* she is at the beginning of the story? Who do we *know* she is by the story's climax? Your answers should reveal a change of insight in the reader/audience.

3. Change

Principle: Character change puts dimension into action.

An age-old puzzle known as the Ship of Theseus Paradox asks: "If a ship is repaired slowly over time so that eventually every part is replaced, is it still the same ship, deserving the same name? If, on the other hand, the ship were lost at sea but another were remade to its exact specifications, does it need a new name or is it essentially the same?"

In both cases not a single board, cleat, or sail is left from the original. Nonetheless, the two ships prompt opposite conclusions: Most people feel that the slowly repaired craft stays the same and should keep its name, but the replacement vessel is new and needs a rechristening.

This archaic puzzle, of course, is not about nautical nomenclature. It's a metaphor for human change. Substitute *identity* for *ship* and it becomes a parable that raises the questions of "Who am I? Who was I? Who will I be? Will fate preserve me or remake me?" Like a ship navigating unknown waters, a complex character sails through random, unexpected, life-battering events that may or may not alter her nature.

Some writers react to character change the same way the public treats the Theseus Paradox: Gradual revisions do not change their character's core identity, while the shock and scar of an explosive event mutates it. Other writers do the opposite: Powerful events never dent their character, although time may slowly evolve her.

As we saw in Chapter Three, every author needs a personal theory of human nature so she can answer the question: "Does damage to my character's life change or not change her core identity?"

Which do you believe? Is a character, like the Ship of Theseus, becoming a more concentrated although essentially unchanged self over time, or is she transforming into a wholly different self that her past self wouldn't recognize? In other words, does your character's every thought evolve her into a minutely different self than she was the moment before? Does every hour she spends with others gradually make her more like them? Or do you believe that these shifts are trivial and that at heart your character always stays who she is?

The Theory of Perpetual Identity

The theory of perpetual identity holds that a child at birth is a clean slate and could become almost anyone, but as life inscribes her with experience, she develops unique patterns of action/reaction that hold her mind together and create her persistent identity. Shifts in characterization take place around this stable center. Once the pattern is set, her choices and actions in the story's future events make her more and more specific, more and more herself.

In *Middlemarch*, George Eliot expressed her belief in perpetual identity with this often quoted image: "Even while we rave on the heights [we] behold the wide plain where our persistent self pauses and awaits us."

In tellings about a protagonist's search for identity, characters such as Jimmy Porter in John Osborne's play *Look Back in Anger* and James McBride in his memoir *The Color of Water* recognize their outer changes, but at the same time feel that their past belongs to them and, in a sense, is them. In fact, the act of retrospection itself implies a constant identity. If a character's core self didn't persist through time, it couldn't exist in the present to look back at its past.

Many writers believe that the core self secures itself against a steady succession of changes in its outer life—bodily changes, personal and social changes in relationships, career moves, housing moves, and the like. Constantly changing circumstances do not change its essence—least of all, its moral nature.[1] For example, Alex (Malcolm McDowell), the protagonist of Stanley Kubrick's *A Clockwork Orange* (a film adaptation of Anthony Burgess's novel), both inflicts and suffers hideous pain but stays steadfast, even happily, the same.

The Theory of the Changing Identity

Animals obey instincts; humans analyze theirs. Wolves never worry about what it means to be a wolf, they just wolf. But the self-aware human mind frets over its urges and intuitions, charts the push and pull of instinct and reason, all in an effort to become a better or at least a different version of itself. For this reason, many writers believe that change is not only possible but essential.

Change, when it occurs, arcs along a character's defining dimension. In John Milton's epic *Paradise Lost*, for example, the protagonist's core contradiction is Good/Evil. The story traces a positive to negative arc as Lucifer, Angel of Light (Good), compelled by pride, gathers an army of like-minded angels and tries to overthrow God. After three days of war he's hurled out of Heaven and down to Hell, where he takes the name Satan, Angel of Darkness (Evil).

Other examples: The dimension Kindness/Cruelty arcs from positive to negative in Chuck Tatum (Kirk Douglas) in Billy Wilder's *Ace in the Hole*, but in the reverse direction in Amir in *The Kite Runner* by Khaled Hosseini. Generosity/Greed swings from negative to positive in Ebenezer Scrooge in Charles Dickens's novella *A Christmas Carol*, but in the reverse for Bobby Axelrod (Damian Lewis) in the Showtime series *Billions*. Multiple dimensions could crisscross with irony: In Aravind Adiga's novel *The White Tiger*, Balram Halwai goes from law-abiding citizen to criminal (positive to negative), while he also changes from impoverished laborer to a corporate executive (negative to positive).

The value-charge in a changing self can pivot in one of two directions: positive or negative.

Positive Arcs

Definition: A positive arc, as the name implies, ends on a positive charge. It could open with a character in either a positive or a negative state, and then move in alternating positive/negative cycles that increase their impact to a climax that fulfills the character's desire.

A positive arc, therefore, often begins when a character senses a negative state within herself. At first, she resists change, but revelations of yet more bitter truths eventually overcome her reluctance until she finally reaches the top of a moral slope.

Examples:

In John Patrick Shanley's play *Doubt: A Parable*, Sister Aloysius arcs from an autocrat blinded by self-righteousness (Arrogance) to a woman shamed by doubt (Humility).

In Danny Rubin's screenplay for *Groundhog Day*, Phil Connors (Bill Murray) evolves from an immature, self-absorbed egoist incapable of love (Selfishness) to a mature, compassionate, heartful lover (Selflessness).

In J. M. Coetzee's novel *Disgrace*, David Lurie, a manipulative seducer and pretentious intellectual (Self-deception) slowly deconstructs his life and finally accepts his place in a world beyond his control (Self-awareness).

Here from the series and films *Sex and the City* are four positive arcs that take characters from incomplete to complete:

Carrie Bradshaw

Carrie (Sarah Jessica Parker) is a pop journalist who writes about sexual and romantic relationships in New York City. Despite her intelligent study and careful observations of these issues, her emotions dominate her choices and behaviors. Carrie opens the series self-conscious and insecure. Over the course of six seasons and two films she arcs to self-possessed and secure.

At the beginning of the series she seeks acceptance and reassurance from her friends and the men in her life, particularly Mr. Big (Chris Noth). Her neuroses become obsessions such as having a key to her lover's apartment and equal space in his bathroom cabinet. She's aware of her behavior and blames it on her tendency to "get carried away." "Just tell me I'm the one," she begs Big at the end of Season 1. She's flawed but empathetic, thanks to her self-deprecating humor.

She searches for true love and commitment but doubts that she's the marriage and family type. Mr. Big, who she meets in the first episode of the series, is her first and only great love. Despite her many other affairs, she feels that Big is her soul mate. At the end of the sixth and last season, Big announces that he is coming back to New York City from California to be with Carrie. At the climax of the first film they marry. Question: Has she arced to self-possession on her own, or has marriage done it for her?

Samantha Jones

The hypersexual Samantha (Kim Cattrall) is the oldest of the four friends and owns her own PR firm. As a self-proclaimed "Try-Sexual" (meaning she'll try anything once), most of Samantha's story lines revolve around her sexual escapades. Passion is her passion, with or without romantic ritual, but she never loves anyone other than herself. She seems incapable of love, and so the series arcs her through a Redemption Plot.

Although sexually narcissistic, among her friends Samantha is the most loyal and least judgmental. She engages in a few serious relationships, one of them lesbian, but rarely dates anyone more than once or twice. In Season 6, however, two things happen: She gets involved with Smith (Jason Lewis) and is diagnosed with breast cancer.

She faces her cancer with great courage and wit. No matter how ugly the therapy, Smith stands by her through the worst of times. She loves him for it; in the first film, set four years later, she lives with him in LA and does her best to stay in a committed relationship.

But despite her tender feelings for Smith, she finds herself madly attracted to her hypersexual neighbor. She finally questions her feeling and concludes that she loves herself more than Smith. They break up. In the second film, she's back to her old self, having sex on the hood of a guy's Mercedes.

Samantha undergoes a double arc: loveless sexual obsession (her true self) to committed sexless love (her false self) back to loveless sexual obsession (her truest self).

Charlotte York

Charlotte (Kristin Davis) is a Connecticut blueblood, prom queen, cheerleader, track star, teen model, equestrienne, Smith College grad, art dealer—aka a WASP. She undergoes an Education Plot from naïve to worldly.

She's blindly romantic, always searching for her knight in shining armor. The least cynical of her friends, she believes love conquers all. She distains the libertine antics of her friends, convinced that dating has rules. Her friends are often envious and even in awe of Charlotte's overall optimism about love. Yet she occasionally surprises them with dirty talk and her love of oral sex.

Her belief in romance leads her to decide not to have sex with her fiancé until their honeymoon, only to discover that her "perfect" husband is impotent. She eventually divorces him due to his twisted relationship with his mother.

Although Charlotte is initially put off by her divorce attorney's constant sweating, messy eating, bald head, and hairy body, she sleeps with him when he confesses his intense attraction to her. Harry (Evan Handler) gives her the best sex of her life. She tries to keep their relationship strictly sexual, but because of Harry's deep caring, she finds herself falling in love.

Initially, she tries to reform him to fit more closely with her image of the ideal man, but when she realizes how much pain she's causing him, she accepts Harry the way he is. In fact, she converts to Judaism because of Harry's avowal to only marry a Jewish woman.

Only when Charlotte realizes that she must put aside her romantic ideals and accept Harry on his own terms does she find a love that fulfills her romantic ideals. The man who is the antithesis of the perfect man becomes her ideal mate. She undergoes an arc from a real-life disaster with Mr. Right to ideal love with Mr. Wrong.

Miranda Hobbes

Miranda (Cynthia Nixon), a Wall Street lawyer, overvalues work and undervalues men. She arcs through a double Education Plot, changing her attitudes toward both. In the early seasons, she treats men with distrust and resentment, finding them immature and unrealistically romantic.

Then Miranda meets Steve (David Eigenberg), a bartender. What starts as a one-night stand grows into sharing an apartment. Economic differences cause arguments, so they separate but keep a friendly sexual relationship. When Steve loses a testicle to cancer, Miranda sleeps with him to convince him that women will still find him attractive whether he has one ball or two.

As a result, she gets pregnant but decides against an abortion. Pregnancy softens her character and she tells Steve that she'll take full responsibility, raise the child, and let him visit the boy if he likes. Motherhood stresses this workaholic, but she finds ways to balance career and a child. She and Steve try to raise their son as platonic partners.

At the boy's first birthday party, Miranda blurts out her love for Steve and to her delight, Steve declares that she's "the One." They marry.

In the second film, Miranda is so overworked that she misses her son's school activities. What's worse, her misogynistic boss disrespects her. Steve convinces her to quit and find a fulfilling job at a firm where she's admired and appreciated. Miranda arcs from imbalance to balance in both work and love.

Negative Arcs

A negative arc could begin with a character in either a positive or negative state, and then alternate positive/negative cycles that deepen in impact until ending in tragedy. This arc, of course, shapes the lives and deaths of Shakespeare's greatest dramatic characters: Antony and Cleopatra, Macbeth and Lady Macbeth, Brutus and Cassius, Coriolanus, Richard III, Hamlet, Othello, King Lear—all of whom complete themselves in a tragic climax.

Negative arcs often begin with a character living in youthful fantasies or naïveté. Reality punctuates her dreams, but she insists on her beliefs until she descends into a pain-filled, irreversible truth: Ibsen's Hedda Gabler, Strindberg's Miss Julie, along with the protagonists of almost every play by Tennessee Williams.

A Good-to-Evil arc could start with a sweet little girl and end with a serial killer (*The Bad Seed*, a play by Maxwell Anderson), or begin with a hard-working white collar engineer and end in a violent psychic breakdown (*Falling Down*, a film by Joel Schumacher) or open with an idealist and arc him into a mass murderer (*Ostland*, a novel by David Thomas).

In Thomas Hardy's novel *Jude the Obscure*, Jude Fawley, a manual laborer, homeschools himself in classical Greek and Latin in hopes of becoming a university scholar (Fantasy). But lower-class deprivations and upper-class bigotries quash his dream. He spends his entire working life cutting stone until he dies in bitter poverty (Reality).

The backstory of George Lucas's *Star Wars* saga mirrors Lucifer's fall.

In it, a Jedi knight, Anakin Skywalker (Good), seeking power over life and death in hope of saving the woman he loves, moves from the realm of light to the infamous dark side. Burnt and dismembered in battle, he joins the empire and takes the name Darth Vader (Evil).

In Patrick Marber's play *Closer*, Dan, Anna, Larry, and Alice search for loving, intimate relationships (Meaningful). All four cycle through years of meeting, making love, partnering up, and breaking up, finally ending in loneliness and discontent (Meaningless).

Character arcs, positive or negative, seldom trace a smooth line but more likely move in dynamic zigzags. If a story's values never change their charge, the telling freezes into a portrait. Imagine if everything that happens runs positive, positive, positive, finally leaving the cast beaming in delight. Or if nothing but grim scenes surge further and further downhill until they crush the characters at the bottom. Repetition is the writer's mortal enemy.

Change from a Character's POV

When your character looks back on her life, who does she see? Herself or someone else? Is she still the same? Better? Worse? Unrecognizable? Does she hate, like, or ignore who she was, who she is, who she will be?

Attitudes toward oneself span from narcissism to self-love to self-respect to self-indifference to self-criticism to self-hate to thoughts of suicide. Two contradictory visions bracket this spectrum: Life-as-Fate and Life-as-Destiny.

Life-as-Fate: If your character looks backward, rarely forward, she may feel trapped in a fate not her own. She may never satisfy her own desires, only the demands of others. She feels lost and out of contact with her true self, an identity hidden somewhere in her subconscious.

As this child of fate surveys her past, does she feel that instead of evolving, she has turned into someone she doesn't know? Do her old beliefs, values, and goals seem lost? Do past desires and behaviors baffle her? Does she wonder how she could have done the things she once did? Do her past deeds seem alien, if not incomprehensible? Does change seem so great that she can't imagine how she could have ever been who she was? In other words, is she self-alienated?

Life-as-Destiny: If your character looks forward, rarely backward, she lives life on her own terms, freely choosing her own path. She never doubts that she is her core self. Destiny implies a destination, and hers awaits in the future, drawing her toward fulfillment.

As this child of destiny progresses to adulthood, does she identify with her changed self? As her teenage anger softens into midlife contentment, as her dedication to career gradually drains away, as arthritis slowly ages her, does she look back and feel that although she's evolved physically and emotionally, at heart she's essentially the same? Has her original psychological makeup evolved naturally? Do her past desires influence present actions? In other words, is she self-empathetic? How does your character see herself over time?

For some characters, change brings clarity. In Frank Darabont's screenplay for *The Shawshank Redemption*, Red (Morgan Freeman) sees his past without distortion or rationalization and wishes he could go back in time to his young self, who had committed a terrible crime, and shake sense into him.

For some characters, change brings confusion. In D. H. Lawrence's novel *The Rainbow*, Ursula Brangwen reviews her life in bewilderment. Every phase seems so different yet always herself: "But what did it mean, Ursula Brangwen? She did not know what she was. Only she was full of rejection, of refusal. Always, always she was spitting out of her mouth the ash and grit of disillusion, of falsity."

For some characters change brings anger. In Samuel Beckett's play *Krapp's Last Tape*, Krapp at age sixty-nine listens to recordings he's made over the decades. In his youth he believed in a lifelong identity. No more. When he listens to his past voices, he knows they were once him, but he sneers at them all and empathizes with none. Like a snake leaving his skin behind, year after year he sloughs off his earlier selves until he's left with a bitter old man, the final Krapp.

Whether change happens fast or slow, inward or outward, by chance or by will, all characters interpret change idiosyncratically—some accept, some deny, some take no notice. In general, however, change elicits four possible reactions:

1. A character may feel that change is merely cosmetic and she'll be back to her old self soon.
2. She may feel transformed into a better self.
3. She may view the past as the grave of the better woman she once was and left behind.

4. She may discover her true self, the self she repressed since child-hood. Now, for better or worse, she can finally live who she really is.

Change from an Author's POV

What is your personal take on character change? How do your characters react to it? Some writers believe in the permanence of identity, others in deep change. Some reveal true character, others keep it a mystery; some arc characters, others do not. In all cases, however, how an author connects a character to her past shapes the course of her identity.

A healthy past, for example, strengthens the link between past and present and keeps identity whole; a traumatic past weakens and fragments it. Once damaged by abuse, the core self holds on to its sanity by clinging to its memories, struggling to keep them alive and true. In this case, the past may inflict itself on a character with various results. Here are four possibilities:

1. Obsession: A trauma constantly reenters the mind with the sharp-edged impact of its original experience, unshaded and unblunted by time—PTSD, for example. Because a psychological scar never forms, each remembrance tears open the same wound.
2. Repression: The conscious mind buries a painful memory in the subconscious where it festers, fueling neuroses, warping identity.
3. Fantasy: If a trauma refuses to fade, the mind copes with its pain by rewriting the past into alternative events it never lived but fantasizes it did.
4. Balance: The mind courageously faces the truth with neither excess nor distortion.

Does the cause and timing of change alter your character's sense of self? If change comes suddenly (a kitchen accident scalds her face and hands), would physical disfigurement shred her identity? If change comes slowly by deliberate choice (each day she poisons her husband just enough to make him sick, as punishment for an insult, but over time she slowly decides he doesn't deserve to live), is she exposed for who she always was, or does a changed self replace the old? Fine authors develop unique, idiosyncratic approaches to character arcs.

Change from the Reader's/Audience's POV

At a story's beginning, as exposition piles up, readers and audiences absorb the surfaces, discovering who the characters seem to be. Twin curiosities about character revelation and change hold interest to the last moments: Who are these characters at heart? Who might they become?

Understanding the necessity to pace and build a reader's or an audience's interest, the writer must time a story's events to first conceal, then reveal, the next change and ultimately complete a complex character.

4. Completion

Principle: The finest works of story art fulfill their protagonist's need and desire at the limits of human experience.

The terms *need* and *desire* may seem synonymous, but in my view, they name two very different aspects of character, seen from two very different points of view.

Desire: a character's persistent purpose, her unreached goal. Throughout a story's telling, as the protagonist struggles to put her life back in balance, she pursues her object of desire as far as her emotional and mental powers can reach.

Need: an empty inner space, a potential that craves realization. At the inciting incident, the writer recognizes an incompleteness in her protagonist. She's raw material for a superb character but lacking the unique experience that would fulfill her unique potential. She, therefore, needs to complete her humanity.

At the climax, the events she creates do just that. The story's final turning points put the protagonist's emotional and mental capacities under enormous pressure. With her last actions, she experiences herself to the limit of her capacities as her author explores and expresses her core self at her greatest emotional and mental depths. She thus becomes a completed character—nothing left to reveal, nothing left to change.

Characters are never aware of their need. Only their author sees it; only their author knows what's latent in her character; only the author can imagine her character in her most complete state.

Characters who do not change—action heroes, cartoon figures, comic roles—have no need. They are unchanging yet fascinating. In *Curb Your*

Enthusiasm, Larry David is the same obsessive at the beginning of each season as he is at the end. Episode after episode, he blindly pursues his slavish mania for propriety, acting out his rigid, hysterically funny self. This same pattern carries over, sequel after sequel, for the superheroes in Marvel's cinematic universe.

In character-driven genres (see Chapter Fourteen), however, stories open with their principals, especially protagonists, internally incomplete. Their lives to date have never called on them to use their capacities (intelligence, morality, talent, willpower, emotional forces such as love and hate, even courage and cunning) to their limit. But during the story's clashes the characters' actions and reactions do that work. At climax, their instinctive need to complete their humanity propels them to the end of the line, the limit of human experience.

Examples of completed characters:

In Euripides's play *Medea*, Princess Medea discovers that Jason, her lover and father of their two boys, has abandoned her for another woman. Medea not only poisons the other woman and the other woman's father but, to punish Jason, murders their children as well. She escapes with her sons' bodies and buries them in hiding so Jason can never say a prayer over their graves. With this revenge, Medea propels herself to a stunning extreme.

At the climax of Sophocles's *Oedipus Rex*, Oedipus's discovery that he has unwittingly murdered his father and married his mother so horrifies him that, raging with grief, he gouges out his eyes. This bolt of emotion numbs all thought, leaving Oedipus in shock and unfinished.

Twenty-three years later, however, Sophocles, at age ninety, completed his character. In *Oedipus at Colonus*, Oedipus thinks to the heart of his complicity and realizes that his pulsing pride and lack of self-awareness shaped his fate. In short, he should have known better. Once he accepts his guilt, he completes himself and dies in peace.

In Kim Ki-duk's *Spring, Summer, Fall, Winter...and Spring*, an apprentice Buddhist monk evolves from a cruel child to a lustful teenager to a wife-murdering felon to a repentant convict to a Buddhist master—an arc that ends in an inner gravity of genuine change, life-worn wisdom, and completion of self.

In *The Sea, The Sea*, a novel by Iris Murdoch, Charles Arrowby, a playwright and director, pursues his lifelong obsession with romance, never understanding that his first, true, and only love is and always has been himself. He finally exhausts his limited humanity, trapped in a cul-de-sac of self-deception, completely blind to himself.

In *Network* by Paddy Chayefsky, adapted for stage by Lee Hall, TV anchorman Howard Beale (Peter Finch on-screen, Bryan Cranston onstage), makes headline news by declaring that modern life is bullshit. Beale's prime-time rants bring higher and higher ratings as he spirals deeper and deeper into insanity. Eventually, his message about meaninglessness becomes meaningless. As his ratings fall, the network has him assassinated on camera. He dies, but not until all of his dimensions have been exposed and exhausted.

When is Michael Corleone completed? At the end of *The Godfather Part II*? Some think yes; I think not. Over the first two films, Michael makes others suffer, but he doesn't burn in real hell until *The Godfather Part III* completes him.

In the finale of *The Leftovers*, the love story between Nora and Kevin climaxes quietly as they hold hands over a kitchen table. For three seasons, Nora's cynicism keeps her from believing in Kevin, and Kevin's intimacy aversion keeps him from believing he deserves Nora. In between their personal episodes, Nora travels sideways to a parallel universe in search of her lost family, while Kevin dies and rises from the dead, again and again. Once they realize that the only way to make sense of the senseless is to believe in their love, they reach completion.

COMPLETING A CHARACTER

To sum up: For some characters, a fierce longing to make their mark on the world, an unquenchable thirst to find purpose, drives them to complete themselves. For others, an inner fear of fragmentation or a fervent curiosity about their natures propels them. In both cases, the uncompleted construct themselves inwardly by testing themselves outwardly. They take grave risks to pursue something they value supremely but cannot control fully . . . even when they reach it.[2]

The vast majority of characters, however, rarely question how deeply they've gone into life, how much wider they might go, if they'll ever experience themselves to their fullest. Instead, the writer does that for them by taking key measurements and asking key questions.

Writing to fulfill a character's need to complete begins with the recognition that we are all born with excess capacity, with far more thought and feeling than life will ever demand, with powers we will never use. So study your character in those days just before the story begins and ask: Given my character at this point in her life, given the small percentage of mental and emotional aptitude she's used thus far and given the depths and breadths she might someday touch, what does her humanity lack?

With that answer in hand, then ask: What does she need to complete herself? What specific event, should it happen to her, would propel her toward fulfillment of her promise? That turning point becomes your story's inciting incident.

After that ask: What events would carry her to the limits of her greatest thoughts, her deepest being? What pressures, conflicts, choices, actions, and reactions will take her humanity to its fullest? These answers become the story you tell.

Once characters reach completion, they often reflect on the ironies that scarred and yet fulfilled their humanity. We'll close with their thoughts:

> *To-morrow, and to-morrow, and to-morrow, creeps in this petty pace*
> *from day to day to the last syllable of recorded time . . .*
> —*Macbeth in* The Tragedy of Macbeth

> *Yes, she thought, laying down her brush in extreme fatigue, I have had*
> *my vision.*
> —*Lily in Virginia Woolf's* To the Lighthouse

> *And soon now we shall go out of the house and go into the convulsion*
> *of the world, out of history into history and the awful responsibility of*
> *Time.*
> –*Jack Burden in Robert Penn Warren's* All the King's Men

> *I'm thinking of aurochs and angels, the secret of durable pigments, pro-*
> *phetic sonnets, the refuge of art. And this is the only immortality you*
> *and I may share, my Lolita.*
> —*Humbert Humbert in Vladimir Nabokov's* Lolita

> *Mediocracies everywhere—now and to come—I absolve you all. Amen.*
> —*Salieri in Peter Shaffer's play* Amadeus

It's old light, and there's not much of it. But it's enough to see by.
— *Elaine in Margaret Atwood's* Cat's Eye

It seems that destiny has taken a hand.
— *Rick Blaine in* Casablanca

12

THE SYMBOLIC CHARACTER

No matter how completed or limited, all characters mean more than themselves. Every figure you create is a metaphor for either a social identity (mother, child, boss, employee) or an inner identity (good, evil, wise, naïve) or a combination of the two. These roles form casts that can be divided into two grand affinities: Realism and Symbolism. Some storytellers create casts inspired by daily observation, and then set them to cope with everyday hell; other writers, such as the creators of the DC Comics and Marvel universes, work with an awareness of a symbolic dimension in their casts, costuming them in imaginary characterizations.

For writers of Speculative Fiction—Fantasy, Sci-Fi, Horror, Superhero, Supernatural, Magical Realism, and the many subgenres of each—the symbol weighs more than its personification. For writers of conventional Realism—dramas and comedies that center in the down-to-earth problems of families, personal relationships, social institutions, legal systems, and moral psychology—the personification counts for more than the symbol.

Symbols evolve involuntarily during the writing. No author, no matter his talent, can deliberately create an all-new symbol from scratch. They are timeless. You can only borrow them.[1]

Symbols arise in this way: As the mind sees, hears, or touches an object, it instinctively asks, "What is this thing and why is it what it is?" Intellect and imagination then peer beneath the surface, as it were, looking for intrinsic structures and hidden causes; over time the insights they capture become idealized into meaning-rich, power-compressing icons.

Examples: Inspired by curvatures found in nature, the mind pictured the perfect geometric circle, and then elevated this abstraction into a symbol for the Cycle of Life. Pregnant women exude the energy of replicating DNA that our ancestors deified as the Earth Mother. The ocean's turbulence reminds sailors of an angry, punishing father who the Greeks then reimagined as Poseidon. Edible plants and animals became the ritual of meal taking that avant-garde chefs perfected into Haute Cuisine. This movement from particular to general to ideal generates the luminous, often fantastic images of symbolism. And where do writers find these visions? In their dreams.

Dreaming in symbols is an evolutionary adaptation the pre–homo sapiens psyche acquired hundreds of thousands, perhaps millions, of years ago. Its adaptive purpose is to protect sleep.

When you toss and turn at night, what pours through your brain? Racing thoughts: those hopes and hungers, dreads and fears, passions and angers, longings and lovings—the unresolved conflicts a weary mind cannot control.

Hindus symbolize the human mind as the chattering monkey— the yak, yak, yak, yak, yak, yak of thoughts running through the brain without pause every minute of every hour of every day and night. This prattle keeps you awake until the pineal gland secretes its melatonin and you drift into sleep. Dreaming then compresses your streaming thoughts inside symbols, giving intelligence a chance to rest and the body a chance to heal.

In the way a piston concentrates heat by reducing the volume inside a cylinder, a symbol creates power by compacting multiple meanings into a single image. A bearded figure, for example, dressed in robes, seated in a great chair, looking down from above symbolizes the *Father*. This image radiates complex ideas of judgment, wisdom, insight, and absolute authority, along with fear of punishment, guilt over broken rules, gratitude for protection, and adoration rooted in respect and dread. This grand mix of meanings and emotions condenses inside one image.

SYMBOLIC CHARACTER SPECTRUM

The spectrum of Symbolism in character creation spans from brightest to dimmest, beginning with the radiance of archetypes, followed by the glow of allegories, then the muted shades of types, and finally the gray outlines of stock characters.

Principle: Archetypes turn essences into characters

Humanity invented archetypes as instinctively as birds weave nests and spiders spin webs. The symbolic power of an archetypal image is so universal it can be endlessly varied in its details yet never lose its basic pattern. No matter how an archetype's veneer shifts from culture to culture, from animation to live action, its presence commands fascination.

Archetypes inhabit four major components of storytelling: events, settings, objects, roles:

1. Events such as the Sacred Birth, the Fall from Grace, the Battle between Good and Evil.
2. Settings such as the Desert as ground for meditation, the Garden as the miracle of fertility, the Castle as the seat of authority.
3. Objects such as Light as the symbol of Hope, Red as the color of Passion, or the Heart as an icon for Love.
4. Roles such as Star-Crossed Lovers, the Outcast wandering in exile, the Wizard waving a magic wand.

An archetypal character, like a stone sculpture, is the same inside as out. The Earth Mother, for example, concentrates all aspects of motherhood—giver of life, nurturer of innocence, forgiver of failings—into one rock-solid identity. She has no subtext. She never pretends, never jokes, never thinks an ironic thought. No hidden wishes contradict her pronouncements; no secret feelings complicate her actions. She simply mothers.

Archetypes expand and contract. The Hag, the Crone, and the Wise Woman are all variations of the Earth Mother. They may or may not have magical or supernatural powers; they may or may not be disagreeable, malicious, or malevolent; they may or may not be helpful. Compare the Wicked Witch of the West with the Good Witch of the North in *The Wizard of Oz*.

To a greater or lesser degree, a character, realistic or fantasized, stands in for his ancient original. Although rooted in its archetype, once on the stage, page, or screen, the character then diminishes the ideal because perfection can only be imagined, not performed. To freshen these repetitions, the writer must invent ingenious new traits of characterization.

Character archetypes are limited in number, but from Plato to Carl Jung to today's writers of Speculative Fiction no one agrees on what that number is. Many are drawn from religion: God, Devil, Angel, Demon; some are found in domestic life: Mother/Queen, Father/King, Child/Prince/Princess, Servant; and others are inspired by social conflicts: the Hero, the Rebel, Monsters (Villains), Tricksters (Clowns), and Helpers (Sage, Mentor, Magician).

This last archetype, the Helper, has given us Gandalf in *The Lord of the Rings*, Obi-Wan Kenobi in *Star Wars*, Merlin in many versions of the King Arthur myth, and the Fairy Godmother in even more tellings. And, of course, one role can combine two or more archetypes. Prospero, protagonist of Shakespeare's *The Tempest*, combines Wizard, Mentor, Ruler, Hero, and Villain.

Because an archetypal character in Speculative Fiction is dimensionless, he's incapable of change: A superhero may resist the task, but in time he'll put on his cape and fly to the rescue. Therefore, the purer the archetype, the less we care about his past or future, the less we imagine him outside his immediate scenes, the less we discern his inner life, the more predictable become his actions.

Because the complex character of Realism is dimensional and changeable, the archetypal role and the myth he rode in on become less important. Nonetheless, whether grounded or imaginary, a character vibrates with greater intensity when he strikes an archetypal chord in the subconscious mind of the reader or audience. If, on the other hand, the reader/audience thinks the conscious thought, "Oh, he's a symbol for...!," if they recognize a character as symbolic, the role flattens and its impact drains away. Therefore, veil symbolism behind a never-seen-before characterization. Fascinate the reader/audience with whom the character seems to be, then quietly smuggle your archetype in below reader/audience awareness and let it slip into their subconscious, where they will feel its presence without knowing or caring why.

Principle: Allegories turn values into characters

Like an archetype, an allegorical character is also made from a single substance but with less density. Whereas an archetype concentrates all facets of a universal role (Hero, Mother, Mentor) into a single persona, an allegorical character embodies only one facet, positive or negative. In the moral universe of an allegorical setting, the cast personifies a pattern of values. In the medieval morality play *Everyman*, for example, each character personifies an aspect of human existence such as Knowledge, Beauty, Strength, or Death.

In the alternative worlds of Jonathan Swift's satire *Gulliver's Travels*, populations represent values such as Pettiness, Bureaucracy, Absurd Science, and Obedience to Authority. William Golding set his novel *Lord of the Flies* on an island where schoolboys collectively represent humanity, while individually they symbolize values such as Democracy versus Tyranny, Civility versus Savagery, and the Rational versus Irrational Mind. Pixar's *Inside Out* created an allegory inside its protagonist's subconscious mind by selecting five emotional values and writing them into the characters Joy, Sadness, Anger, Fear, and Disgust.

Other examples: a lion as Wisdom in *The Chronicles of Narnia* and as Cowardice in *The Wizard of Oz*; Lord Business as Corporate Tyranny in *The Lego Movie*; an enormous stuffed whale as the Apocalypse in Laszlo Krasznahorkai's novel *The Melancholy of Resistance*; Tweedledum and Tweedledee as Difference-Without-Difference in *Alice Through the Looking Glass*. The allegorical cast of *Steven Universe* (Cartoon Network) take their identities from gemstones.

Principle: Types turn a behavior into a character

Stories, especially those told in the genres of Realism, need not include an archetypal or an allegorical character, but few can be cast without a type or two.

A type is an animated adjective. Disney's *Snow White and the Seven Dwarfs* (adapting a Brothers Grimm fairy tale) turned seven adjectives into the characters Sleepy, Bashful, Grumpy, Happy, Sneezy, Dopey, and Doc (smart).

These nondimensional supporting roles act out a single trait of behavior such as muddled, caring, blaming, fretting, artistic, shy, jealous, panicked, cruel, or a single trait of temperament such as the indifferent clerk, the talkative cabby, the unhappy little rich girl. All adjectives have an opposite charge of value—happy versus miserable, daydreamy versus vigilant, whining versus stoic—thus doubling the number of possible types.[2]

The first storytellers typed characters according to their social role: king, queen, warrior, servant, herdsman, etc. But in the *Nicomachean Ethics*, Aristotle began studying people by personality. He used adjectives such as Excessively Vain, Great of Soul, Choleric, Good Tempered, Officious, Contentious, and the like.

Aristotle's student, Theophrastus, expanded this idea in his *The Study of the Character*. He lists thirty brief, trenchant types, giving us an insightful portrait of his time and humanity at large. All thirty, however, are negatively toned: Superstitious, Lying, Nervous, Pretentious, Buffoonish, Flattering, Boring, Bragging, Cowardly, and so on. He could have listed correspondingly positive examples: Rational, Truthful, Calm, Modest, Wise, Sincere, Entertaining, Discrete, Heroic, but I suspect negative types were great fun for his readers. The comedy writer Menander cast many of Theophrastus's types in farces with titles such as *The Grouch*, *The Peevish Man*, *The Misogynist*, and *The Man Nobody Likes*.

To elevate an extra into a type, simply give him a specific behavior. A nondescript teenager steps out of the crowd and takes on a role when, despite his best efforts to control himself, he constantly giggles with embarrassment.

For example, three familiar types:

The Fanatic

The Fanatic may be a bored misfit, an untalented artist, or a chronic discontent, but in all cases, he rejects his meaningless life and hates himself for who he is not. In search of a new identity, he joins a movement that gives him a new name, new uniform, and new vocabulary. So equipped, he becomes a fanatic for the thing he loves and a hater of anything opposed to it. At rock bottom, the angry fanatic projects his self-loathing onto something or someone foreign.[3]

For thought-provoking examples, study Daniel Balint (Ryan Gosling) in Henry Bean's *The Believer*; Freddie Quell (Joaquin Phoenix) in Paul Thomas Anderson's film *The Master*; Syndrome (Jason Lee) in Brad Bird's film *The Incredibles*.

The Hipster

The Hipster is the opposite of the fanatic. He obsesses on the only thing he loves: himself. He wears forgotten fashions (Hawaiian shirts), collects antique things (portable record players), and takes up pointless hobbies (home brewing). The hipster wants to be one of a kind, not with fresh ideas of his own but from things no one else wants. To deflect mockery, he brags about his failure to do anything meaningful. To preempt criticism, he adopts an I'm-Only-Kidding smirk and lives ironically by hiding in public.

For hip examples, consider Jeff Bridges as *The Big Lebowski*, Jon Heder as *Napoleon Dynamite*, and Oscar Isaac as the title character in *Inside Llewyn Davis*.

The Cool

Cool describes an emotionally controlled, never eager or needy, detached, and self-possessed type. He stands still, quiet and opaque, depriving the reader/audience of insight. We sense that he has a secret past, but we never know for sure. Gracefully skilled, he has found a unique way to make a living, but only he knows what it is. A morally ambiguous realist, he lives by his own code in an absurd world. He doesn't need or want applause; he knows his worth. We sense his depth but can only guess what's behind his eyes.[4]

Examples of cool: The enigmatic murderess Juliette Fontaine in *I've Loved You So Long* suffers decades of silence for her secret; Amy in *Gone Girl* impersonates many lethal selves, none of which are her; Clint Eastwood played cool in films such as *Play Misty for Me* and *High Plains Drifter*.

Principle: Stocks turn a job into a character

Types act out a behavior; stocks take a job. Fictional societies require citizens playing social roles, defined primarily by their work.

People in the insecure gig economy—grad students waiting tables, elderly greeters at Walmart, artists doing something other than their art—cannot control their future. Because their jobs contradict what they want out of life, they may become too interesting and dimensional to play stock characters.

Instead, people in secure positions tend to work in a field small enough that they can control its machinery: lawyers, house painters, doctors, golf club pros, and the like. Job security may dull their inner creativity, as well as their empathy for clients, homeowners, patients, and club members, but professions such as these, placed around the principals, become stock roles.

The first stock characters were given props onstage so audiences could identify them: Shepherds held a crook, ambassadors carried the caduceus, kings a scepter, heroes a sword, old men a staff.

The Roman satirist Plautus used and reused farcical stocks: Rich Miser, Clever Slave, Stupid Slave, Slave Dealer, Prostitute, Braggart Soldier, and the hanger-on parasite that today we would call a Groupie.

As they carry out their tasks, stocks make no choices: Doctors deliver bad news to families, lawyers explain provisions in a will, beggars beg. Whether clichéd or freshly drawn, the great advantage of stock characters is an instant recognition of purpose that lessens the need for exposition. The reader/audience knows why a stock has entered a story and his task in the telling. As they do their job, however, stocks needn't be dull. A stock can be worth his moment in the light if you give him a one-of-a-kind characterization, the unique technique he uses to carry out his task.

Stock roles go in and out of fashion. Prosperity preachers replace hippie gurus; Russian spies exit, Middle East terrorists enter; man-made monsters are out, people with genetic mutations are in; space aliens are passé, zombie hordes are hip.

Because stocks must act within their job and types within their type, they make very few, if any, choices. For that reason, they constantly risk becoming clichés. A cliché is a once-superb idea that's been copied to death and is now done without originality.

As Henry James pointed out, clichéd characters are used but never used up. Are the old miser, young spendthrift, penny pincher, gambler, drunk, and teetotaler never to appear again because they've been done before? Of course not. In the hands of an imaginative writer, a stock can be wonderfully idiosyncratic. Arnold Schwarzenegger's assassin in *The Terminator* is a menacing villain, type and stock, but the melding of machine/human gave him a characterization like no other.

In fact, over recent decades, the origin stories of superheroes make them seem more and more like super-stocks doing their job. Archetypal twentieth-century creations, such as Thor, a Norse god; Wonder Woman, a Greek goddess; and the godlike Superman are born super;

while twenty-first-century heroes turn super by accident (a radioactive bug bites Silk, a random mutagen infects Ms. Marvel) or by scientists doing it themselves (Iron Man builds his own supersuit). *Galaxy Quest* satirizes this trend when stock actors become archetypes for stock aliens.

Principle: Stereotypes turn prejudice into character

Stereotyping begins with a fallacy: "All Xs are Y." The wealthy, for example, often stereotype the poor as lazy; the poor stereotype the too-rich as cruel. Prejudices, for that reason, are worse than clichés. A cliché is a very good idea someone had a very long time ago. Since then, writers have drummed this invention into a cliché, but still it holds a truth. Stereotypes, instead, distort the truth.

A stereotype models itself after an archetype but reduces grandeur to bias: The Earth Mother becomes the Jewish mother, the Wise King becomes the mean boss, the Warrior Hero becomes the street hustler, the Goddess becomes the hooker, the Magician becomes the mad scientist.

So why do stereotypes persist? Because they're easy to write. Realistic characters demand work from the writer, reader, and audience.

REALISTIC VERSUS SYMBOLIC CHARACTERS

Realism and Symbolism create characters at opposite ends of the cast spectrum—one rooted in fact, the other in abstraction. In between these two extremes run the mixtures and mergers of qualities that make possible every character ever imagined. So, let's separate these two poles to see what they are and how they influence character creation.

The Symbolist tradition began in prehistoric myths. Mankind's earliest storytelling symbolized the forces of nature (sun, moon, lightning, thunder, seas, mountains) into gods, demigods, and other supernatural beings. In these myths, gods create the cosmos and, with it, human beings. Paraphrased from epoch to epoch, culture to culture, myths travel mouth to ear with slight loss of meaning because they are not literature. In myths, words mean little, symbolic characters and actions everything.

The Realist tradition dates back to Homer's vivid depictions of warrior psychology and blood-spattered battles in the *Iliad*. Realism seeks to portray life as lived, unclouded by false beliefs or sentimental beautifications. Its straightforward dramatizations avoid symbolic dream fiction to emphasize hard-edged thought fiction—characters living in the as-is rather than the as-wished-for.

The key differences between realistic and symbolic characters number at least ten:

1. Truth: Factuality Versus Wish Fulfillment

Realism grapples with a factual world in which wishes almost never come true; whereas the symbolic genres of speculative fiction—myths and fantasies, both ancient and modern—put wish fulfillment into action. The heroes and superheroes of today, with or without magical powers, live in a strictly moral universe where Good always triumphs over Evil, love conquers all, and death does not end life.

Other symbolic genres, such as fables and legends, treat wishes as dark and dangerous, so they tell cautionary tales that teach moral lessons. "The Fox and the Grapes" by Aesop, "Hansel and Gretel" by the Brothers Grimm, and the legend of the House of Atreus are three classic examples. Modern fables warn of a dystopian future: George Orwell's *Nineteen Eighty-Four*, Margaret Atwood's *The Handmaid's Tale*, Naomi Alderman's *The Power*.

2. True Character: Complex Psychology Versus Imposing Personality

Symbolic tellings incite conflicts between characters rather than contradictions within characters. As a result, symbolic characters have remarkable, imposing personalities, while realistic characters develop complex psychologies. Compare Batman (aka Bruce Wayne) to Saul Goodman (aka Jimmy McGill).

3. Level of Conflict: Outer Versus Inner

Symbolic characters take action against external antagonistic social and physical forces, while realistic characters often battle self-doubt, self-deception, self-criticism, and other such inner confusions and invisible demons.

4. Complexity: Solid Versus Dimensional

Like the archetypes that inspire them, modern mythical characters have traits but no dimensions, desires but no contradictions, a text but no subtext. They are one-piece symbols, inside and out.

Multidimensional realistic characters, on the other hand, string dynamic contradictions between their public, personal, private, and hidden selves.

5. Detail: Scarcity Versus Density

The Symbolist writer of fables, legends, and myths focuses on the essential. He simplifies the density of reality by avoiding meticulous traits of characterization.

The Realist author, on the other hand, gathers telling details that enrich and specify his characters. Compare, for example, the smooth outlines of the animated family in *The Incredibles* with the painstakingly particularized family in *Six Feet Under*.

6. Comprehension: Hard Versus Easy

Realism calls for concentration and perception. A character seems real in proportion to how much we consider his total self. The more contradictory yet consistent, the more changeable yet unified, the more unpredictable yet credible, the more specific yet mysterious the role, the more real, fascinating, and intriguing he becomes. He makes us work to understand him but rewards us with insight once we do. Consider Vicomte de Valmont (*Dangerous Liaisons*), Thomas Sutpen (*Absalom, Absalom!*), and Jimmy McGill (*Better Call Saul*).

The symbolic characters of myth, legend, and fable are instantly and easily understood. The more generalized, predictable, and text-bound the role, the less surprising, less intriguing, and less real he becomes. Consider Albus Dumbledore, Mad Max, and Superman.

7. Worldview: Skeptical Versus Sentimental

Realism encourages characters treated with tough-minded sentiment; Symbolism often sweetens its roles with sentimentality.

Sentiment is a feeling that flows when a creditable motivation compels a powerful action: a parent risking everything for a child, as in playwright Henrik Ibsen's *Ghosts* and Alvin Sargent's screenplay for *Ordinary People*.

Sentimentality, however, manipulates emotion by using phony causes to trigger false effects. The forced happy ending, for example, is a device as antique as Hans Christian Andersen's "The Little Mermaid" and as yesterday as Steven Spielberg's *War of the Worlds*.

8. Endings: Irony Versus Simplicity

The writers of Realism grapple with life's constant duality: The steps you take to achieve something are exactly what's necessary to make sure you never get it, while the steps you take to avoid something take you directly to it. Whether climaxing in grief or joy, Realism turns a double effect: Positive endings demand great sacrifice, while tragedies bring insight and wisdom. Reality is relentlessly ironic and characters suffer accordingly.

With the exception of authors like Philip K. Dick, myth, fable, and legend resist irony; they cast characters who act out straight, pure, and positive stories.

9. Character Dynamics: Flexible Versus Rigid

Realism reveals the truths hidden in its characters and then often flexes their inner natures with change. Symbolic roles possess one rigid quality through and through, and therefore have nothing to reveal or change.

Realism is skeptical; myths wishful. Test myths against reality, and their archetypes are exposed for the wish fulfillments they always were.

In the early twentieth century, psychologist Carl Jung based theories about the collective unconscious on archetypes drawn from myths. Expanding on Jung, Joseph Campbell concocted a monomyth popularly known as "the hero's journey," hoping to replace Christianity with his personal brand of spiritualism. Hollywood actionsmiths hammered Campbell's pseudomyth about the hero's quest into a template to mass-produce summer hits.[5]

10. Social Dynamics: Flexible Versus Rigid

The class structure in Symbolist genres tends to cast a ruler at the top, peasants at the bottom, the rest somewhere in between. Realism moves power through its cast with fluidity, even if the telling is set in a monarchy or dictatorship.

CASE STUDY: *GAME OF THRONES*

David Benioff and D. B. Weiss, adapting George R. R. Martin's *A Song of Ice and Fire* to the longform screen, brought harsh realism to high fantasy. Between the black-and-white outlines of Symbolism, they drew characters in every possible shade of gray. They merged the autocracy of myth with the freedom of fiction to create a vast cast of 160 roles, representing all degrees of Realism and Symbolism plus all possible points on the political compass.

On the extreme Right, the tyrannical Cersei of House Lannister, Protector of the Seven Kingdoms. On the progressive Left, the graceful Daenerys of House Targaryen, Mother of Dragons.

Cersei embodies retrogressive, incestuous, matriarch, monarchical despotism. Temperamentally, she is pro-feudalism and anti-change. Daenerys embodies the future-leaning, humanistic spirit of justice and progress. Temperamentally, she's anti-feudalism and pro-change. Daenerys denies myth; Cersei lives myth.

Within this polarized world, the writers array the meritocracy of the Night's Watch, the equalitarianism of the Unsullied, the fanaticism of the Sparrows, and the democracy of councils in which equals cast votes to make decisions. Death, however, has no politics, so when the Night King and his horde of White Walkers invade, the tension between Symbolism and Realism fades into the question of who lives and who dies.

HOW TO MAKE THE OLD NEW

You hope to invent characters unlike any ever seen, but for thousands of years, storytellers have created, re-created, and recycled characters by the millions...literally. You write in this tradition, and therefore your character's core identity will echo an archetype, an allegory, a type, or a stock.

Your task is to create within the known (otherwise no one will know how to respond to your work) and yet make your characters unique, fresh, and unlike any ever met before. Try one of these four paths:

1. Within the genres of Speculative Fiction, create plausible motivations for implausible actions.
2. Within the genres of Realism, create characters who live off-center lives and see people and actions in an off-center way.
3. In either subset, give characters radical experiences that shock old beliefs into the new.
4. In either subset, add a sense of immediacy by writing in-character. In prose, write from the POV of a character who has lived these events in the past. On-screen or onstage, take the POV of a character living them in the now.

13

THE RADICAL CHARACTER

The Realism/Nonrealism/Radicalism Triangle

Fiction's conflicting treatments of reality create a triangle of character possibilities: In one corner, Realism gives characters the powers they have in ordinary life; in a second corner, Nonrealism gives them powers far beyond the ordinary; at the third corner, Radicalism warps the powers found in the other two. All three extremes meet and overlap within this triangle, creating an infinite variety of characters.

REALISM: CONVENTIONAL CHARACTERS IN CONVENTIONAL WORLDS

The literary movement known as Realism began two centuries ago in reaction to the operatic excesses of Romanticism. Realism works from the ground up, but in truth, its style of offhanded underplay is as artificial as the high-style overplay it replaced.

Realist writers gather close observations of people and behavior, stir these inside the imagination, filter this concoction through the latticework of the mind, and finally crystallize it into a character who lives in a world that echoes ours. She has a unified self, moral balance, rational perceptions of reality, interactions with other characters, willful pursuits of desire, capacity to choose and act with purpose, and flexibility to change. This protagonist, surrounded by a cast of similar roles, acts out a story that by cultural conventions readers and audiences accept as everyday reality. You have seen and read these works all your life.

NONREALISM: CONVENTIONAL CHARACTERS IN UNCONVENTIONAL WORLDS

Nonrealism places the conventional characters of Realism inside extrarealities powered by forces such as the supernatural in *Pirates of the Caribbean*; the magical in *Harry Potter and the Philosopher's Stone*; the coincidental in *1Q84*; the metaphorical in *Babe*; the paranormal in *The Dead Zone*; the transnormal in *Six Characters in Search of an Author*; an opaque bureaucracy in *The Trial*; dream power in *Alice's Adventures in Wonderland*; futuristic science in *Do Androids Dream of Electric Sheep?*; time travel in *Somewhere in Time*; time warps in *Looper*.

Some of these extended realities are populated by characters who sing (*La Traviata*), dance (*The Sleeping Beauty*), or sing and dance (*The Book of Mormon*). Nonrealism often eliminates the "fourth wall" to let characters talk to theatre audiences (*Hair*), film audiences (*Wayne's World*), or television audiences (*Fleabag*).

Nonrealism grows out of either conscious fantasies during the day or subconscious dreams at night. Once these imaginary settings and casts inspire a story, they play as grand metaphors for idealized worlds, expressing humanity's wish fulfillments.

The fictional worlds of Realism and Nonrealism vary extremely, but nonetheless, they share two things in common: (1) No matter how bizarre or real a setting may seem, once folded into a fiction, it develops rules of causality, of how and why things happen, patterns that operate like the laws of physics to shape what can and cannot occur. (2) Characters who live in both real and unreal worlds believe in them. From the cast's point of view, everything they see and hear seems as real as pain.

They may at first, like Phil Connors in *Groundhog Day*, doubt their world and test its laws, but in time a fictional reality becomes their reality and they behave in a more or less normal way. This is the nature of storytelling. The world of Homer's *Odyssey* contains gods and monsters, but Odysseus deals with them as any hero would.

Conventional characters exist in social, cultural, and physical settings that are either Realism's imitations of reality or Nonrealism's imagined reinventions of reality. The behaviors and motivations of conventional characters demand credibility; the meanings of their stories are ultimately clear and expressed with emotional impact; their dialogue strives to be instantly understood; their tellings bring freshly observed details and insights into human nature.

The note to take here is that the fully expressed character built around a unified dimensionality is standard in both Realism and Nonrealism. These characters inhabit the hits and best sellers of page, stage, and screen.

Therefore, think carefully about the tastes of your readers and audiences and which reality they want: Realism or Nonrealism. Because in all probability, they do not want Radicalism.

RADICALISM: UNCONVENTIONAL CHARACTERS IN UNCONVENTIONAL WORLDS

The more a writer loses faith in meaning, the more she feels a pull toward Radicalism.

From the very first, philosophers assumed that life had meaning and that finding that meaning is mankind's chief goal. This pursuit wound its way through the centuries, but then by the nineteenth century, Nietzsche, Kierkegaard, and other voices warned of a rising tide of meaninglessness. This trend deepened as psychoanalysis, led by Freud, Jung, and Adler, discovered disunities within the self and the near impossibility of knowing your true identity, let alone finding a meaning to guide it. Two world wars and a dozen genocides later, nihilism found its voice in postmodern works of theatre, cinema, and prose of the absurd that revolutionized storytelling and character.

Radicalism finds both the outer and inner life meaningless, so it reverses everything: instead of continuity, fragmentation; instead of clarity, distortion; instead of emotional immersion, intellectual exertion; instead of involvement, distance; instead of progression, repetition.

Unconventionality is Radicalism's convention. Whatever's orthodox, the Radicalist does the opposite, but, ironically, that doesn't set her free. As Martin Heidegger pointed out: "Opposition is invariably comprised of a decisive, and often even perilous, dependence."[1]

Radicalism is to character what Cubism is to portraiture. The writer, as if painting a Picasso-esque portrait, exaggerates, shatters, shrinks, distorts, and rearranges selves, yet somehow the reader/audience still sees a character.

Radical settings are highly symbolic, but their rules for causality are radically inconsistent. In Jean-Luc Godard's film *Weekend*, anything can happen for no reason; in Samuel Beckett's play *Waiting for Godot*, nothing happens, again, for no reason. These reimaginings, needless to say, demanded new and very radical characters.

Radical characters have little relationship to anything beyond themselves—not god or society, not family or lovers. They are either isolated and static (Tom Stoppard's play *Rosencrantz and Guildenstern Are Dead*) or mobbed and frantic (Marlon James's novel *A Brief History of Seven Killings*). Their dialogue often degenerates into babble (David Lynch's film *Inland Empire*).

The medium for expressing radical characters with relative ease is prose. The novelist, in first or third person, can reach into the mind of a character and emulate her splintered, skipping-stone thoughts, sketching out her wildly subjective, often paranoid anxieties and impressions, her instant impulses, fragmented desires, and fractured personality. This technique was foundational to everything Samuel Beckett wrote for page and stage.

In *White Noise*, novelist Don DeLillo created characters whose identities are not just in doubt, but absolutely uncertain. Thomas Pynchon's *Gravity's Rainbow* swirls four hundred characters around Tyrone Slothrop, who may or may not be anything that he, other characters, or even the author say he is.

For the playwright and screenwriter, expressing radical characters becomes a bit more difficult because the physical presence of an actor gives a role a sense of solidity.

In *Happy Days*, Samuel Beckett worked against the actor effect by burying his only two characters, Winnie and Willie, up to their necks in dirt and debris.

In *Holy Motors*, Cinema of the Absurd filmmaker Leos Carax has his protagonist, Oscar, perform nine different impersonations, ranging from an old female beggar to a Chinese gangster to the husband and father of chimpanzees.

CREATING A RADICAL CHARACTER

To radicalize a character, simply empty out her conventional aspects. Below are nine possible deletions that lead characters toward the extreme:

1. Subtract Self-Awareness

The self-aware dramatic character can step back from the struggle and think the thought, "You know, this could get me into real trouble," and then, despite the threat, go on. But when you subtract self-awareness, dramatic characters turn into comic obsessives.

The comic mind is ruled by a blind obsession—single-minded as a stone, persistent as the sea, repetitious as rain. To create a farce, the comedy writer locks the character into her fixation, then exploits it at every opportunity:

In *A Fish Called Wanda*, Archie Leach obsessively fears embarrassment, yet stumbles into one red-faced humiliation after another.

In the *Pink Panther* films, Inspector Clouseau obsesses on perfection as a detective, yet blunders through his investigations, one pratfall after another.

In *Curb Your Enthusiasm*, Larry David obsesses on proper social behavior, and yet finds himself surrounded with people who constantly break his petty rules.

In *Bridesmaids*, Annie Walker obsesses on her one and only friendship, and yet ruins the relationship at every turn.

Conventional comic obsessives, like the above, have a commonsense interest or two that rounds out their natures. But not the radical character. Radicals push beyond obsession into the absurd limits of monomania. To radicalize a comic character, take away everything except her obsession, then trap her inside it and never let her out:

In *The Maids*, Jean Genet traps the maids in their sadomasochistic games.

In *Exit the King*, Eugene Ionesco traps Berenger in his fear of death.

In *Rosencrantz and Guildenstern Are Dead*, Tom Stoppard traps Rosencrantz and Guildenstern in Hamlet's story.

In *A Behanding in Spokane*, Martin McDonagh traps Carmichael in an endless search for his missing hand.

2. Subtract Depth

The opposite of a full, complex, and revealed character is a role that's emptied out—a character whose humanity shrinks into an inner void, putting her just a step or two away from the radical.

In *Falling Down*, Ebbe Roe Smith peels away William Foster's (Michael Douglas) sanity.

In *Capote*, Dan Futterman extracts Truman Capote's (Philip Seymour Hoffman) morality.

In *The Imitation Game*, Graham Moore amputates Alan Turing's (Benedict Cumberbatch) core self.

Despair swallows the humanity of all three of these men, leading their lives to the brink of absurdity.

3. Subtract Change

Complex, multidimensional protagonists undergo arcs of change; flat characters do not. Flat characters contract into themselves, eliminating their ties to other characters.

In genres of Realism, flat characters are revealed but incapable of change—for example, Jude and Tess in Thomas Hardy's novels *Jude the Obscure* and *Tess of the d'Urbervilles*. Their only change is a downward slide from hopeful to hopeless.[2]

In genres of non-Realism, heroes and villains, with or without superpowers, are also flat. Characters in action-filled, speculative fictions change the world but never themselves. They personify Good or Evil and obey ancient storytelling traditions by staying either good or evil until they die.

In both non-Realism and Realism, unchanged characters suggest that the possibility of change, no matter how remote, exists. If Hardy had allowed Jude to become the classical scholar of his dreams, Jude's arc to fulfillment would be profound and moving. If Bruce Wayne got fed up with the public's lack of respect for Batman and decided to use his skills to build an evil empire, the change would be shocking and yet fascinating. I would watch that sequel.

So if flat characters in conventional genres change, their change surprises, yet seems credible and meaningful. On the other hand, if a radical character living in a radical world were to change from flat to complex, the switch would seem false.

In *Waiting for Godot*, two aimless characters, Vladimir and Estragon, sum up the flatness of their natures with the refrain: "Nothing to be done." But if one were to turn to the other and say, "Enough waiting. I don't think Godot will ever show up. Let's go find jobs and make something of our lives," and off they went, excited by the chance to change, Samuel Beckett's existential masterpiece would collapse into silliness.[3]

In novelist Will Self's trilogy of *Umbrella, Shark,* and *Phone,* flat characters fragment into five different points of view. Shards of thought express variations of dissociative identity disorder, drug-induced hallucination, and autism-spectrum discord. If the author unified these pieces into whole characters, they would corrupt his wild creation.

4. Subtract Identity

Prior to the twentieth century, authors wove their characters' identities from the cultural threads that encircled them: gender, class, family, age, religion, nationality, education, profession, language, race, taste in art, and the like. When a character said, "I am a—," what followed were nouns drawn from her immediate world. This ancient practice continues today, reenforced by identity politics.

The Modernist movement, however, reversed that pattern. It turned away from conflicts between characters to tell tales located in the inner life and the search for an ever-lasting private truth. Modernist characters turn their back on the world, hoping to find a core self waiting quietly within, surrounded by infinite freedom of thought and the beauty of creativity.

By the end of the century, however, postmodernists found that the inner life offers no such refuge. The outer and inner worlds are just two versions of hell. In Samuel Beckett's novel *The Unnamable,* the protagonist declares that he's "shut the door, at home to no one," including himself. A character homeless within himself suffers derealization or depersonalization or both. Derealization is the sudden perception of the world as unreal; depersonalization is the sudden perception of yourself as unreal.

Derealization is the side effect of despair, often magnified by drugs and alcohol. Depersonalization is the side effect of physical and psychological trauma or extreme loneliness. A prisoner condemned to solitary confinement over time inevitably loses his identity. When finally taken out in a straitjacket, his first question (if he can still speak) is "Who am I?"

Derealization strips a character of the power to empathize, to see the humanity in others; depersonalization severs self-empathy, a character's power to feel her own humanity.

How many different ways can a character lose self-empathy and with it, her identity? Here's a brief list:

(A) Loss of an Identity Source

A character draws both characterization and true character from her surrounding culture. If an outside power destroys the sources of her identity, she vanishes with them.

In *Wide Sargasso Sea* by Jean Rhys, Antoinette Cosway, a Creole/Jamaican heiress, marries an Englishman. He takes her from her island home to his, then insults her race and poisons their marriage with adultery. Locked in an attic and stripped of all sense of self, she goes mad.

In *Things Fall Apart* by Chinua Achebe, a Nigerian tribal champion fights against English colonists and missionaries, but his tribe converts to Christianity and turns against him. Stripped of his ancestral identity, he commits suicide.

(B) Rejection of an Identity Source

If a character hates her ancestry and so turns against her religion, ethnicity, gender, or any other personality-shaping influence, she alters, if not utterly erases, her identity.

In *Look Back in Anger* by John Osborne, Jimmy Porter feels heroic energies pulsing through him, but now that the British Empire has collapsed, he realizes that his chance for an epic life is lost. He's an ordinary working man who will never be part of a great enterprise, never live the courageous identity he craves.

In *More Happy Than Not* by Adam Silvera, teenager Aaron Soto hires a psycho-technology company to erase his gay identity. The company removes a few memories, but gayness isn't a memory, it's genetic.

(C) Trauma

Damage caused by ordeals or genetic abnormalities such as schizophrenia can shatter a character's identity.

In *The Bourne Identity*, Jason Bourne suffers traumatic amnesia and goes in search of his identity.

In *The Three Faces of Eve* and *Alias Grace*, doppelgängers and multiple personalities give the protagonist different identities, none of them hers.

In *Blue Jasmine*, Jasmine Francis revenges her husband's adultery by betraying him to the FBI for embezzlement. Soon penniless, her identity crumples as she suffers a pathological, delusional breakdown.

(D) Identity Theft

An impostor slowly steals a character's identity until no one believes that she is who she says she is.

In *Single White Female*, Hedy Carlson suffers a soulless, deep-seated emptiness. To find a fulfilling self, she imitates her roommate and then steals her identity.

(E) Obsession

When fanatics obsess, they take actions that seem out of character. Shocked, they step back from what they've done and excuse it with "I wasn't myself." In fact, their choice under pressure revealed exactly who they are.

In *Lust, Caution*, the Japanese army occupies Shanghai in 1942. As part of an assassination plot, a beautiful young rebel seduces the head of the secret police, but their passion becomes her sexual obsession. When given a chance to kill, she suddenly shocks herself by choosing not to end his life but to save it.

5. Subtract Purpose

Many radical characters turn their backs on the world. They flee the turmoil of relationships by withdrawing into the mental life, thinking that there they will enjoy freedom, creativity, and quiet self-awareness. Instead, their mediations meander pointlessly; they find creativity pretentious and self-knowledge painful. When involuntary memories pop up from the past, they either deny their truth or draw a blank. Stuck between the inner and outer life, they try to flee both and live in neither. When radical characters crave company, it's to escape their acute anxieties about modern afflictions, existential minutiae, and meaningless inner boredom. They are purposeless.

In Beckett's *Krapp's Last Tape*, Krapp's doctor has warned him that bananas are bad for his health. So Krapp peels a banana, sticks it in his mouth, then stands for minutes on end, staring into space, unable or willing to bite down, a banana protruding from his face.[4]

Radical characters are purposeless and thus trapped: trapped in an incomplete play (*Six Characters in Search of an Author*), in mindless repetition (*The Chairs*), in maniacal politics (*The Arsonists*), by an unknown menace (*The Birthday Party*), in conformity (*Rhinoceros*), by death (*Exit the King*), in Shakespeare's play (*Rosencrantz and Guildenstern Are Dead*), in bureaucracy (*The Trial*), in a police state (*Pillowman*), in mundanity (*The Flick*), in the Amazon jungle (*The Encounter*), in a neighbor's backyard (*Escaped Alone*). Like an improv actor on *Whose Line Is It Anyway?*, these characters are stuck onstage and cannot escape their playwright's premise.

For many twenty-first-century writers, political absurdity has blurred their sense of purpose. Gridlock inside an artist often paralyzes the creatures she creates—static characters who feel that nothing redeems life—not love, not art, not knowledge, not God, and certainly not sex. Thus, the perfect metaphor for today's loss of purpose is the zombie. Like zombies, radical characters long to live no life at all. Were it possible, they would inhabit a zombie zone of nothing.

6. Subtract Unity

A complex character is one person who acts in two directions: She loves and hates, tells truth and lies. These cohesive contradictions unify her, whereas the unstable shards of a radical role fragment the character.

In today's participatory theatre, for example, when a cast interacts with its audience, their roles splinter into character and performer: *Brute Force*, *Sleep No More*, *66 Minutes in Damascus*.

In Isabel Waidner's novel *Gaudy Bauble*, objects become characters and then compound themselves: A face printed on a sweatshirt multiplies into an army of transsexuals.

7. Subtract Maturity

The daily task of the mature mind is to mediate between the world around her and the instincts inside her, balancing these two hostile powers and negotiating an inner peace.[5]

The radical character is an eternal child who surrenders to the world (obedience) or to her impulses (violence) or to both at once (the violent savage who obeys orders).

In Haruki Murakami's *The Wind-up Bird Chronicle*, when Toru, the novel's childlike protagonist, isn't searching for his cat, or his wife, he's ruminating at the bottom of a well.

The risqué send-ups staged by Madison, Wisconsin's Broom Street Theater, such as *Oklahomo!* and *The Ballerina and the Economist*, show little interest in maturity.

The same is true of screenplays by Broom Street alumnus Charlie Kaufman. *Human Nature*, for example, features a psychologist who teaches table manners to mice.

8. Subtract Conscience

An evil character commits unregretted acts of brutality because she has no conscience to restrain her. Characters of conscienceless evil motivate power struggles in a wide variety of genres such as Crime, War, and Action/Adventure, as well as Political and Family Dramas. When stakes are high, people know how to vacate their conscience. It's commonplace.

Radical evil takes brutality to another level: As the Marquis de Sade explains in *Philosophy in the Bedroom*: "Through cruelty one rises to heights of superhuman awareness and sensitivity to new modes of being that cannot be reached any other way."

The core psychology of radical evil is Sadism: the belief that the common objectives of torture (information and confession) distract from the unutterable pleasure and transcendent purity of the torturer's experience. Radical evil seeks grotesque pleasure.

Acts of radical evil nauseate into disgust. Disgust is a gut reaction to rot, to foul-tasting, foul-smelling feces, gore, pulp, puke. Physical disgust reacts against these rank animal spillages to protect the body from poisons; social disgust reacts against moral rot to protect the soul from evil. Profoundly evil characters turn your stomach...literally.

In *Lord of the Rings*, Lord Sauron is not radically evil. He is, in fact, rather elegant. He fights to maintain power, but he's not sadistic, so he provokes no disgust.

In contrast, O'Brien, the Party enforcer in George Orwell's dystopian *Nineteen Eighty-Four*, locks a wire enclosure around Winston Smith's head, then fills the surrounding cage with ravenous rats scrabbling to eat the man's face. O'Brien, content in his pleasures, watches as this horrific psychic torture rips through his victim. O'Brien is radical evil.

9. Subtract Belief

Here's a useful question to ask of any role you create, conventional or radical: How crazy is my character? Sane in a sane world? Insane in a sane world? Sane in an insane world? Or insane in an insane world? The first three possibilities encompass characters found in Realism and non-Realism; radical characters inhabit the fourth.

Patricia Highsmith's Tom Ripley falls into the second category. The world around him is sane, but he is not. He's a psycho-sociopath who kills when necessary. To Ripley, *necessary* means getting what he wants by paying for it with someone else's life.

Lewis Carroll's Alice fits the third case. She's sane, but the world around her is not. This well-bred, snobby little girl needs to make sense out of an insane world, or she'll never find her way home.

What makes Ripley and Alice conventional characters is their trust that the world makes sense. A radical character lacks any such belief. Radical characters cannot find meaning in either their outer or their inner lives, and they certainly do not believe in anything spiritual.

Belief is a personal interpretation of reality. Religious belief trusts that a god created reality and gave it moral imperatives. Patriotic belief trusts in the righteous and tradition-bound reality of a nation-state. Scientific belief trusts that mathematical laws of causality hold reality together. Romantic belief trusts that love is the ultimate value. With beliefs such as these, conventional characters find purpose in their lives.

Radical characters, having no belief to buoy them, despair in the face of absurdity.

In *Perfume*, a novel by Patrick Suskind, Jean-Baptiste finds people, himself included, disgusting and meaningless. Void of belief, he makes the ultimate escape from absurdity by enticing a starving mob into ripping him apart and cannibalizing him in the street.

THE FUTURE: UNCONVENTIONAL CHARACTERS IN CONVENTIONAL WORLDS

The postmodern avant-garde died decades ago and was replaced by a retro-garde. Postpostmodernist theatre, films, and novels of today simply recycle the twentieth century, exhausting its every minimal or maximal device ad nauseam. As a Beckett character might say, "Nothing that hasn't been done." So, instead of copying the past, the leading edge of twenty-first-century storytelling satirizes the present.

In classical satire, clear-minded narrators ridiculed lunatic societies. Jonathan Swift perfected this technique in *Gulliver's Travels*. Seventy years ago, Samuel Beckett ridiculed reality itself with radical characters in absurd settings. Today's writers reverse both Swift and Beckett. They place radical characters in a conventional setting, and then draw us into empathy despite our better natures.

The Black Comedy protagonists of *The White Tiger* by Aravind Adiga, *A Behanding in Spokane* by Martin McDonagh, *Birdman* by Alejandro Inarritu, *The Sellout* by Paul Beatty, and *All Grown Up* by Jami Attenberg are criminal or lunatic or criminally lunatic.

In fact, the utmost radical characters now star in their own longform series: the anxiety disordered and clinically depressed protagonist of *Mr. Robot*; the charming cannibal of *Santa Clarita Diet*; the psychotic, drug experimenters in *Maniac*; the darkly obsessed comedians in *I'm Dying Up Here*; Villanelle, the lovable serial killer in *Killing Eve*; Barry, the actor/assassin in *Barry*; and Jimmy McGill, the criminal criminal lawyer in *Better Call Saul*.

As writers push the limits of empathy, they ask their readers and audiences to identify with more and more crazed and dangerous characters. The answer to the question "How dark is too dark for the contemporary reader/audience?" seems further and further away.

PART 3

THE CHARACTER UNIVERSE

The next three chapters look at character from three different angles: the casts in various types of stories, the actions characters take within a story, and character from the point of view of readers and audiences.

14

CHARACTER IN GENRE

Nothing in the art of storytelling compels a writer to do anything in a rule-driven way. The genres impose no dictates; they simply follow traditional, conventional patterns. Like trends in music or painting, readers and audiences come to know their favorite genres, expecting and enjoying these designs. They naturally want to reexperience them but each time with a satisfying difference.

Here, for example, are three sets of event expectations:

1. The Crime Story: (a) A crime will be committed. (b) The injustice will be discovered. (c) The protagonist will seek to identify, apprehend, and punish the criminal. (d) The criminal will fight against his discovery and punishment. (e) The protagonist may or may not restore justice.
2. The Love Story: (a) The lovers will meet. (b) They will fall in love. (c) Powerful forces will oppose their love. (d) The lovers will combat these forces. (e) Their love will triumph or fail.
3. The Education Plot: (a) The protagonist will lead an unfulfilling life. (b) His sense of emptiness and meaninglessness will weigh on him, but he will not know what to do. (c) He will meet a "teacher character." (d) The teacher will guide or inspire him. (e) The protagonist will develop a new understanding that gives his life meaning and purpose.

The ways courts define crime, the ways families encourage or oppose romance, the ways intellectuals define meaning evolve over time. When a society's beliefs undergo change, genre conventions develop innovative ways to express these evolving ideas. The writer, sensitive to the changing world around him, keeps, cuts, or reinvents these conventions. But any innovation must anticipate the public's expectations. Because readers and audiences love their genres, bending or breaking conventions must add newer, clearer meaning and emotion to the telling.

Genre conventions, properly understood, do not limit expression but make it possible. Love Stories can't be told if lovers never meet. Crime Stories can't be told if crimes go undiscovered. An Education Plot can't be told if a protagonist leads a happy, satisfying life. Without conventions, the story arts would not exist.

The genres divide into two basic classes:

1. Primary genres that create content: characters, events, values, and emotions.
2. Presentational genres that express content: comic or dramatic, gritty or poetic, factual or fantasied, and the like.

THE ORIGIN OF PRIMARY GENRES

The primary genres evolved in reaction to life's major levels of conflict: Physical, Social, Personal, Private.

In reaction to physical conflicts, storytellers first told origin myths of how gods created the skies, the earth, the seas, and humanity. Once belief in the supernatural gave reality a sense of order, storytellers moved from gods to heroes and invented the Action/Adventure Genre. These fictions acted out life-and-death battles against storms, floods, lightning, and voracious beasts.

But the most lethal threat to anyone's life comes from other human beings, so storytellers developed additional genres based on social, domestic, and intimate levels of conflict. These conflicts generated arcs of outer change. Last, struggles within the mind gave rise to arcs of character change.

Few stories are so pure that they engage their characters on only one level of conflict. In most tellings, levels mix, merge, and multiply, but let's separate the levels of conflict to see how they generate primary genres.

Self Versus Nature

The Action/Adventure Genre: The first action tales pit heroes against the powers of nature personified as gods: Odysseus battles a hurricane driven by the breath of Poseidon; Lot flees Yahweh's volcanic fire and brimstone; Gilgamesh slaughters the Bull of Heaven, and thousands more.

The Horror Genre: The Greeks exaggerated nature into monsters such as the Hydra, Chimera, Minotaur, Cyclops, the vampire Mormo, the werewolf Lycaon, and the gorgon Medusa—each a nightmare of imagination.

Self Versus Society

The War Genre: Warfare has raged ever since the first man picked up the first club, but Homer launched this genre with the *Iliad*'s telling of the Trojan War and Achilles in battle.

The Political Genre: When Athenians instituted democracy around 500 BC, political power struggles immediately became subject matter for tragedies such as *Antigone* as well as farces such as *The Wasps*.

The Crime Genre: Crime detection as a genre took root with Edgar Allan Poe's master investigator C. Auguste Dupin in "The Murders in the Rue Morgue." The genre captured the reading world when Arthur Conan Doyle gave it Sherlock Holmes.

The Modern Epic: Spurred by the rise and fall of twentieth-century dictators, writers revamped the ancient quest epic into a fight for freedom that pits a lone hero against an all-powerful tyrant. This wide-ranging underdog/overdog genre spans both realism and nonrealism: *Lord of the Rings*, *Nineteen Eighty-Four*, *Spartacus*, *Star Wars*, *The Handmaid's Tale*, *Braveheart*, *Game of Thrones*.

Social Drama: Political upheavals in the nineteenth century exposed social problems such as poverty, corruption, and gender inequality. This genre identifies these conflicts and dramatizes their possible cures. Novelists like Charles Dickens and playwrights like Henrik Ibsen spent their literary lives exposing social injustices. Today, Social Drama is a magnet for Oscars.

Self Versus Intimates

At the level of intimate relationships two genres act out conflicts between families and lovers:

Domestic Drama: From *Medea* to *King Lear* to Wally Lamb's novel *I Know This Much Is True* to Christopher Lloyd's sitcom *Modern Family*, family stories, dramatic and comic, are an ancient and unending genre. They dramatize the loyalties and betrayals that bind or shred families.

The Love Story: The idealization of romantic love began as an effort to civilize male rage. In the late Middle Ages, an epidemic of rape swept through Europe, and so in reaction, troubadours, the pop culture of their day, told stories and sang songs praising the virtues of chaste, chivalric love. Since then, waves of Romanticism followed by tides of anti-Romanticism have buoyed and swamped Western culture and the love stories it tells.

A subgenre of the Love Story, known as the Buddy Story, dramatizes the intimacies of friendship rather than romantic love. Examples: *My Brilliant Friend* by Elena Ferrante, *A Coupla White Chicks Sitting Around Talking* by playwright John Ford Noonan, *Butch Cassidy and the Sundance Kid*, *Thelma and Louise*.

Self Versus Self

Stories of deep psychological complexity arc a character's inner nature from who he is at the inciting incident to who he becomes by the climax. But what exactly can a writer change within a character? One of three qualities: morality, mentality, humanity.

Morality: How does a protagonist treat other people?

Responses to life's temptations either strengthen or corrupt a character's moral nature, changing him for better or worse, making him more honest or lying, more kind or cruel, more giving or selfish.

Mentality: How does a protagonist think and feel about reality and his life in it?

The genetic imperative against suicide makes us wait for death, but beyond that pause, existence has no intrinsic meaning. Faced with the relentlessness of time and randomness of luck, each complex character must answer a deeply private question: Does my existence have a purpose beyond survival? Is my life meaningful or absurd? In stories told at the level of an existential conflict, a protagonist either discovers a positive reason for living or surrenders to meaninglessness.

Humanity: How does a character's human potential change? To a fuller or lesser self?

The most subtly complex stories engage and change a character's humanity. They raise the most difficult questions a writer ever asks: Does my character evolve or devolve over time? If so, what need or lacking in the character's humanity does the telling fulfill or fail to fulfill? Does he grow or hollow out? Answers to these questions will come as you carry out two major tasks:

(1) At the beginning of a story, a character's overall humanity could be profound or shallow depending on an intricate weave of qualities such as wisdom versus ignorance, compassion versus indifference, generosity versus selfishness, emotional calm versus impulsiveness, and the like. In the planning stages of a story, imagine the relative maturity and fullness of your character's inner world, and then measure its propensity for positive or negative change.

(2) Once you have a grip on the depth and breadth of your character, reveal his nature at the inciting incident and the events that follow, arcing it over an expanse of story.

You can execute these two tasks in only one way: Put your character under pressure, then, as he pursues his desire, give him choices of action that reveal who he is now and set up who he will become. At the story's climax, the character will either heighten or diminish his humanity, becoming either a fuller or lesser human being.

THE SIXTEEN PRIMARY GENRES

Primary genres cause critical change in a character's life on either the outer levels or in the inner life. As a result, primary genres are divided into two basic sets: Plots of Fortune and Plots of Character.

To cause and express change, primary genres contain four core conventions: core value, core event, core emotion, core cast. The next two sections examine the sixteen primary genres—ten of fortune, six of character—with their quartets of key conventions:

The Ten Plots of Fortune

Plots of Fortune change the outer conditions of a character's life for better or worse. His fortunes could swing up or down between winning and losing, poverty and riches, loneliness and togetherness, and the like.

Genres under Plots of Fortune have numerous subgenres, some a dozen or more: Action, for example, has sixteen; Crime, fourteen; Love, six. This list outlines only the mother form without her children.

1. The Action Genre

> Core Value: Life Versus Death
> Core Event: Hero at the Mercy of the Villain
> Core Emotion: Excitement
> Core Cast: Hero, Villain, Victim

These three characters form a triangle of moral archetypes. The essential trait of the hero is altruism; of the villain, narcissism; of the victim, vulnerability.

Heroes change the world but not themselves. Their shades of power run from superhero (Superman) to action hero (Jason Bourne) to everyman hero (Captain Phillips). Superheroes employ extrahuman powers to battle extrahuman villains and monsters; action heroes test their strengths against conventional villains; everyday heroes have no special skills, except the willpower to suffer pain and risk out of necessity.

Villains range from supervillains to master criminals to street gangs. They use violence without hesitation because they're indifferent to the humanity of their victims; the hero has to be provoked to violence because he cannot be indifferent to anyone's humanity, including the villain's. To the villain, heroes and victims are just objects—a means to an end; to the hero, no one, not even the villain, is an object.

Unlike criminals in crime stories, the action villain cannot be bought off. He has a project that defines his life, a perfect crime that's more important than himself. This scheme is both opaque and mysterious (otherwise it's just lawbreaking) and extremely disruptive (otherwise ordinary cops could handle it).

The vulnerable victim wears many faces: a child, a lover, a family, a small town, a nation, the planet Earth, and the universe. They are essential to the telling. Without victims, heroes cannot be heroic, nor villains villainous.

In a genre as ubiquitous as Action, repetition wears archetypes to the nub. This pattern, for example, is older than the Bible: the hero's miraculous but humble birth, an early proof of his superhuman power, his rapid rise to prominence, his betrayal by a trusted companion, his triumph over evil, his sin of pride and fall from grace, his atonement, self-sacrifice, and moral triumph.

Recent heroes have added idiosyncratic variations to this template: Spock, Ellen Ripley, James Bond, Harry Potter, Wall-E, Gracie Hart, and Daenerys Targaryen.

2. The Horror Genre

Core Value: Survival Versus Damnation
Core Event: Hero at the Mercy of the Villain
Core Emotion: Terror
Core Cast: Monster, Victim

The Horror Genre eliminates the Action hero and focuses on the monster-victim conflict. The Action hero inspires excitement; the Horror monster provokes terror. Action keeps the reader and audience at a safe emotional distance; Horror assaults the subconscious. Think of Action as a force, Horror as an invasion.

Action villains obey the laws of nature; monsters either break these laws with a supernatural power or bend them with power of an uncanny magnitude.

The Action villain is a narcissist; the Horror monster is a sadist. The villain possesses the spirit of greed; the fiend possesses the spirit of evil. Wealth, power, and fame will satisfy a villain, but the monster inflicts pain and prolongs suffering because the agony of his victims gives him sublime pleasure.

3. The Crime Genre

Core Value: Justice Versus Injustice
Core Event: Hero at the Mercy of the Villain

Core Emotion: Suspense
Core Cast: Antihero, Villain, Victim

The twenty-first-century Crime Genre, for the most part, has abandoned the action hero for the antihero. Like the Action hero, the antihero never arcs, but unlike the Action hero, the antihero's core self is layered and complex.

An antihero is a moral realist capable of both virtue and vice. The difference is that he sees it in himself and so hardens on the outside to protect a better self within. He appears too cool to feel anything, but at heart he has a passion for justice. An antihero carries a villainous version of himself deep within as he struggles to obey his private code and keep his morality intact. He knows that a life spent coping with crime will slowly deaden his soul, but head down, he plows ahead.

4. The Love Genre

Core Value: Committed Versus Lost Love
Core Event: An Act of Love
Core Emotion: Longing for Love
Core Cast: Lovers

If love doesn't hurt, it isn't real. The only act of genuine love is an act of anonymous self-sacrifice—a deed taken in silence, without hope of recognition or reward, that costs the lover but benefits the beloved. The rest, no matter how deeply felt, are simply gestures of affection. The great test in writing a love story is the creation of an original act of love that is unique to your characters and deeply moving to your reader/audience.

5. The Domestic Genre

Core Value: Unity Versus Breakup
Core Event: A Family Unites or Splinters
Core Emotion: Longing for Togetherness
Core Cast: A Family

The cast of a Domestic Story may or may not be blood relatives, but no matter how the group was formed, the members mutually support, protect, and commit, even if they don't love each other.

6. The War Genre

Core Value: Victory Versus Defeat
Core Event: The Decisive Battle
Core Emotion: Harrowing Fear
Core Cast: Soldier, Enemy

A successful military strategy hinges on the courage to carry it out. This genre calls for characters who think and act in the face of fear.

7. The Social Genre

Core Value: Problem Versus Solution
Core Event: Recognition of a Crisis
Core Emotion: Moral Indignation
Core Cast: Social Leader, Victim

The Social Genre identifies social problems such as poverty, racism, child abuse, or addiction, and then dramatizes the need for a cure.

8. The Political Genre

Core Value: Powerful Versus Powerless
Core Event: Power Won or Lost
Core Emotion: Hunger for Victory
Core Cast: Two Combative Parties

In a battle for partisan power, the official beliefs of the characters are virtually irrelevant. In political warfare, the weapon of mass destruction is scandal: bribes, backstabbings, and, above all, secret, illicit sex.

9. The Modern Epic Genre

Core Value: Tyranny Versus Freedom
Core Event: An Act of Rebellion

Core Emotion: Moral Outrage
Core Cast: Tyrant/Rebel

In nonrealistic epics, such as *Lord of the Rings, Star Wars, The Princess Bride*, and *Game of Thrones*, tyrants never survive, but heroes do. In realistic epics, such as *Spartacus, Nineteen Eighty-Four, Braveheart*, and *Lord of the Flies*, tyrants always survive; heroes never do.

10. *The Enterprise Genre*

Core Value: Success/Failure
Core Event: A Professional Loss
Core Emotion: Rooting for Success
Core Cast: Protagonist/Social Institution

In this genre, the ambitious—scientists, athletes, entrepreneurs, and the like—strive to achieve. This genre finds a natural home in autobiographies such as Chris Gardner's *The Pursuit of Happyness* and *Unstoppable* by Maria Sharapova.

The Six Plots of Character

Plots of Character change the inner nature of a character from better to worse or the reverse in terms of his morality, mentality, or humanity.

As set out in Chapter Twelve, stock characters come into a story to carry out their prescribed tasks and no more. They are exactly who they seem to be. Multidimensional characters, on the other hand, conceal their inner selves behind social masks. Choice by choice, action by action, their true natures reveal themselves but do not change. These roles populate the casts of the ten plots of fortune listed above, while characters undergoing true psychological change inhabit the half-dozen story forms that follow.

These six genres express the dynamic triumphs and tragedies of the ever-changing human spirit. As we noted, to arc a character from one kind of person to another, a story can change one of just three inner qualities: Morality, Mentality, Humanity.

Morality Plots

Every society maintains particular judicial and personal codes that tell its people how to treat each other. These codes span various spectra from legal to illegal, good to evil, right to wrong, kind to cruel, and the like. Religions regulate even more detailed codes of moral and immoral behavior. Despite best efforts, however, the golden rule is more bent than kept.

Every author designs a unique morality for each story he tells, which is a subset of his personal code, which is a subset of his culture's code, which is a subset of the Golden Rule ideal imagined by the public as they read or watch. The author works with the protagonist's behavior toward other people, guided by values such as Ethical/Unethical, Valuable/Worthless, Right/Wrong, Kind/Cruel, Truthful/Liar, Compassionate/Indifferent, Loving/Hateful, Charitable/Selfish, Good/Evil. Stories in the Redemption and Degeneration Genres dramatize the morality of their protagonists as it arcs along a path from either negative to positive or positive to negative.

1. The Redemption Plot

> Core Value: Morality Versus Immorality
> Core Event: An Act of Redeeming Morality
> Core Emotion: Hope for Change
> Core Cast: Protagonist

What people do, they become. The Redemption Plot arcs a protagonist's morality from negative to positive. When a protagonist's treatment of other human beings changes from cruel to kind, deceptive to truthful, unethical to ethical, his moral action at the climax redeems his previous immoral deeds.

In Ernest Lehman's screenplay for *The Sweet Smell of Success*, a failing hustler meets a ruthless mentor who offers him a lucrative career...if he sells out. Ultimately, the hustler's nagging conscience defeats his ambition. He restores his better self...but at a price.

In Fyodor Dostoevsky's *Crime and Punishment*, Raskolnikov, a delusional intellectual, murders an old woman, thinking that this deed will somehow make him exceptional, even heroic. The cruel absurdity of his action eats at him until he confesses and finally begs forgiveness.

In David Mamet's screenplay for *The Verdict*, attorney Frank Galvin redeems his prior corruption when he defeats an even more corrupt law firm.

In Annie Mumolo and Kristen Wiig's screenplay for *Bridesmaids*, Annie Walker's selfish jealousy arcs into a rewarding friendship.

2. The Degeneration Plot

> Core Value: Immorality Versus Morality
> Core Event: Act of Irreversible Immorality
> Core Emotion: Dread of Loss
> Core Cast: Protagonist

When a character's treatment of other human beings changes from ethical to unethical, good to evil, moral to immoral, he corrupts his core self. This movement from positive to negative morality arcs the Degeneration Plot.

In Anthony Minghella's screen adaptation of the Patricia Highsmith novel *The Talented Mr. Ripley*, Tom Ripley arcs from petty con man to identity thief to multimurderer.

In *The White Tiger* by Aravind Adiga, Balram Halwai arcs from hardworking servant to corrupt entrepreneur, using murder, theft, bribery, and the assassination of his own family to get what he wants.

In *Hand to God* by playwright Robert Askins, Jason (aka Tyrone) arcs from innocent teenager to surrogate Satan.

In *Better Call Saul*, created by Vince Gilligan and Peter Gould, Jimmy McGill (aka Saul Goodman) arcs from an attorney with criminal clients to a criminal with gangster clients.

Mentality Plots

A character's mentality contains faculties such as knowledge of the people, history, and the world around him, plus all of his personal and professional experiences, awake and dreaming, together with his IQ, EQ, and willpower. The sum total of these elements creates a character's sense of reality and how he sees himself in it. His underlying attitudes shape his choices of action, plus the reactions he expects and his feelings about the results. At rock bottom, his mentality determines whether he finds life meaningful or meaningless.

In the Education and Disillusionment Plots, the writer works with a character's view of reality as it affects his attitude toward life, expressed in values such as Meaningful/Meaningless, Proud/Meek, Educated/Ignorant, Theistic/Atheistic, Optimistic/Pessimistic, Trusting/Distrustful, Contented/Depressed, Self-respect/Self-disgust. `

3. The Education Plot

> Core Value: Meaning Versus Nihilism
> Core Event: Discovery of Meaning
> Core Emotion: Longing for Meaning
> Core Cast: Protagonist, Teacher

Today's crisis of meaninglessness drives ever-rising rates of suicide and addiction. Human beings want lives that matter, significance beyond survival. When meaning evaporates, they despair; when they find meaning, they live with purpose.

The Education Plot expresses this change from negative to positive by moving the protagonist from someone who finds life meaningless to someone who learns what's worth living for. The Education Plot takes its name from its emphasis on learning experiences that lead to an inner discovery.

Hamlet is the ultimate Education Plot. Two inner selves pull Hamlet in opposite directions: His princely self longs to revenge the murder of his father, while his core self asks, "What's the point?" One person can't move in two directions at once, so Hamlet wars within. Because he hates the state of the world, he alienates everyone; because he's lost within, he alienates himself. Between the two, life seems pointless. But ultimately, he finds meaning in a surrender to fate: "There's a special providence in the fall of a sparrow ... the readiness is all."

In *Fahrenheit 451* by Ray Bradbury, Guy Montag turns against his illiterate ignorance and embraces the beauty of written knowledge.

In *The Sympathizer* by Viet Thanh Nguyen, the protagonist comes to realize that revolutions invariably betray the revolutionaries who created them. Even so, a true revolutionary lives for only one thing: the next revolution.

In *Lost in Translation* by Sofia Coppola, two self-critical characters arc from meaningless isolation to a meaningful embrace of love.

In *Up in the Air* by Jason Reitman and Sheldon Turner, the protagonist's story begins and ends on an empty note, but in between he arcs from self-deceived to self-aware.

4. The Disillusionment Plot

> Core Value: Meaning Versus Nihilism
> Core Event: Loss of Belief
> Core Emotion: Dread of Meaninglessness
> Core Cast: Protagonist

Stories in the Disillusionment Plot move their protagonist from optimism to fatalism, from someone who finds life meaningful to someone who can no longer imagine his future.

In *The House of Mirth* by Edith Wharton, Lily Bart traps herself in a contradiction: She hates the snobbery and vacuity of elite society but, in truth, cannot live without the comforts of wealth. Her dilemma ends with an overdose of sleeping pills.

In *The Fall* by Albert Camus, Jean-Baptiste falls from self-admiration to self-disgust to self-destruction as he realizes that his life is false—always has been, always will be.

In *American Pastoral* by Philip Roth, Seymour Levov realizes that no one lives truthfully—not even himself within himself. The good life, therefore, is an impossibility.

In Graham Moore's screenplay for *The Imitation Game*, legal authorities force computer genius and war hero Alan Turing to undergo chemical castration because he's homosexual. Realizing that society will never let him live an honest life, Turing commits suicide.

In Dan Futterman's screenplay for *Capote*, Truman Capote, intent on writing a best seller, spends seven years cultivating and then exploiting the trust of two imprisoned murderers. Disillusioned by his cynical exploitations, he never writes another novel.

Humanity Plots

The most profound stories are always, to some degree, Humanity Plots. While Morality and Mentality Plots change a protagonist's empathies and beliefs, a Humanity plot arcs his total being. A character's humanity includes not only his moral principles and mental attitudes but his maturity, sexuality, spirituality, courage, creativity, willpower, judgment, and wisdom, plus his sensitivity to beauty, insight into others, insight into himself, and much more.

From the point of view of readers and audiences, Humanity Plots hook curiosity with the most thought-provoking concern of all: Will the protagonist become a fuller or lesser human being? Will he enrich or deplete his core self? Will his humanity evolve or devolve?

Every complex character you create contains a unique set of qualities. You lay the foundation for an arc of humanity by first listing and measuring your character's capacities. Before your protagonist enters the story, establish his state of need by asking: "What are his principal qualities? How far has he evolved to this point in his life? What is his potential for change? How much more could he evolve and grow? What events would lift him to the fullest experience of his humanity? If the story arcs to the negative, how far could he devolve and decay? What turning points would strip his humanity to the bone?" The story you tell answers these questions.

In the Evolution and Devolution Plots the writer calls on values such as Child/Adult, Dependent/Independent, Addicted/Sober, Impulsive/Prudent, Weak/Strong, Callow/Sophisticated, Self-indulgent/Self-controlled, Normal/Neurotic, Sane/Psychotic.

5. The Evolution Plot

> Core Value: Full Versus Emptied Humanity
> Core Event: A Triumph of the Core Self
> Core Emotion: Longing for Fulfillment
> Core Cast: Protagonist

Works in the Evolution Plot arc a character's humanity from negative to positive, giving him a chance to live life at its fullest. One of the most popular of these tellings is the coming-of-age-story, a revolution from immaturity to maturity that elevates the protagonist from child to adult.

In *A Separate Peace*, a novel by John Knowles, a teenager, Gene, harbors a childish jealousy against his best friend, the gracefully athletic and poised Finny. When Finny dies, Gene's childish self dies with him. The protagonist loses his friend but finds maturity.

Films such as *Stand by Me*, *Big*, and *Beasts of the Southern Wild* evolve juveniles into grown-ups. Other maturation arcs begin with a character who looks grown up but is at heart a juvenile.

In Steve Kloves's screenplay for *The Fabulous Baker Boys*, pianist Jack Baker lazes through life like an unkempt kid. But once he decides to abandon the ease of pop and face the rigors of jazz, he finds his inner adult.

In *The Hustler*, a novel by Walter Tevis, Fast Eddie Felson, a pool hustler enjoying a delayed adolescence, eventually finds his manhood—but only after his selfish indifference to the woman he loves triggers her suicide.

As we saw in Chapter Eleven, evolution to the limits of humanity often swivels around an epiphany, a sudden "I get it!" In that moment the protagonist lives life to its limit as he undergoes his most profound experience of head and heart, of emotion and perception, of thought and feeling. A price, however, must be paid for this peak experience, and that often costs life itself.

In the final scene of Ibsen's *Hedda Gabler*, Hedda realizes that she will always have to live through men, that these men will always have power over her, and therefore she will never achieve greatness on her own. At the pinnacle of awareness and in the depths of rage, she puts a gun to her head.

Dark ironies such as *Oedipus Rex*, *Othello*, *Anna Karenina*, *The Iceman Cometh*, and *The Killing of a Sacred Deer* climax in the moment the protagonist experiences life lived to an absolute limit and with their death or resignation, the fulfillment of their humanity.

6. The Devolution Plot

> Core Value: Full Versus Lost Humanity
> Core Event: Surrender of the Core Self
> Core Emotion: Dread of Emptiness
> Core Cast: Protagonist

Works in the Devolution Plot arc a character from positive to negative, stripping his humanity with every choice and action he takes. In one of its most frequent tellings, addiction devolves the protagonist.

In Hubert Selby's novel *Requiem for a Dream*, four protagonists shred their humanity with drugs, as does Jackie Peyton in *Nurse Jackie*, and Edith Piaf in *La Vie En Rose*. In *The Lost Weekend* and *The Days of Wine and Roses*, characters destroy themselves with alcohol. In *Madame Bovary* and *Anna Karenina*, addiction to romance kills the soul.

In Ebbe Roe Smith's screenplay for *Falling Down*, William Foster, a weapons engineer, loses his family and his job. As he walks across Los Angeles, laying waste to the cityscape along the way, his humanity progressively disintegrates.

In Woody Allen's *Blue Jasmine*, guilt, lies, poverty, and rejection combine to devolve Jasmine's sanity.

Sudden change in a character often comes off as temporary, superficial, and easy to reverse, but when cause and effect link over time, change seems permanent and inevitable. Notice that most of the previous examples of both evolution and devolution span or at least imply years, if not decades, of gathering change.

THE TEN PRESENTATIONAL GENRES

To bring the primary genres to life and express their characters vividly, storytellers developed various techniques of performance, illustration, point of view, style, and tone. These methods shape the ten presentational genres:

1. Comedy: Any principal genre can inspire laughter. Dramas in the principal genres easily flip into comedies, even spin off into farce.
2. Musical: Any principal genre can be sung and danced.
3. Science Fiction: Any genre can be set in a futuristic world or an alternate reality.
4. History: Any genre can take place in a previous time period.
5. Fantasy: Any genre can happen in a timeless world or magical reality.
6. Documentary: Any genre can be told factually.
7. Animation: Any genre can be animated.
8. Autobiography: Any genre can dramatize a memoir's protagonist.

9. Biography: Any Plot of Fortune can place a biographical subject's outer life at its center. The author then decides whether or not to use a Plot of Character to portray an inner life only he can imagine. Don DeLillo's *Libra*, about Lee Harvey Oswald, and Joyce Carol Oates's *Blonde*, about Marilyn Monroe, arc their subjects through the Devolution Plot.

10. High Art: *High Art* is the presentational style common to the art film, experimental theatre, and avant-pop fiction. These works begin with a principal genre but then run its characters through fragmented happenings told from unreliable points of view in discontinuous time frames. To these macro distortions they often add micro executions of mixed media, hyperimages, and graphic symbols.

GENRE COMBINATIONS

When a work's central plot and subplot(s) combine various genres, character complexity expands with a natural ease. In the classic example, a Crime Story central plot spliced with a Love Story subplot instinctively pulls the inner life of a detective protagonist toward the tough qualities called for in police work and then the tender touches needed in romance.

Genres can either mix or merge.

Mixed genres crosscut two or more story lines. The plots' counterpointing themes enrich the work's overall meaning and at the same time add facets and dimensions to their characters.

For example: David Mitchell's novel *Cloud Atlas* intercuts six stories in six different genres taking place in six different times and settings: Education Plot, Disillusionment Plot, Evolution Plot, Political Drama, and two subgenres of Crime: the Thriller and the Prison Drama. The principal characters in all six echo one another from epoch to epoch, story to story.

As the author said in an interview on BBC Radio 4: "The characters, except one, are reincarnations of the same soul in different bodies throughout the novel identified by a birthmark...[*Cloud Atlas's*] theme is predacity—the way individuals prey on individuals, groups on groups, nations on nations, tribes on tribes...[I] reincarnate that theme in a different context."

Mixed designs multiply the number of genre conventions the writer must master and the reader/audience will expect, and at the same time, they expand the work's cast in number and variety. A cast as massive as *Cloud Atlas*'s puts tremendous creative demands on its author. Some readers use margin notes to keep track of the complicated population.

Merged genres combine plotlines so that one story takes place inside of another to motivate and complicate it.

Two examples:

The overall genre of Russell Harbaugh's *Love After Love* is Domestic Drama, a Plot of Fortune. Members of an already troubled family suffer their father's death, raising the major dramatic question: Will the widow and her two sons unify as a family or fall apart?

The answer to that question, however, depends on the arcs of three stories running inside each principal character: A Love Story for the widow and two Evolution Plots tracing her sons' struggles to reach adulthood. In other words, the three inner story lines motivate the climax of the Domestic Drama: The family stays together because their humanities evolve and they find love after love.

Quentin Tarantino's *Once Upon a Time in...Hollywood* both merges and mixes genres. A Buddy Plot between actor Rick Dalton (Leonardo DiCaprio) and stuntman Cliff Booth (Brad Pitt) merges with an Evolution Plot arcing within Dalton. Dalton struggles to find the inner strength to overcome his alcoholism and save his acting career, but his codependent friendship with Booth blocks his path to self-control. The conflict between these two story lines raises the major dramatic question: Will these men sacrifice their relationship for the sake of Dalton's future or stay drinking pals to the bitter end? Meanwhile, a life-and-death Crime Story crosscuts with these two merged stories, climaxing all three with a home invasion by the infamous Manson gang.

When genres merge, the course of one story determines the outcome of another. This blending reduces the size of the cast (one character plays protagonist in two genres) as well as the number of conventions (one inciting incident launches two genres as the lovers meet during a bank robbery).

15

CHARACTER IN ACTION

Every character has her self-stories. These are the three tales she tells herself as she looks back on her past identities, as she reflects on her present state, and as she looks forward to her future self. Her future story becomes the most important because it shapes and governs the course of your work.

Somewhere in her childhood, while immersed in her upbringing, her schooling, her culture, she dreamed up a wished-for life with an ideal identity, an ideal beloved, an ideal career, an ideal way of life—the way things *should* happen to her. Over time, she constantly rewrote and rationalized her past to give herself reasons for how she became who she's become. When she asks, "Who am I? How did I get here? And how will I fit into this world?" her self-story gives her answers that pull her many selves into a unity.[1]

Put into action, her self-story gives her a one-of-a-kind modus operandi (to borrow a term from the Crime Genre), a unique way of doing things.

A character's MO goes beyond the collection of characterization traits—voice, gesture, dress, mood—that create her personality. It gives her the pattern of tactics that she habitually uses to pursue her object of desire, to live out her ideal future. Her one-of-a-kind MO guides her efforts to cope with both positive and negative eventualities—how she intends to go about getting what she wants, plus how she plans to escape the things she fears. Over a lifetime, a character may abandon the MO of her youth, but more often than not, she simply reshapes it under the pressures of family, work, and, of course, love.[2]

When your story's inciting incident throws your protagonist's life out of balance, she will pursue rebalance by trying to impose her self-story on the forces that oppose her will and desire. In other words, she will do things her way, in her unique MO. So, to put your character into action, first conjure her self-story, then imagine her future as she wants it to be and focus her MO through it.

Character MOs tend to cluster around various themes. To give you a sense of what's possible, I've listed three of the most common premises with examples taken from plays, series, novels, and films. I give each an additional twist that might propel the story forward.

HOLLYWOOD THEMES

Many people try to live daily life as if it were a movie. They find their personal goal in their favorite story; they then identify with its characters and model their real-life MOs on fictional behaviors. Writers recycle these behaviors back into stories, and as a result, certain MOs drive both fact and fiction, real people and make-believe characters. Below are just five:

The Mystery Lover

Because the protagonist finds everyday life boring, her MO seeks a mysterious, enigmatic lover.

Examples: Scottie Ferguson in Alfred Hitchcock's *Vertigo*; Jerry in Paul Theroux's novel *A Dead Hand*; Arthur in the Susan Hill–Stephen Mallatratt play *The Woman in Black*; Dale Cooper in David Lynch's TV series *Twin Peaks*.

Twist: It turns out that the mystery figure has nothing to hide or say. To attract lovers, she simply feigns inscrutability.

The Alien Adventurer

The protagonist feels estranged from normal society, so she creates an outlandish version of herself and seeks others who are as weird or even weirder than herself—the more alien, the more exciting.

Examples: The unnamed narrator of Pam Houston's short stories in *Cowboys Are My Weakness*; Martin in Edward Albee's play *The Goat, or Who is Sylvia?*; Lars in Nancy Oliver's screenplay for *Lars and the Real Girl*; Cosmo Kramer in the Larry David–Jerry Seinfeld sitcom *Seinfeld*.

Twist: We often assume that eccentricity hides a fascinating personality, but suppose the protagonist discovers that her partner's tattoos, scarring, and pastel-streaked hair are just a futile tactic to seem interesting.

The Fairy Tale

The protagonist plays a fairy-tale prince or princess.

Examples: Mrs. Hardwicke-Moore in Tennessee Williams's play *The Lady of Larkspur Lotion*; Claire in Ronald Moore's series *Outlander*; Xiao in Tong Hua's novel *Bu Bu Jing Xin*; Buttercup in William Goldman's screenplay for *The Princess Bride*.

Twist: The fairy-tale world becomes grotesque as the prince transforms into a knave and the princess into a witch.

The Documentary

A common MO among intellectuals is the compulsive analysis of personal relationships that turns dating into a Discovery Channel documentary. Similar to the Heisenberg Uncertainty Principle, the act of observation affects passion, reducing it to a sex manual.

Examples: Alvy Singer in Woody Allen's *Annie Hall*; Alexander in Philip Roth's novel *Portnoy's Complaint*; the four co-protagonists of Darren Star's series *Sex and the City*; Laura and Danny in David Eldridge's play *Beginning*.

Twist: As they dissect their feelings and behaviors, flirtation morphs into a science project, a fetish they find more titillating than pornography.

The XXX-Rated Flick

Sadomasochists take pleasure in both brutality and humiliation. These characters seek to inflict or suffer abuse so they can either degrade their victim or be degraded or both at once.

Examples: Solange and Clair in Jean Genet's play *The Maids*; Severin in Leopold von Sacher-Masoch's novella *Venus in Furs*; Erika in Michael Haneke's *The Piano Teacher*; Lorne Malvo in Noah Hawley's anthology series *Fargo*.

Twist: The sadist's fear of death drives an MO that enjoys debasing victims. The infliction of suffering gives the abuser a temporary sense of godlike power over life and death. But in time the law of diminishing returns reverses everything: The more and more she humiliates her victims, the less and less pleasure she feels. Instead, she suffers more and more boredom, less and less power, until the dread of death becomes so unbearable, she inflicts violence against herself.

POLITICAL THEMES

Politics is the name we give to the use, abuse, and hierarchy of power inside social organizations—governments, corporations, religions, hospitals, universities, and the like, even down to families, friends, and lovers. Whenever human beings gather to do anything, there's always an uneven distribution of power—in short, politics.

Tyranny

The protagonist's MO leads her to play the ruler and oppress others as her subjects.

Examples: Violet Weston in Tracy Letts's play, *August: Osage County*; Tony Soprano in David Chase's series *The Sopranos*; Tony Montana in Oliver Stone's screenplay for *Scarface*; Thomas Cromwell in Hilary Mantel's trilogy of novels *Wolf Hall*, *Bring Up the Bodies*, and *The Mirror and the Light*.

Twist: In a master-slave relationship, the slave revolts and turns tables on the tyrant. Second twist: The slave, now master, suddenly suffers the stress of earning money and paying bills. She tries to get her old job back, but her ex-master stays put, now enjoying her stress-free, worry-free life.

Democracy

The protagonist advocates balanced power.

Examples: Valentine Smith in Robert Heinlein's novel *Stranger in a Strange Land*; Longfellow Deeds in Frank Capra's film *Mr. Deeds Goes to Town*; Jon Snow in David Benioff and D. B. Weiss's series *Game of Thrones*.

Twist: A father cares for his family with a gentle, balanced hand, but to them he seems weak. They crave discipline. Because life scares them, his wife cheats on him and his kids run wild, subconsciously hoping he'll bring down his fist.

Anarchy

A character uses power so impulsively that personal, family, and social chaos follows.

Examples: Bernard in Marc Camoletti's farce *Boeing-Boeing*; Larry David in his sitcom *Curb Your Enthusiasm*; General Jack D. Ripper in Terry Southern's screenplay for *Dr. Strangelove*; the King of Dunces in Alexander Pope's narrative poem *The Dunciad*.

Twist: A chaotic character leading a chaotic life fails to get what she wants, so she decides that from now on she will take only logical steps. She imagines a rational future, uses rational actions to achieve her desires, then suffers the boredom that comes with that, and so discovers that what she really wants out of life is the excitement of chaos.

OBJECT THEMES

Characters incapable of intimate relationships often tend to treat people like objects. If they value another person, it's not for who they are, but for how they serve a purpose. Of the many variations of this MO, here are four of the more common.

The Collector

This character collects beautiful things in a treasure chest of houses, cars, artworks, and lovers.

Examples: Frederick in John Fowles's novel *The Collector*; Andrew Wyke in Antony Shaffer's play *Sleuth*; Alfie in Bill Naughton's screenplay for *Alfie*; Nick Ruskin in James Patterson's novel *Kiss the Girls*.

Twist: The collector is collected.

The Player

This character treats life as a game (however deadly) and uses other people as players (wittingly or unwittingly) in it.

Examples: George and Martha in Edward Albee's play *Who's Afraid of Virginia Woolf?*; the Bliss family in Noel Coward's comedy *Hay Fever*;

Frank Underwood in Beau Willimon's series *House of Cards*; Tomas in Milan Kundera's novel *The Unbearable Lightness of Being*.

Twist: The player is played.

The Obsessive

Like the collector, the obsessive prefers things to people; unlike the collector, the obsessive's MO focuses on only one thing, constantly and repetitiously. Anything can become an addiction:

Sex: Sada and Kichizo in Nagisa Oshima's *In the Realm of the Senses*.

Religion: Matt Jamison in Tom Perrotta's novel *The Leftovers*, the basis for the longform series.

Drugs: Mimi Marquez in Jonathan Larson's rock musical *Rent*.

Alcohol: Geoffrey Firmin in Malcolm Lowry's novel *Under the Volcano*.

Art: Martin Clay's obsession with a lost Bruegel in Michael Frayn's novel *Headlong*.

Love: Ted Stroehmann in the Farrelly brothers' *There's Something About Mary*.

Himself: Dorian Gray in Oscar Wilde's novel *The Picture of Dorian Gray*.

Twist: The obsessive finally gets what she wants and hates it.

The Businessman

This single-minded boss tries to run his business like a machine and treat his workers and customers like discs and chips.

Professor Henry Higgins in George Bernard Shaw's play *Pygmalion*; Basil Fawlty in John Cleese's twelve-episode series *Fawlty Towers*; Henry Graham in Elaine May's screenplay for *A New Leaf*; Alfred Lambert in Jonathan Franzen's novel *The Corrections*.

Twist: The business goes bankrupt.

SCENE CREATION: CHARACTER IN ACTION

Definition: *Action* means anything a character does, verbally or physically, in thought or deed, inwardly or outwardly, that pursues a desire. Without desire, action becomes activity—boring, time killing, thumb twirling.

To put a character into action, the writer answers these key questions in each scene: "What do these characters want at the moment? What actions do they take to get it? What surprising counteraction blocks their way? How do they react to that? What do they do next?"

Let's take these questions in sequence:

What does my character want?

Two desires, present and future, propel a character through any scene: She desires (1) an immediate effect (what she wants to happen now) that will take her a step toward (2) her long-term desire (the rebalancing of her life). If the character's current wish fails, her future darkens; if it succeeds, her life moves in a positive direction. Actors call the character's immediate desire the Scene-Objective and her overall desire the Super-Objective.

To compose a scene around its turning point, first discover your protagonist's scene-objective, what she wants to accomplish immediately as a step toward her super-objective. Then with that immediate goal in mind, take her point of view and put her into action.

What is her first action?

As a scene begins, each character calls on familiar MOs and favorite tactics—gestures and words that have worked in the past. Each relies on her best sense of probability, a semiconscious expectation that runs like this: "Given this situation, if I do *xxx*, in all probability *yyy* will happen, and that reaction will take me a step toward what I want."

A character's life experience has taught her what reactions to anticipate from people in a range of circumstances. Over time, a sense of probability develops within a character. The relative sophistication of her expectations depends on the number of years she's lived, the breadth of her experience, and the depth of her insight into the cause-and-effect of things. For this reason, every character's sense of probability is unique; every character tests the world in her distinctive way; every character's first action is a tried-and-true tactic that she thinks will trigger a useful reaction.

What counteraction blocks her?

But instead of causing the helpful reaction the protagonist hopes for, the action she takes to get what she wants provokes an unexpected, antagonistic counteraction that blocks her from getting it. At each turning point, what a character thinks will happen when she acts collides with what in fact happens. Her beat-by-beat, moment-by-moment subjective expectations are constantly violated by the objective reality of the people and world around her.

These antagonistic counteractions could come from physical forces, institutions, another character or group, dark impulses within herself, or a combination of such powers.

What surprises spring from counteractions?

When a counteraction strikes from out of the blue, surprise jolts the protagonist. She suddenly discovers hidden reactions in places she thought she knew but now sees in a whole new light. The impact of this surprising counteraction may change her situation to an unforeseen positive, but more often the value at stake in a scene pivots to the negative.

How does change affect her?

A dynamic pivot around a turning point not only gives us insights into a character and her setting but moves emotions as well. *Emotion* is the side effect of a changing charge in value. Whether the emotion is positive or negative depends on the direction of that change.

When a living value changes from negative to positive, a character naturally experiences a positive emotion. The change from slavery to freedom, for instance, would lift a character out of misery into joy. Conversely, when change arcs from positive to negative, a character's emotions descend with it. The change from companionship to loneliness, for example, could induce intense suffering.

Values don't necessarily need external conflicts to bring about change. The mind can sometimes reverse a charge all on its own.

Imagine a character living in a state of calm inner trust. She does not fear the future. She believes that no matter what happens, she will cope. But then, for some irrational reason, the dread of something bad heading her way slowly seeps into her mind. Her thoughts fill with a gnawing suspicion that in an unknown future an as-yet-unknown person in an unknown way will violate her.

In this case, the value Safety/Threat slides from positive to negative, and as it does, the character undergoes the icy emotions of anxiety. In an extreme case, she could lose all control and plunge into paranoia.

What would she do next?

From the inciting incident on, the protagonist pursues her object of desire, doing all she can to follow her self-story, her ideal sense of how to rebalance life. But things will get worse before they get better. Her path will be blocked by forces of antagonism that gain ever greater power and sharper focus, putting her in more and more jeopardy, forcing her to dig deeper and deeper into herself for better and better actions.

Throughout this conflict, the character will try to live up to her best sense of who she is, to the ideal identity she created in her self-story. But as her actions escalate to meet ever more intensely negative counteractions, the pressure may become so great that her core identity cracks and her morality, mentality, or humanity bends for better or worse. The story then enters one of the six genres of character change. (See "The Six Plots of Character" in Chapter Fourteen.)

Putting a character into action may force you to reconsider previous choices. As new scenes inspire new ideas for behavior, you may want to redesign a role's characterization; as new turning points call for new tactics, you may reconceive her true character. All to the good. The scene-by-scene interplay of action and reaction evolves original inspirations into the cohesive mergers of complex characters and superb stories.

16

CHARACTER IN PERFORMANCE

What do audiences and readers want from a cast of characters? Discovery and recognition.

Discovery: Audiences and readers want to venture into a story the way explorers push into a wilderness. They seek the anthropological excitement of discovering a tribe they've never seen before. For no matter how exotic or familiar the setting, its inhabitants are always strangers. Eccentric traits and intriguing behaviors mark these roles, and so the reader/audience wants to know them and understand them. As Aristotle said, the greatest of all pleasures is the pleasure of learning without being taught.[1] Through stories and their characters, the reader/audience gains effortless insight into human nature and the real-life consequences of its desires and actions.

Recognition: Once in the setting, the reader/audience wants to discover himself. At the heart of the story's protagonist, and perhaps other characters as well, he recognizes a humanity that reflects his own—not in every way, obviously, but in some essential quality. In other words, empathy with a complex character is like looking into a mirror.

An empathetic character opens an emotional door to an intimate, even primal, deeply felt yet fascinating identification. Without empathy, the reader/audience sits on the outside looking in, feeling little, learning less.

Discovery and recognition allow readers and audiences to travel through thousands of fictional realities, to live lives they could never live in worlds they could never know, to experience feelings light-years beyond their daily existence.

To explore how character performance achieves this for readers and audiences, let's start with seven common character functions.

SEVEN FUNCTIONS OF CHARACTER IN PERFORMANCE

1. To Expand the Reader's/Audience's Intellectual Pleasure

The violation of expectation sparks insight, but it's a character's unique traits and surprising yet believable behavior that adds fascination to the society and setting that surrounds him.

2. To Develop Empathy in the Reader/Audience

Empathy is key. Without an emotion-deepening sense of shared humanity, readers and audiences become indifferent and disinterested.

3. To Drive Suspense

Suspense is emotional curiosity—the merger of the reader's/audience's interest in a character's nature with their concern for his well-being. Pure curiosity without concern turns a character into an intellectual case study; pure concern devoid of curiosity becomes mindless longing.

To sustain plot-long suspense, a character's actions must be various but within limits. If he can do only one thing, he generates no suspense, but if he can do anything, even the impossible, then once again, no suspense.

4. To Create a Puzzle Within a Puzzle

A story is a mass of questions: Why is this happening now? What will happen next? How will this turn out?

A complex character offers readers and audiences yet another set of questions, taking them into psychological depths: Who is he? What does he think he wants? What does he really want? Why does he want these things? How do his desires contradict each other? Who will he become?

By adding puzzle piece after puzzle piece, a character creates a second line of psychological suspense that runs parallel to the story's overall plot-driven suspense.

5. To Surprise

Not only do unexpected counteractions from a character's world startle the reader/audience, but so do the character's reactions to them. The surprising ways he copes with change gives readers and audiences insights into his nature. Ideally, therefore, with every turning point, a character's reaction to the unexpected, followed by his choice of action, no matter how big or small, should seem unpredictable and yet in-character, making surprising yet retrospective sense.

6. To Bring Out Dimensions in Other Characters

As we'll see in the next chapter, in a well-designed cast, characters illuminate and develop one another.

7. To Inspire Insight into Human Nature

Characters, no matter how realistic or fantasied, induce inner visions in readers and audiences. Searching through the natures of characters encourages them to explore not only themselves but the innerness of the people around them.

THE READER/AUDIENCE/CHARACTER CONNECTION

Feelings of fear, rage, love, hate, suspicion, defiance, and submission have evolved to cope with life's deadliest threat: other people. That's a sensible adaptation. What isn't logical is the way we disconnect these energies from reality and aim them at people who do not exist. Emotion helps us survive in reality, but what's the point of making ourselves vulnerable in a fiction?

As noted, characters serve an educational purpose. People, both real and imagined, are puzzles to be solved. Characters arouse our curiosity and then satisfy it as we perceive what's in their minds, giving us valuable insights into ourselves and others.

That makes sense. It's our emotional connection that seems strange. Crying over the charred victims of a forest fire is a logical reaction in real life, but why do we shed tears for the characters who perished in *The Towering Inferno*? How do imagined beings in imagined worlds cross the line from fantasy to actuality and break the hearts of audiences and readers? How do unreal beings spur real, even painful, emotions?

The Power of *As If*

Between our two inner domains of rational thought and instinctive emotion sits a third realm. When it wishes, the mind can leave reality behind and relax into the imaginary landscape of *as if.*

The power to pretend, to think in an *as if* mode, is an evolutionary adaptation that enhanced survival. The shift to a hypothetical gear gives the self a chance to rehearse reality before it happens as a means to survive when it does happen. The first art, for example, far older than cave painting or figurative carving, was dance—an ancient *as if* ceremony that mimicked hunting and killing as preparation for real life-and-death violence.

The same is true of stories and their characters. When we connect to people who do not exist, we experience trial emotions—love prior to actual romance, fear prior to actual threats, grief prior to actual loss. Emotional immersions in the *as ifs* of fiction prepare the mind for the real thing; they rehearse survival and equip us for life.[2]

Reader/Audience POV

From an audience's or a reader's point of view, the emotions they feel for characters seem simple and natural, but for the writer, creating and shaping these experiences calls for a skillful balancing of one aspect with another.

First of all, life contains just two basic emotional experiences: the pleasureful and the painful. Each of these, however, comes in infinite shades and strains—the pleasureful such as joy, love, beauty, and sensuality versus the painful such as grief, rage, terror, and sadness. Varying qualities of emotion depend on two different reader/audience reactions to character: sympathy and empathy.

Sympathy, aka Likability

When the reader/audience feels that a character is "likable," sympathetic feelings flow. A pleasant and agreeable character becomes someone they would like as a neighbor, a coworker, or an acquaintance, someone worth a chat now and then. And of course, the reverse is also true. If a reader/audience dislikes a character, then their feelings turn to irritation, even contempt, which may be exactly what the writer wants.

Empathy, aka Identification

The moment a reader opens a book or a storygoer takes a seat, he begins searching the story's world for the best place to put his emotional interest. As setting and cast appear, he quickly sorts positives from negatives, worthy from worthless, boring from interesting, right from wrong, good from evil, seeking the Center of Good.

He seeks the "good" because, like all human beings, he's aware of his flaws and weaknesses, but on balance, he's convinced that he's more true than false, more just than unjust, more fair than unfair—his intentions sincere. Because he considers himself essentially positive, he naturally seeks the story's center of good as a mirror of himself.[3]

When he senses a link between a quality within himself and the same quality living inside a cast member, he identifies with that character. Empathy, his sense of "someone like me," turns this character into a person he might want to have as family, friend, or lover, or even become himself.

Empathy is instinctive; it happens spontaneously and subconsciously. Antipathy needs a conscious choice. When the mind spots moral or aesthetic repulsiveness in a role's inner nature, it refuses to identify, and any chance for empathy withers into an aversion or no feeling at all.

Once a reader or audience goer senses a kindred spirit, he instinctively roots for that character's success. He experiences the telling, to some degree, as if it were happening to him. He lives in parallel to the character as he vicariously performs the character's actions and experiences the character's emotions.

The Primacy of Empathy

When facing a work of story art, people become moral philosophers. They measure the behavior of characters against ethical standards higher than the ones they enforce in themselves. In the struggle between what a person should do versus must do, audiences lean toward the should as they seek the center of good.

This is why when two intelligent, sensitive people experience the same story and yet come away with opposite reactions, it has little to do with the telling and everything to do with empathy. One empathized with the protagonist and so loved the story, subconsciously sweeping away all flaws so as not to spoil his pleasure. The other felt antipathy toward the protagonist, and so hates the story and finds its flaws painful. In other words, one identified with the center of good; the other either couldn't find it, or if he did, he was repelled by it.

The center of good doesn't name a glow of kindness or sweetness. Empathetic characters often wage private wars between moral and immoral impulses. Rather, the phrase refers to the positive light at the heart of a character that shines in contrast to the negative shades surrounding it. To make certain that empathy flows where it's needed most, the storyteller anchors this positive charge in the central plot's protagonist.

Placement of the center of good within a character is just one of many delicate graces an author must manage while shaping the reader's/audience's emotions. Here's a short list of five such balancing acts:

A Balance of Good

Consider Mario Puzo's *Godfather* trilogy: It maps out a criminal universe of gangsters, crooked cops, and corrupt politicians. The Corleone family, however, has one positive quality: loyalty. They stick together and defend each other. Other mafia families back-stab in constant cycles of betrayal. That makes them the bad bad guys, while the Godfather's family's loyalty makes them the good bad guys. When the audience senses that positive charge, empathy flows and they find themselves identifying with mobsters.

To take the center of good a step deeper, look at the cast design of Thomas Harris's novel *The Silence of the Lambs*. The reader finds an empathic center in Clarice Starling, the protagonist, but they also find one in a first circle role, Hannibal Lecter. To begin, the author surrounds Lecter with a darker world: The FBI manipulates Clarice while it lies to Lecter; Lecter's psychiatrist and jailer is a sadist and publicity hound; the cops Lecter kills are fools. Then Harris radiates powerful lights from within the character: Lecter is massively intelligent; he feels compassion for Clarice; his dry wit is a delight; his schemes are brilliant and pulled off with cool courage; he lives in a hellish asylum, yet stays amazingly calm and gentlemanly. As a center of good forms inside Lecter, the reader identifies with him, thinking and shrugging: "So he eats people. There are worse things. Offhand I can't think what, but there must be. Because if I were a psychopathic, cannibalistic serial killer, I'd want to be just like Lecter; he's amazing."

A Balance of Power

At an early point in your story's development do this: Put your protagonist in one hand, so to speak, and weigh his capacities for action, intelligence, imagination, will, maturity, and other such strengths. Then in your other hand, weigh the sum total of power in all the sources of antagonism he will have to confront through the telling.

Start with impulses and contradictory desires at war within him; he may well be his own worst enemy. On top of his inner conflicts, stack the problems he'll confront in his personal relationships. Next, add antagonisms from the institutions that surround him—employment, government, church, and the like. Lastly, top it off with forces in the physical world: the chaos of traffic, extreme weather, lethal diseases, not enough time to get things done, too far to go to get what he needs, and the brevity of life itself.

When you weigh your protagonist's individual capacities against the sum total of antagonistic forces he will face from all levels of his life, you should see that the odds against achieving his object of desire are enormous. He is an underdog.

At heart, everyone on this planet thinks of himself as an underdog. The poor and weak obviously are, but even rich, powerful top dogs whine and wallow in self-pity over government regulations and taxes. Virtually everyone feels that life is an uphill battle against persistently negative forces, starting with the fact that, sooner or later, your time will be up. For that reason, the reader/audience will not empathize with an overdog such as

Mark Zuckerberg (Jesse Eisenberg) in *The Social Network*. To draw empathy to the heart of your story, therefore, place your protagonist at the center of good, array very powerful forces against him, and cast him as an underdog.

A Balance of Intensity

Some characters we love for a lifetime, others we dismiss. The vividness of a character in the reader's/audience's imagination, along with the intensity of their caring, depends on the strength of identification. To feel an intense link, they imagine what it would be like to be the character and sense his thoughts and feelings. This, of course, depends on a willingness to empathize. Some characters we swallow whole; others we only taste and judge. An author must create a role both complex enough to hold a reader's/audience's conscious interest and human enough to capture their subconscious empathy.

A Balance of Focus

Drawing empathy away from the telling's central character to a supporting role instead risks defocusing the reader/audience. On the other hand, each subplot has a subcenter of good in its protagonist. These additional story lines often magnify overall involvement.

Readers and audiences can identify with a great variety of roles. When a cast draws its storygoers into multiple lines of empathy, they focus on several at once or alternate between them. A diverse cast gives them the chance to visit different mental landscapes and to empathize with or be repelled by what we discover inside.[4]

Game of Thrones, for example, follows three major story arcs: The first takes Cersei Lannister as protagonist against the royal families who fight to usurp her or win independence from her rule. A second arc takes Daenerys Targaryen as its protagonist and follows her quest to reclaim the Iron Throne. A third arc takes Jon Snow as the protagonist leading the Night Watch into battle against the Night King and his White Walkers.

These three crosscutting central plots spawned numerous subplots of family conflict, political drama, and love story, along with plots of character redemption, degeneration, evolution, and devolution. Practically every major character had a subplot, and with that, a subcenter of good.

A Balance of Attitudes

When a cast of characters reacts to one of its members, their response radiates social signals such as empathy, antipathy, likability, animosity, or indifference. If the reader/audience empathizes with the cast, they're encouraged to feel what the cast feels. If they dislike the cast, that's their cue to feel the opposite of whatever the cast feels.

The Bridges of Madison County, for example, uses a scene in a diner to shape the audience's attitude toward adultery. When a known adulteress enters the coffee shop, the protagonist (who's contemplating adultery himself) offers her a seat at the lunch counter. As she takes it, the locals whisper and glare at her until, humiliated, she turns and walks out.

The two adulterers are attractive, intelligent, and polite; the townies who stare at them are snarly faced and ignorant, each misshapen in his or her own special way. The audience senses that if they join this adultery-hating crowd, they too might seem repulsive and obnoxious. To escape that, they send their empathy where the writer wants it, to the good-looking sinners.

The Danger of Empathy

Even though human beings are genetically disposed to empathize, their feelings toward characters vary greatly by intensity and depth from story to story, reader to reader, audience to audience. People motivated by self-interest are less sensitive to the inner states of characters; others with strong empathetic natures are more sensitive.[5] Taken a step too far, the overly empathetic fall prey to the narcissists who exploit them. By making us gravitate toward people "like me," empathy also causes prejudice and impairs judgment. It leads us to prefer attractive people to ugly, nepotism to merit, short-term victims of an immediate disaster to long-term victims of disease or starvation. It discourages quiet observation, listening, and judgment.[6] On the other hand, without empathy to deepen involvement, sympathy alone twists into sentimentality.

Sentiment Versus Sentimentality

As noted previously, sentiment is a balanced emotional response in proportion to the events that caused it. Sentimentality is an imbalanced, undermotivated, overexpressed indulgence that's out of proportion to the events that caused it: for example, a brave smile through trembling tears shed over a child's better-than-average report card.

In the climax of *Game of Thrones*, Season 8, Episode 5, "The Bells," Jaime Lannister fights his way to the trapped and terrified Cersei. Just as the Red Keep collapses around them, he takes her in his arms and says, "Look at me. Just look at me. Nothing else matters. Only us." He sacrifices his life so that she won't die alone. This act, in proportion to his love, moves an honest sentiment.

In *Schindler's List*, a black-and-white film set during the Holocaust, a little girl wearing a bright red coat walks through the horrific liquidation of Krakow. Later, Oskar Schindler sees the child's dead body wrapped in her red coat and the sight moves him to change from selfish, callous materialist to noble, self-sacrificing hero. This is wish fulfillment and as phony as a villain stroking a kitten to show that, evil as he is, he can feel something for a pet. As Carl Jung pointed out, cruelty seduces its victims with the syrup of sentimentality.

Reader/Audience Interpretation

A story asks its reader/audience to interpret not only the events in front of them, but offscreen, offstage, or off-page happenings as well. They must add up what has occurred since the previous scene that led to the present, and they must infer the future this present event may bring. Without their ability to interpret, involvement is impossible.

The same is true for subtext. To discover the truth of a character's motivations, readers and audiences must look past his words and deeds, his choices and actions, and seek hidden causes and meanings.

Interpretation, however, depends on an understanding of desires and values. To react fully and grasp a clear meaning, the reader/audience must sense a character's immediate desire in each scene, and how these scene-by-scene desires feed into his end goal at the climax. To understand what a character wants, however, the reader/audience must also understand the values at play in each scene and the core value that drives the story.

A misunderstanding of a story's values causes a misunderstanding of character desires, which leads to misinterpretation. If readers or audiences cannot sort out what's at stake in your character's life, what's positive from what's negative, then they may misunderstand what the character wants or why he wants it. Their bewilderment leads to mistaken readings that distort the meaning you want to express.

Case Study: Heart of Darkness

Set in Africa in the 1890s, Joseph Conrad's novella *Heart of Darkness* follows riverboat captain Charles Marlow up the Congo on a mission for a Belgian trading company to bring back a cargo of ivory and the company's agent, Kurtz, who they fear has gone rogue.

During the voyage, Marlow questions people who know Kurtz, and everything he hears seems contradictory. Some fear and distrust him, hinting at a sinister nature. Others claim he's a civilized and charismatic artist and musician. One thing is certain: Kurtz knows how to inspire the slaughter of elephants and pile up their tusks by the ton.

In one possible interpretation, Marlow is a psychological detective, fascinated by the enigmatic Kurtz. This makes the story's core value Insight/Ignorance and the discovery of the real Kurtz Captain Marlow's object of desire.

In a different reading, Marlow is a lost soul, adrift in moral confusion. His fellow Europeans think that colonialism brings civilization to the "dark continent," but Marlow suspects that this is a convenient self-deception to rationalize their greed. He hopes that Kurtz understands this, too, and has rebelled against his employers by choosing the virtues of primitive nobility over perverse civilization. In this case, the story's core value becomes Purity/Corruption, and Marlow's object of desire is to prove that human nature, in its primal state, is innately good.

When Marlow reaches Kurtz, however, he discovers that the once-civilized gentleman has turned into a vicious tyrant worshipped like a god by brutalized, terrified tribesmen. Kurtz's embrace of the primitive has not unleashed his nobility but his barbarity.

Different values create different meanings: In the first interpretation, when Marlow discovers the radically changed Kurtz, he realizes that because the core self evolves, it's impossible to know another person's true identity. In the second interpretation, Marlow gains a deeper, more universal insight into the innate savagery of human nature.

Key point: Once the reader/audience grasps the story's essential subject matter, its core value, that perception grounds their interpretation of character.

Reader/Audience Perception

In addition to the emotions they feel and the meanings they interpret, readers and audiences also perceive characters on different levels (text versus subtext), at different points in the chain of events (free will versus fate), and from different angles of awareness (mystery versus suspense versus dramatic irony). During the creative process, an author needs to work with his characters from each of these three points of view:

Text Versus Subtext

Feeling empathy is not the same as perceiving subtext. Readers and audiences read the minds of characters they hate as well as love. Rather than simply following a story with interest, they become simultaneously aware of what's going on at two levels: outward sayings and doings versus inward thinking and feeling—text versus subtext.

As Dostoevsky noted, the implied inner life of a complex role is symphonic. When one character tells another what's on his mind, readers and audiences hear just two or three notes, but then perceive an orchestra of thoughts and feeling playing within. The two modes of character performance activate this perception in two very different ways:

On page, the creativity of the writer and the imagination of the reader combine to generate characters. Onstage and on-screen, the actor, supported by directors, lighting and set designers, cinematographers, editors, makeup artists, and composers, work in concert to bring the writer's creation to the audience.

In terms of characterization, audiences watching the screen or stage see characters from head to foot as they move through their social and physical settings. They absorb an enormous amount of detail, leaving little work for the imagination. The reader, on the other hand, notes details, some concrete, some metaphorical, then adds his own personal experiences scattered through a lifetime, and finally pours these ingredients into his imagination, stirring the bits and pieces together to concoct a characterization.

In terms of true character, when watching performances onstage or on-screen, the imagination peers past the actors' eyes, past words and gestures, past intentions and self-deceptions, searching for the truth rising up from the subconscious. It sees the character form ideas in his conscious mind, but then hold them unspoken beneath the surface of his persona.

First-person prose often puts the character's conscious thoughts, although unspoken to other characters, on the page. Now the reader must penetrate the written text to scan the protagonist's subconscious. The inner life of the rest of the cast comes filtered through the narrator's perceptions. How much that warps the true thoughts and desires of these characters alters from author to author.

Third-person prose varies perceptions. Some writers show and imply, others tell and explain. Writers who show dramatize surface behaviors and imply a character's inner life; those who tell portray a character's thoughts and feelings directly on the page. Hemingway's *The Old Man and the Sea* is an example of the first; Virginia Woolf's *Mrs. Dalloway* is an example of the second. Today, most third-person prose mixes showing with telling, implying with explaining.

Free Will Versus Fate

As noted previously, when we begin a story and look forward to its ending, the protagonist's course to the future seems open to all possibilities. But when the story ends and we look back to the beginning, events seem predetermined. Now that we know him in depth, we feel that his psychology could not let him act any way other than he did. Given the innate powers of the physical and social world that surrounded him, what happened *had* to happen. He was at the mercy of an invisible but inevitable fate.

In storytelling, the perception of determinism versus free will depends on the reader's/audience's location in time: before, during, or after events. Before things happen, we're ignorant of what lies ahead, so the characters seem free to choose and act. But after things happen, we look back and discover that a multitude of interconnected forces flowed into everything. The outcome now seems destined. The writer, therefore, needs to pace character arcs, scene by scene, sequence by sequence, act by act, so that our curiosity at the beginning is satisfied at the ending by a retrospective insight into their fate.

Mystery / Suspense / Dramatic Irony

Characters struggle through invented events in invented worlds unaware that they live in a fiction; to them the telling is their life. Readers and audiences, meanwhile, sit outside story-time, knowing events before, during, or after the characters experience them. This split in awareness creates three storytelling strategies: Mystery, Suspense, Dramatic Irony.

Mystery puts characters ahead of the reader or audience. In the classic Murder Mystery, for example, someone goes to a closet for a shirt, opens the door, and a dead body falls out. This twist puts the victim's killer ahead of the storygoer. The murderer knows who did it, but he's not talking. Therefore, the ever-curious reader/audience, knowing less than the characters, runs from behind, looking ahead, following events wherever they lead, trying to find out what the characters already know.

Stories ruled by mystery, especially those propelled by master detectives, draw sympathy but no empathy. Sherlock Holmes is likable but not like us. We can't identify with him because his brilliance touches perfection.

Suspense puts the reader/audience in the same moment as the cast. The instant events happen, they impact both characters and storygoers. The reader/audience may anticipate certain turning points and characters may hide certain secrets, but overall, each knows the past and present, while neither knows the future. Thus, the major dramatic question (MDQ) becomes "How will this turn out?" Ninety percent of all storytelling employs this strategy.

Dramatic Irony puts the reader/audience ahead of the characters, knowing future events before they happen to the cast. This strategy shifts the MDQ from "How will this turn out?" to "How and why did these characters do what I already know they did?"

Two films by Billy Wilder, *Double Indemnity* and *Sunset Blvd.*, open with their protagonists riddled with bullets, then flash back to the choices and actions that cost them their lives. Because the filmgoer knows the ending from the very beginning, he watches from a godlike perspective, knowing that the schemes the protagonist thinks will enrich him will ultimately kill him.

Stories set during renowned historical events or told about famous people automatically position the reader/audience in dramatic irony. But then to some degree, no matter the telling's strategy, the reader/audience often knows things characters don't. For example, anything said, done, or planned in any scene that does not contain the protagonist instantly gives us greater knowledge than him because we were there and he wasn't.

However, other than biographies and murder mysteries, the exclusive use of either dramatic irony or closed mystery is relatively rare. Instead, most writers merge all three: Suspense shapes their overall strategy, but within its arc, characters that hide secrets know more than the storygoer, while readers and audiences reacting to flashbacks know more than the characters in them.

The political and romantic plotlines in *Casablanca* fill the film with suspense, but within that tension, a flashback to the young lovers' meeting in Paris adds a layer of dramatic irony. As the audience watches Rick and Ilsa's romance, they know the dark future that awaits the lovers. Later, the telling shifts to mystery when Rick chooses his final action but keeps it secret from everyone, including the audience.

More recently, in *The Sympathizer*, a first-person novel by Viet Thanh Nguyen, an espionage chief holds a double agent captive and forces him to write out his life story and, above all, tell the truth. The prose we read is that "confession." Suspense hangs on the MDQ: Will the spy tell the truth or lie? And will his choice save him or kill him?

As the narrator's confession weaves back and forth over three decades, mysteries surrounding hidden assassination plots entice the reader, while, at the same time, dramatic irony haunts every page. We realize that even though the protagonist faced death, he must have survived or we couldn't be reading his book.

The Power of First Impressions

Let's end this chapter with a look at beginnings:

While creating starting points—images that establish locations, chapters that open novels, actions that trigger scenes—be alert to the power of first impressions. When the reader/audience encounters something new, his thoughts rush ahead, driven by curiosity, anticipating the worst or best or both, wondering where this new thing will lead. This is particularly true the moment a character enters the telling, and absolutely true when it's your protagonist.

Resist the urge to plant your protagonist on page one. Instead, intrigue the reader or audience by withholding the protagonist until the most effective scene, and then give him an entrance.

In the opening scenes of *Casablanca*, characters raise questions about the protagonist, finding him charismatic yet aloof, renowned yet mysterious. When the camera finally settles on Rick Blaine, he's dressed in a white tuxedo, playing chess against himself. After all those setups, the audience naturally wonders, "Who is this guy?"

No matter where you bring in your major characters, fame them with an entrance that introduces them with impact:

In David Lean's *Lawrence of Arabia*, Sherif Ali first appears as a distant speck on the horizon, then rides slowly toward us, growing larger and larger against a blazing desert sky.

In Eugene O'Neill's *Long Day's Journey into Night*, Mary Tyrone wanders into her living room, mumbling in a morphine haze.

In Ralph Ellison's *Invisible Man*, a man sits in a basement lit by a hundred blindingly bright bare bulbs strung from the ceiling. He calmly tells the reader that he's stealing electricity from the city.

In Season 1, Episode 1 of Phoebe Waller-Bridge's *Killing Eve*, a sweet-faced child sits in an ice cream parlor eating a sundae. From across the room, Villanelle smiles at her and the kid gleams back. Then as Villanelle heads for the door, she smacks the girl's ice cream into her startled face.

In William Golding's *Darkness Visible*, the Luftwaffe pulverizes World War II London. Then out of the raging bomb-blasted inferno, a child emerges naked, horribly burnt and disfigured.

In the Jerry Herman–Jerome Lawrence–Robert E. Lee musical *Mame*, Mame blows a bugle atop a curved staircase, then slides down the banister.

Ideally, the entrance of a complex character intrigues us about his future and invites insight into his core self.

PART 4

CHARACTER RELATIONSHIPS

No one reveals her complete self to anyone. Each of us exposes only certain facets to others, holding back the rest, keeping big secrets at home. The same is true for self-knowledge. No one shows all of herself to herself. Blind to who we really are, certain truths are perceived only by other people.[1]

As in life, so in fiction. One character may link to another through a shared academic interest or religious feelings or romantic love, but never all aspects equally at once with any one person. However, if you surround this character with a cast, each member geared to draw out a specific aspect, her traits and dimensions will reveal themselves as she encounters the various cast members. The writer's problem, therefore, is how to design a cast so that by the climax, the reader/audience knows the characters better than the characters know themselves.

Principle of Character Relationships: Every cast member draws traits and truths out of every other cast member.

Part Four puts this principle to work as it guides the mapping and designing of a cast.

17

CAST DESIGN

No one travels to her destiny down a razor-straight road. Each of us winds through a maze of social and personal intersections, navigating crossroads and cloverleafs, the entrances, exits, and U-turns of relationships. A character's core self, therefore, is never the sole determiner of her fate. Her instincts push her toward one set of desires, while the tides of physical, social, and personal oceans pull her toward others. Because people impact one another, we design casts around links and oppositions that define each other's qualities. Within these conjoined yet contrasted dealings, a cast forms.

Inside a well-formed cast, traits and dimensions create counterpoints that distinguish each character from every other character. While interacting within scenes, or talking or thinking about each other in separate scenes, roles reveal and clarify one another by contrast and contradiction. What's more, as characters interact face-to-face, they provoke actions and reactions in each other that reveal the positive/negative charges of their dimensionalities.

As focus shifts from character to character, this system shapes how they help and hinder each other, what they want or refuse, what they will or will not do, who they are, and how each character exposes the traits and dynamics of the others. When incompatible desires fester into conflict, the links between characters break, transforming relationships.

So as a writer develops her story, she constantly compares and contrasts characters, arranging similarities and differences, creating patterns only she can see. Hamlet desperately searches for meaning, but Shakespeare always knew where his prince would finally find it.

Therefore, just because a character appears in your imagination doesn't mean she's earned a place in your cast. Each role must play a part in a creative strategy that enhances the storytelling. The reader's/audience's full psychological involvement comes not from the protagonist alone, but from the tensions between resemblances and differences among all cast members. If characters are opposed on just one axle—good versus evil, or courageous versus cowardly—they trivialize each other, and interest in them wanes. But if they are opposed in complex ways, they arouse curiosities and empathies that draw energy and concentration from the storygoer. This calls for thoughtful cast design. The next five sections explore five examples from the major storytelling media.

CASE STUDY: *PRIDE AND PREJUDICE*

Jane Austen's basic cast design embraces the five Bennet sisters. Austen places Elizabeth, her complex protagonist, at the center and gives her four visible traits: cool rationality, social charm, self-esteem, and independence. To span Elizabeth's dimensions, Austen then opposes these outer features with four inner qualities of impulse, private convictions, humility, and romantic longing.

These four contradictions—Rational/Impulsive, Social Charm / Private Conviction, Self-Esteem/Humility, Independence / Romantic Longing—set her dimensions and come into play as Austen links Elizabeth to a quartet of sisters: Jane, Mary, Kitty, and Lydia.

The personalities of her four siblings depend on their outer traits only. None of the four are dimensional; instead, each is flat and exactly who she seems to be. In a design of mutual oppositions, each sister's traits define and highlight one of Elizabeth's dimensions, while Elizabeth's dimensions counterpoint their traits. These distinctions clarify and individualize all five characters.

1. Elizabeth and Jane

Elizabeth's core dimension pits intellect against impulse. At the novel's inciting incident, she's a woman with patient, mature insights into people. But when she meets Mr. Darcy, an impulsive, prejudicial judgment about the prideful gentleman (thus the title *Pride and Prejudice*) suddenly

Elizabeth's Four Dimensions

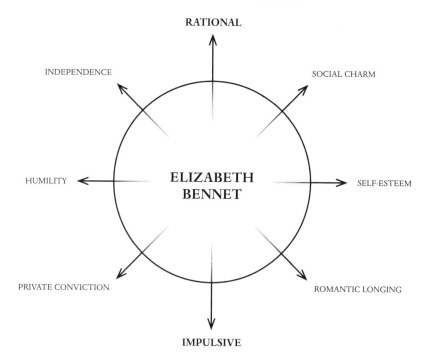

contradicts her normally balanced acumen, turning her against Darcy and setting their story on its rocky road to love when she at last realizes that her private convictions are in fact prejudices, that her self-esteem is a synonym for pride, and that she and Darcy mirror each other.

In clear contrast to Elizabeth's sophisticated skepticism, Jane, her older sister, innocently trusts in the goodness of people. Jane's fawn-like naïveté sharply diverges from her clear-eyed sister and leads to unfortunate choices.

2. Elizabeth and Mary

Elizabeth's second dimension counterpoints her charming wit with moral conviction. Deep within, Elizabeth holds unambiguous ethical beliefs, but rather than bore or antagonize friends and family, she keeps them unseen and unspoken behind her smiling charisma.

Mary, on the other hand, irks people with her moralizing pedantry and pretentiousness. As a result, she has, unlike Elizabeth, no social life.

3. Elizabeth and Lydia

Elizabeth's third dimension contradicts her spirited sense of self-worth with restrained, unaffected modesty.

Lydia, conversely, puts her animal spirits on constant display, making her frivolous vanities and flirtations all the more immodest.

4. Elizabeth and Kitty

Elizabeth's fourth dimension pits her willful independence against her equally strong romantic attraction to Mr. Darcy.

Kitty is her opposite: dependent, needy, weak willed, and easily reduced to tears.

Elizabeth's intelligent, self-possessed calm contradicts the weak, frantic insecurities of her four sisters. In the scenes between the sisters, each evokes the contrasting traits of the others, so that the five become distinctive and memorable, all the while keeping Elizabeth solidly at the novel's center.

Like Elizabeth, dimensions in highly complex characters crisscross between all four levels of self: social, personal, private, hidden. The more dimensions in a character, the more relationships she needs to delineate her complexities. Therefore, to activate your imagination as you develop each character and explore the interplay of your cast's traits and dimensions, I suggest that you lay out a map of your cast's traits and dimensions.

Cast Map

To map your cast's interconnections, create three concentric circles. At the center of it place your protagonist. Because contradictions need performance time to reveal themselves to the reader/audience, give this character a majority of dimensions. The four-dimensional Elizabeth Bennet, for example, centers the cast map of *Pride and Prejudice*.

Around the first circle, distribute major supporting and servicing players, noting their traits and dimensions. Then counterpoint them with the protagonist. For example, the three-dimensional Mr. Darcy and Elizabeth's four sisters:

Darcy (Prideful/Chastened, Arrogant/Kindhearted, Self-deceived/Self-aware), Jane (Innocent), Mary (Pedantic), Kitty (Immodest), Lydia (Dependent). Elizabeth brings out the three positive sides of Darcy.

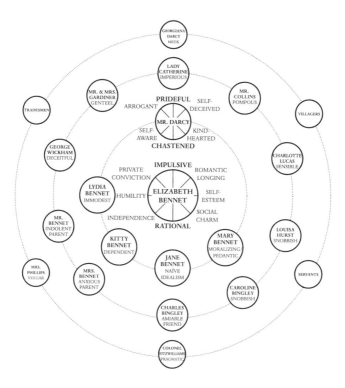

Because dimensions draw interest to a character and consume storytelling time to express, limit second circle roles to their distinctive traits only. For example: Mr. and Mrs. Bennet (anxious parents), Charles Bingley (amiable friend), Caroline Bingley (snobbish), Charlotte Lucas (sensible), William Collins (pompous), George Wickham (deceitful), Louisa Hurst (snobbish), Lady Catherine de Bourgh (imperious), Mr. and Mrs. Edward Gardiner (genteel).

Third circle parts fill out the periphery: servants, villagers, tradesmen, and distant relatives.

CASE STUDY: *A FISH CALLED WANDA*

A Fish Called Wanda was written by John Cleese and Charles Crichton. The Motion Picture Academy nominated them for Best Original Screenplay and Best Director, giving an Oscar to Kevin Kline for Best Supporting Actor. John Cleese and Michael Palin won BAFTAs for Best Actor and Best Supporting Actor. The British Film Institute ranks it among the greatest British films of the twentieth century. Its inspiration happened over lunch.

One day, as the two worked together on a corporate video, Cleese, who graduated in law from Cambridge University, remarked that he'd always dreamed of playing a barrister. Crichton responded that he'd always dreamed of directing a scene with a steamroller in it. They decided to coauthor a screenplay containing both a barrister and a steamroller.

Cleese then mused this bit of whimsy: A man who loves dogs can't stop killing them. Crichton naturally asked the logical question, Why? Answer: He's actually trying to kill the dogs' owner and keeps missing. Why is he trying to kill the owner? Because she's a witness. A witness to what? A robbery. And on they went to satirize film noir plots into a delightful "crimedy."

Story

Wanda, an American con artist, and Otto, her boyfriend, plan to double-cross George, a London gangster, and his partner, Ken. After the four of them pull a multi-million-dollar diamond heist, Wanda and Otto immediately rat George out to the police, but then discover that he has triple-crossed them by secretly hiding the diamonds.

Wanda gets a lead on George's stash when she discovers a safe deposit box key in Ken's fish tank and hides it in her pendant. Next, the film adds a Love Story subplot when Wanda seduces George's barrister, Archie, hoping to learn the diamonds' whereabouts from him. But then she accidently loses her pendant in Archie's house and Archie's wife, Wendy, mistakes it for a gift from Archie.

George tells Ken to kill the only eyewitness to the robbery, Mrs. Coady, a mean old lady who owns three pocket dogs. Ken tries to knock her off three times over, but each time he accidentally kills one of her dogs instead. He finally succeeds when he crushes the third dog under a massive construction block and the horrifying sight gives Coady a fatal heart attack.

With no witness, George is ready for release from jail, so he tells Ken where he hid the diamonds as they plan their getaway. But in a courtroom hearing, Wanda double-crosses George. Stunned, Archie inadvertently calls her "darling." Wendy, watching from the gallery, realizes that Archie had an affair with Wanda and ends their marriage.

Meanwhile, Otto tortures Ken and learns that the jewels are hidden in a hotel safe deposit box. Otto knows the hiding place and Wanda has the key to the box, so they join forces.

Archie resolves to cut his losses, steal the loot, and flee to South America with Wanda. He pulls her into his Jag and they race to Ken's flat. But when Archie runs into Ken's building, Otto steals Archie's car, taking Wanda with him.

Ken and Archie give chase. Otto and Wanda recover the diamonds, but Wanda double-crosses Otto, knocking him unconscious in a broom closet. Otto recovers and sprints for Wanda's plane, but Archie confronts him on the airport tarmac. Otto is just about to shoot Archie when Ken runs him over with a steamroller. Archie and Wanda reunite aboard the plane.

Here is the *A Fish Called Wanda* cast map, setting out their obsessions and dimensions:

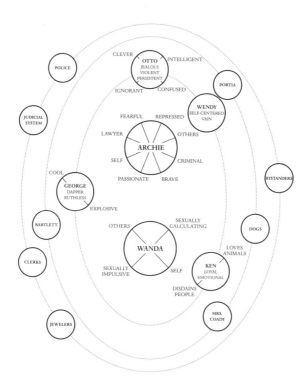

As we saw in Chapter Thirteen, comic characters are marked by a blind obsession, a rigid behavior they do not see in themselves and from which they cannot deviate.

Archie Leach (John Cleese) obsesses on his fear of embarrassment. Once he realizes this, however, he takes on the "Cary Grant" role and becomes the film's romantic lead. (Archie Leach was Cary Grant's real name.)

Archie's three dimensions:

He's fearful and courageous. At first, he's frightened of the mad Otto but eventually finds the courage to face him.

He's a lawyer and a criminal. Many people would not see that as a contradiction, but in Archie's case it is. He's devoted to the law but commits crimes for love.

He's devoted to others but then to himself. He works for his wife, daughter, and clients, denying himself, but once he falls for Wanda, he finally fights for what he wants out of life.

Wanda Gershwitz (Jamie Lee Curtis) obsesses on men who speak foreign languages.

Wanda's two dimensions:

She's sexually calculating and sexually impulsive. Smarter by far than any of the male characters, she uses her charms to manipulate them, occasionally falling prey to her blind obsession.

She's devoted to herself but then to Archie. Money is her only object of desire, but then she falls for Archie and gives him her heart.

Otto West (Kevin Kline) obsesses on Nietzsche.

Otto's two dimensions:

He's intelligent but ignorant. Otto is an ex-CIA operative who quotes Nietzschean philosophy but thinks that the London Underground is a political movement.

He's clever but confused. Otto thinks quickly under pressure and lies with easy skill but loses focus during conversations and can't remember the "middle thing."

Ken Pile (Michael Palin) obsesses on animal welfare.

Ken's one dimension:

He loves animals to the point of obsession but disdains people. He feels a tragic loss when an animal dies, sending him to the pet cemetery in tears and grief, but he happily kills a human being on the street.

George Thomason (Tom Georgeson) obsesses on crime as a white-collar profession.

George's one dimension:

He's icy and volcanic. George is cool, calculating, ruthless, dapper, and devoted to his criminal trade, but when Wanda double-crosses him in a courtroom, his rage exposes him to the world.

Wendy Leach (Maria Aitken) obsesses on her superiority. She's aristocratic, arrogant, and unloving toward others, even her daughter.

Portia Leach (Cynthia Cleese) obsesses on her nose. Her key trait is self-centeredness.

Eileen Coady (Patricia Hayes) obsesses on her dogs. Her dominant trait is irritability.

The rest of the cast contains prosecutors, a judge, jewelers, locksmith, clerks, clients, jailors, and passersby.

Conclusion

Although critics rarely take comedy seriously, all well-told stories make meaning. The controlling idea of *A Fish Called Wanda* is that you, too, could end up in Rio de Janeiro with $20 million in diamonds and the lover of your dreams if you're willing to throw away your career and your family.

CASE STUDY: *SLAVE PLAY*

A play by Jeremy O. Harris

Slave Play is a modern allegory. The title suggests a drama about slavery but also hints at whips and bondage, welts and orgasms. Individually, its characters seem realistic as they grapple with intimate, personal problems, but at the same time they symbolize a range of types caught up in the eternal conflict between the powerful and the powerless.

Jeremy Harris began writing *Slave Play* while a student at Yale University. It opened off-Broadway in 2018 and sparked immediate controversy. The following year it moved to Broadway, where it played to sold-out houses until COVID-19 closed all theatres.

Slave Play raises these questions: What drives racism? Why is America's racial ménage so dysfunctional? Is it nature or nurture? Power-hungry impulses in the human psyche? Or the tyrannical social institutions of segregation and mass incarceration? To seek answers, the play casts four troubled interracial couples.

The play's black characters burn with the history of racial trauma, but their white lovers don't, can't, or won't see it or feel it. Although they genuinely care for their black partners, they either ignore their blackness or find it charmingly erotic. And if the black partners felt safe to express what they suffer, would their white lovers ever see it and get it? Or are black lovers condemned to live forever in their partners' blind spots? The effect of this impasse on the black characters is anhedonia, the inability to feel sexual pleasure.

The play takes place on a former Virginia plantation. Its multiplot design crosscuts three story lines of conflicted interracial couples: Phillip and Alana, Gary and Dustin, Kaneisha and Jim. Two supporting characters in a lesbian interracial coupleship, Teá and Patricia, help build the play's tensions, but their relationship never develops into a plot.

The three acts go like this:

Act One—"Work"

Act One plays out three vignettes of sadomasochistic seduction and copulation. The three couples, dressed in antebellum garb, act out brutal, sexually raw conflicts that seem genuinely nineteenth century, although occasional touches of modern music, modern names, and anachronistic dialogue seep in:

Scene 1: A slave named Kaneisha calls her overseer "Massa Jim" and asks if he is going to beat her. Jim wonders why she'd think such a thing, and Kaneisha replies, "You got that whip, ain'tcha?" Jim has had no training with a whip, so when he tries to crack it, he hits himself in the face. To seduce him, Kaneisha eats off the floor and twerks.

Scene 2: Alana, a sexually frustrated Southern belle, flounces seductively on her canopied bed, flourishing a formidable black dildo. Phillip, her handsome, light-skinned slave, services her lust as she forcibly penetrates his anus with her dildo.

Scene 3: In the plantation's barn, Dustin, a white indentured servant, bales hay in the shadow of Gary, a threatening black overseer. As Dustin rebels, the violence morphs into virtual rape. When Dustin licks Gary's boots, Gary comes, then breaks into tears.

Suddenly, a powerful turning point sends Teá and Patricia, two clipboard-carrying psychotherapists, bursting into the room, revealing that the three vignettes were actually exercises in sex therapy for interracial couples.

Act Two—"Process"

The psychologists believe that their radical remedy, known as Antebellum Sexual Performance Therapy, cures anhedonia as it "helps black partners reengage intimately with the white partners from whom they no longer receive sexual pleasure." But as Teá and Patricia "process" the three couples through their slave-master experiences, the real selves behind Act One's sadomasochistic fantasy roles look each other in the eye and inflict pains far worse than whips, boots, and dildoes. One by one, the six deliver cutting insights into the clashes between their real-life selves and their hidden selves, between what terrifies them and what tantalizes them.

This, for example, from the usually reticent Phillip: "So, like, are you saying that my...um...the reason I can't get it up...the reason I don't come is because of...just, like, racism?" Throughout the play, lines like this inflict the pleasures of pain, causing delight and damage.

As Act Two builds, psychotherapy becomes psychotorture. Rather than curing racist wounds, the therapeutic experiment inflames them. Partner turns on partner; the "process" crashes and burns; masks fall; core selves strip naked. The Phillip-Alana and Gary-Dustin plots climax to bring down the Act Two curtain. This leaves Kaneisha-Jim, the play's dominant story line, to carry Act Three.

Act Three—"Exorcise"

The last act paints a fierce portrait of a racial dilemma. Alone in a bedroom with Jim, Kaneisha struggles to understand her visceral distaste for her husband. He worries that the therapy traumatized her, and he's right but for reasons he doesn't understand.

Initially Kaneisha was attracted to Jim's whiteness because he's British and so unmarred by American prejudices. In time, she came to realize that because he's white, he carries an invisible whip, and because she's black, her hands are empty. The power is his, just as simple as that. This hard truth he denies. She wants him to see it; he won't listen.

At the play's climax, they suddenly replay their sadomasochistic master and slave selves from Act One. When their rape improv becomes too violent, Kaneisha shouts the safe word. As they slowly return to normal, she thanks him for listening. Curtain.

The play reveals the characters' dual identities, dividing them into Act One's symbolic selves, contradicted by Act Two's core selves, merged in Act Three as their core selves fuse with their symbolic selves—two completed characters.

Cast

To shape his cast, Jeremy Harris created a spectrum of character awareness ranging from sharp insight to dull blindness. At one end stands Kaneisha, who's painfully self-aware and black; at the far end is Jim, who's happily self-deceived and white. The other six roles symbolize various mental types along a continuum of attitudes toward blackness: Gary hates being black; Patricia ignores her blackness; Teá intellectualizes her blackness; Phillip transcends blackness; Dustin loves blackness; Alana finds blackness erotic.

Before we map the cast, let's review the eight roles from least complex to the most.

Patricia and Teá

Patricia and Teá, a duet of therapists, speak in mind-numbing psychobabble. When they refer to feelings, they talk about "processing materials in psychic spaces and communication spheres." They indulge in jargon such as "materiality" and "positionality." Black people become "minoritarians"; white society is "heteropatriarchal."

The team researches the abrasive effects of racism, then re-inflicts them on their subjects with blindly dangerous experiments. Although they seem empathetic and caring, the real reason they take notes on psychological pain is to gather data for monographs. To them, science outweighs solace. This inner/outer contradiction between seemingly sensitive beliefs and insensitive science strikes the first dimension in both women.

A second contradiction between true character and characterization, between reality and appearance adds a layer of complexity to each. The light-brown-skinned Patricia secretly feels she's white, mirroring Dustin who's white but claims he's black. The coolly professional but inwardly troubled Teá wishes she were, like Phillip, detached. These unfulfilled wishes give both women their second dimension: a secure professional self versus an insecure personal self.

Phillip

Phillip is powerfully built, mixed-race, model handsome, educated but none too bright. Alana, his white girlfriend, talks for him, keeping him in the background. He believes race doesn't matter and sees himself as a "superhuman dude beyond black and white." Stuck between his dominating partner and his a-racial identity, he suffers anhedonia. His core dimension makes him sexy to behold but at heart unsexed.

Alana

In Act One, Alana plays a nervous, horny, wild plantation dominatrix who yearns to sodomize her house slave and does, confessing, "It was hot for me, really hot." During the next act, however, she reverts to a hand-raising, note-taking student. When this A-type perfectionist finally glimpses the truth of her relationship, that her deliberate blindness to Phillip's race has ruined their love, she suddenly retreats into denial, repeating "It wasn't racial" like a mantra.

Her dimensions pit curiosity against self-deception, and a hypercontrolled manner against an out-of-control sex drive.

Gary

Gary hates being black. His stifled, lifelong, slow-burning rage hides behind a mask of quiet resentment. In Act One's fantasy play, he forces Dustin, his lover of nearly a decade, to lick his boots, and then comes in a shuddering climax. His core dimension pits inner rage against outer cool.

Dustin

Dustin hates being white. He could be Hispanic or Sicilian but swears he's black. His partner, Gary, can't see him as anything but white; still, the narcissistic Dustin argues that the evidence is obvious. When finally forced to confront his truth, Dustin throws a diva tantrum, shouting, "There are shades between!" He wears his dimension on his sleeve: a white man insisting he's black.

Jim

In Act One, Jim plays Kaneisha's reluctant master, but when he orders her to eat off the floor, he shivers with lust. He calls her his "queen" and that, by implication, makes him a king, and kings rule queens.

In the play's last minutes, the truth he's been suppressing arcs into awareness: A white man always has greater power. Finally, he hears Kaneisha plead and gives her the rough sex she wants. As he assured her, "We're on the same ground. Only difference is, I am, you know, your manager." An inner dimension cuts through Jim: Consciously he loves his wife; subconsciously he loves punishing her.

Kaneisha

White demons haunt Kaneisha. Nonetheless, in Act One's fantasy play, she begs Jim to call her "negress." Then mingling fear with lust, she slips into the role of "bed wench." In Act Three, she takes their role-playing even further, forcing Jim to admit that, although genuinely loving, he is a sadistic white devil. As she lures him into playing that part, she arcs from fantasy to reality, revealing that the masochist she portrayed in Act One is in fact her true self. As the contradiction between her improv self and her true self dissolves, she ends the play a completed character.

Given these relationships, the play's cast map looks like this:

Racist society forms the third circle.

Teá and Patricia (sensitive/insensitive, secure/insecure) are on opposite sides of the second circle.

This surrounds three separate inner circles: one containing Gary/Dustin (inner rage / outer cool, hates white / hates black); another with Phillip/Alana (sexed/unsexed, sighted/blind, overcontrolled/out-of-control); and a third holding Kaneisha/Jim (self-aware/self-deceived, loving/punishing, sadist/masochist) that's slightly larger than the other two to signify that theirs is the central plot.

Conclusion

Slave Play's title nails its meaning: Slavery puts sadomasochism into action. The massive wealth that slavery created was simply the side effect of mankind's darkest desire. Money is a means, not an end. The deep-seated cause of slavery—or, for that matter, the oppression of any underclass—is the lust for power and the pleasure of pain, aka sadomasochism.

Flash back to the issue of motivation raised in Chapter Eight: "Why do people do the things they do?" Over the centuries, philosophers and psychologists have sought a single grand answer to that grand question. Sigmund Freud said it was all about sex; Alfred Adler said it was all about power; Ernest Becker said it was all about death. When you think about it, sex and power are actually about death—just two ways to either defeat it by reproducing yourself or control it by defeating your enemies. So I go with Becker.

Sadomasochism follows this path: Fear is a trembling emotion that grips us when we don't know what's going to happen. Dread is a terrible awareness that floods the mind when we know what's going to happen, but there's nothing we can do to stop it. At an early age, we discover that death is a fact of life. Sooner or later, we're going to die and there's nothing we can do to change that fact. Some handle death-dread better than others, but all feel it.

At some point, a child may discover that power makes her feel better... at least for the moment. Perhaps she crushes the life out of an insect and suddenly feels a rush of pleasure. For an instant, a godlike power over life and death ignites her body. She wants to repeat that pleasure, more and more often, to a greater and greater degree. As she seeks power, her personality—at times, at least—leans toward the sadistic, toward someone who bends the dread of death to her will by usurping power over death. Slave owners felt that rush every day; the ultrarich still do.

Or, perhaps the child discovers that she is powerless and always will be but can still enjoy an escape from the anxiety of death if she shelters in the shadow of someone powerful. So long as that person exhibits their power by making her suffer, she feels the masochistic comfort of a temporary release from dread, aka the pleasure of pain. Slaves felt that thrill when they bowed to their masters; employees still feel it when they applaud their boss.[1]

Harris's drama speaks wisely and wittily about personal politics. As will your writing, if you give power room to play. For no matter how you set up your story—a cast of thousands to a pair of lovers—power will ebb and flow. Weigh, therefore, the balance of power in your cast members as you open the telling, then follow the dynamic of change (Who's up? Who's down?) to the final scene. Playing with power as you shape a cast often inspires the unexpected.

CASE STUDY: "BLOODCHILD"

A short story by Octavia E. Butler

"Bloodchild" tells a love story between species.

Isaac Asimov's Science Fiction Magazine published it in 1984. In the years since, it has won both Hugo and Nebula awards; *Locus* and *Science Fiction Chronicle* have also named it Best Novelette.[2]

Backstory

Generations ago, the vestiges of humanity migrated to a planet inhabited by the Tlic, gigantic insects that reproduce by injecting their eggs into animals. When the earthlings landed, the Tlic realized that the human body is the perfect incubation host. The Tlic government then built an encapsulated preserve to protect humans from the planet's egg-laying hordes, but as quid pro quo for survival, each family must select one of its own to bear a Tlic's larvae. The chance of dying when these worms hatch and eat their way out of the host's body is great. Humanity agreed to the deal.

Lien, a widow with four children, chose Gan, her youngest son, to bear the eggs of T'Gatoi, a high government official. T'Gatoi is a loving creature who befriended the family years ago, visiting daily, providing them with the comforts of mildly narcotic drugs. She feels a special maternal caring for Gan.

Story

Inciting incident: The day arrives when the body of someone in Lien's family must accept T'Gatoi's eggs. Gan is intensely aware that when his mother was pregnant, she selected him for this duty. His feelings wait in limbo and confusion. Gan's two sisters, however, feel that hosting Tlic eggs would be an honor, while their older brother, Qui, hates the idea. He once witnessed a man die in agony as larvae ate their way out of him.

Ideally, when the eggs hatch and their worms emerge, the Tlic performs a kind of cesarean section on the human, passing the hungry worms into some animal flesh, saving the host's life. Indeed, that afternoon

Bram, a pregnant man who's been abandoned by his Tlic, bangs on their door and T'Gatoi performs the emergency operation. Gan helps save the man by shooting an animal kept on the preserve and providing nonhuman food for the emerging larvae.

As T'Gatoi pulls worm after worm from the man's body, Gan witnesses the blood-soaked surgery and the victim's hideous suffering. He is so repulsed, he contemplates suicide rather than impregnation. Afterward, T'Gatoi, who must lay her eggs that night, gives him a way out and asks if he would rather have her impregnate one of his sisters.

Now in crisis, Gan must choose: risk a sister's life to save himself or risk his own life as an act of honor and manhood. He chooses to accept his fate and offers his body out of love for his family, humanity, and T'Gatoi. As T'Gatoi impregnates Gan, she lovingly promises she will never abandon him.

Cast

Short stories don't offer the pages necessary to develop a complex cast of great size. In this telling, only Gan and T'Gatoi are complex; the rest have nicely drawn characterizations but no dimensions.

Gan

Gan narrates the story in the first person, giving us access to his inner conflicts and the three dimensions that span within him.

1. He's fearful yet brave. Terror grips him, but his untapped courage waits in reserve.
2. He's self-preserving yet self-sacrificing. He fights against his fate for selfish reasons but finally surrenders to it for moral reasons.
3. He's a child on the cusp of maturity. His opening words set the story with "My last night of childhood..."

T'Gatoi

This nine-foot-tall segmented insect has multiple limbs on each segment and a stinger in her tail that puts people to sleep. Her long friendship with Lien and her wise, patient devotion to Gan gives her a grandmotherly aura. At the same time, however, her genes are driving her to reproduce. She, too, has three dimensions:

1. She's kind but autocratic. Like a zookeeper, T'Gatoi is a generous, caring protector, but also the master of her human charges.
2. She soothes pain yet causes pain. T'Gatoi knows the dread, even death, her species causes human beings. So her guilty conscience moves her to pacify the fear and anxiety in Lien's family with gifts of narcotic pills and injections.
3. She cares but kills. She loves Lien's family, especially Gan, but will end their lives, if necessary, to secure the survival of her species.

The other cast members have no dimensions, just one distinctive trait each.

Lien

Trait: Sadness. The widow Lien knows that her son or one of her daughters will be impregnated with T'Gatoi's larvae that evening, and there's nothing she can do to stop it. A mood of pained resignation seems to age her.

Qui

Trait: Anger. Qui rebels, furious that human beings must submit to Tlic rule.

Gan's sisters

Trait: Submission. Gan's sisters take the opposite view. They believe that being chosen for a Tlic impregnation is a privilege.

Bram

Trait: Terror. Bram screams in a panic as the worms inside him burst out of their shells.

T'Khotgif

Trait: Personal concern. The Tlic who impregnated Bram hurries to him.

Doctor

Trait: Professional concern. He helps T'Gatoi save Bram.

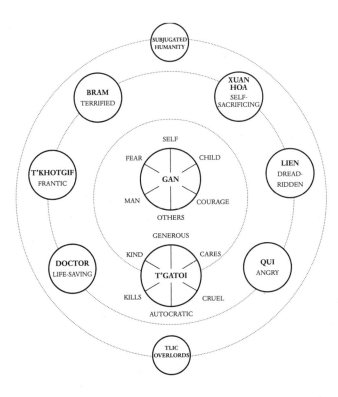

Conclusion

Science Fiction is a presentational genre, home to any of the sixteen primary genres. In the case of "Bloodchild," Gan arcs along an Evolution Plot from immaturity to maturity.

Sci-Fi's distinguishing convention is its setting. Its temporal location may or may not be futuristic, but its society is somehow warped (even dystopian).[3] This disturbance in the natural social order began in the backstory when human folly misused science.

In "Bloodchild," the author never tells us what global catastrophe caused the cast's ancestors to abandon Earth, but their migration reversed nature's balance. On planet Earth, humanity was the dominant species that used various subspecies as food, clothing, and pets. On planet Tlic, human beings are reduced to a subspecies, useful as a nesting place for eggs.

If Science Fiction is your genre, then like Octavia Butler, use its power to invert reality to create an empathetic cast in an unpredictable story that warns of things to come.

CASE STUDY: *BREAKING BAD*

The longform series is a unique medium, as different from prose as cinema is from theatre. Longform tellings, with their open episodes and open seasons, put mammoth casts through years of screen performance. To the writer, longform offers the opportunity to create characters of dimensionality and complexity beyond the reach of any other storytelling form. So before we unravel *Breaking Bad*, let's take a brief look at the medium that made it possible.

The Effects of Length and Cast Size

The smaller the cast, the fewer the relationships between characters, and therefore, the less numerous and various their tactics, behaviors, and desires. The fewer the scenes and less the diverse their turning points, the fewer the choices and actions its characters must make and take. For these reasons, the casts of one-act plays, short stories, short films, and comic books are limited in number and dimensionality.

Conversely, the larger the cast, the greater the ramifications of character relationships and dimensions. In addition, the more numerous and diverse the scenes and the longer the performance time, the greater the variety of desires, choices, and actions characters must take and make. As a result, the casts that fill novels, as well as full-length dramas, comedies, and musicals onstage and on-screen tend to be rich in variety and psychological complexity.

Longform screen works, by reason of cast size and years of performance, take the art of story into complexities of character beyond the scope of any other medium. A thousand-page novel or epic saga, for example, contains about the same event and character development as a single season of longform. Multiseason storytelling tests an author's limits of insight, memory, and human feeling. Therefore, the herculean task for the longform writer is holding viewers' interest in a vast cast of characters through fifty to one hundred episodes told over five to ten years.

The Two Modes of Interest

A story compels interest by drawing on the reader's or audience's conscious curiosity and subconscious concern.

Curiosity: the intellectual need to answer questions, solve puzzles and problems, close open patterns, and learn the hows and whys of a character's life.

Concern: the emotional need to experience the positive charge of values—life, not death; love, not hate; justice, not injustice; peace, not war; good, not evil; and the like.

Neither curiosity nor concern, however, will hold interest if an audience cannot identify with at least one major character in the cast. In fact, the ideal longform work draws empathy to many centers of good, not only in the central plot's protagonist but in the protagonists of subplots as well.

A story's major dramatic question is a specific variation on the universal question "How will this turn out?" MDQs such as "Will Ragnar Lothbrok conquer England?" in *Vikings* or "Will Kendall Roy take over his father's business empire?" in *Succession* hook and hold its audience's curiosity over years.

However, the greatest magnetic force, the one that grips the deepest interest over the longest stretches of time, arises from the psychological depths of major characters in longform tellings. Like the allure of the ocean, the inner lives of complex characters fascinate the audience, inducing multihour binges as they discover unforeseen traits, marvel at contradictions between public selves and core selves, and most important, follow the protagonist's arc until she completes herself with moral, mental, or humanistic change.

The point to remember: Revelation and evolution hold longform audiences to the screen over years of time. What kills that long-term interest? Repetitiousness and rigidity. Once a protagonist has nothing left to reveal, once she is no longer capable of change, once she is emptied out and her psychology exhausted, her behavior becomes predictable and monotonous. With that, the audience dwindles.

Consider *Dexter*: This eight-season series ran on Showtime from 2006 to 2013. Season 1 sets up Dexter (Michael C. Hall) as a psychopathic vigilante hiding behind a likable characterization. Devoid of emotion, compassion, or conscience, he comes to life only in the midst of murder. The next three seasons, however, give Dexter compassion for children, feelings of romantic love, and guilt over unintended consequences. That completes him; everything knowable about Dexter was known by the end of Season 4. Seasons 5 to 8 neither revealed previously unseen traits nor changed his psychology. Plot twists proliferated, but Dexter stagnated until his diehard audience gave up. I hope its proposed renewal as a 10-episode miniseries in Fall 2021 manages the character arc its audience has long desired.

Fifty to one hundred hours of longform performance calls for a protagonist whose complexity goes far beyond three dimensions.

Breaking Bad

by Vince Gilligan

Breaking Bad ran for sixty-two episodes over five seasons. Its creator titled the series after a Southernism that means taking your life down an immoral, violent road. Gilligan sold the series with the now-famous four-word pitch describing the story's arc: "Mr. Chips goes Scarface."

It has a central plot, twenty-five subplots, and a cast of more than eighty speaking roles. In 2013, the *Guinness Book of World Records* declared *Breaking Bad* the highest-rated screen series ever. The three lead actors won nine Emmys among them, while the show itself won another seven Emmys and two Golden Globes as well as two Peabodys, two Critics' Choice Awards, four Television Critics Association awards, and three Satellite awards.

A series prequel, *Better Call Saul*, debuted in 2015, and a movie sequel, *El Camino*, premiered in 2019.

Backstory

Walter White (Bryan Cranston), a polymath scientist, and Gretchen (Jessica Hecht), his girlfriend, teamed with Elliot Schwartz (Adam Godley) to found Gray Matter Technologies. After a falling-out, Walt sold his share and quit. Elliott and Gretchen persevered, and exploiting Walt's corporate-owned inventions, built a highly successful company. In time, Elliott and Gretchen married.

Walt, embittered by his failures, became an Albuquerque high school teacher, married Skyler (Anna Gunn), and fathered two children.

Season 1

Although never a smoker, Walt discovers he has inoperable stage-3 lung cancer. To secure his family's future before he dies, Walt turns to a life of crime. He coerces a former student, Jesse Pinkman (Aaron Paul), to work with him cooking methamphetamine. Jesse buys an old RV to serve as their kitchen. In it, Walt uses commonplace chemicals to create a powerful blue-tinted meth.

When Jesse tries to sell their drug on the street, Emilio (John Koyama) and Krazy-8 (Maximino Arciniega), two low-level drug dealers, horn in. Walt lures them to the RV where he poisons one and later garrotes the other. Walt and Jesse then go into business with Tuco Salamanca (Raymond Cruz), a ruthless, virtually insane gangster.

Season 2

A deadly shoot-out with Tuco leaves Walt and Jesse without a distributor, so they find their way to a criminal lawyer, Saul Goodman (Bob Odenkirk) who hooks them up with a major drug dealer, Gus Fring (Giancarlo Esposito). Gus pays them a huge sum, and Walt adopts the street name "Heisenberg." The DEA, led by Walt's brother-in-law Hank Schrader (Dean Norris), begins to investigate this mysterious crime boss.

Jesse falls in love with Jane Margolis (Krysten Ritter), a heroin addict, and becomes addicted himself. Walt refuses to give Jesse half of Gus's money until he gets off drugs. Jane tries to blackmail Walt into paying up, but she passes out on heroin, and then chokes to death on her own vomit while Walt watches silently from across the room. Walt gets Jesse into rehab. A few days later, he witnesses the midair collision of two passenger jets over the city—a tragedy caused by Jane's distraught, air-traffic controller father, Donald (John de Lancie). The blame is Walt's.

Season 3

At home, Walt's marriage falls apart. When Skyler seeks a divorce, Walt reveals his secret criminal life, pleading that he did it for his family. Skyler, in revenge, seduces her boss, then taunts Walt with her affair.

Walt and Jesse go to work for Gus, cooking meth in a hidden high-tech lab. Soon after, two cartel assassins, seeking revenge for Tuco, attack Hank. He dispatches them and survives, although temporarily paralyzed.

Jesse rebels against Gus because he uses children to sell drugs on the street. Gus replaces Jesse with Gale Boetticher (David Costabile). Walt fears that once Gale learns to cook on his own, Gus will kill both him and Jesse. He tells Jesse to kill Gale, and Jesse does.

Season 4

Gus puts Walt and Jesse back to work cooking meth. Skyler accepts Walt's criminal enterprise and, with Saul's help, buys a car wash to launder Walt's earnings.

Gus wipes out his enemies in Mexico, then turns against Walt. Walt seduces Jesse into murdering Gus. Their first attempt fails, but when Walt offers Hector Salamanca (Mark Margolis) a chance to take revenge on Gus, Hector happily detonates a hidden bomb that kills himself and Gus.

Season 5, Part 1

Walt, Jesse, Mike Ehrmantraut (Jonathan Banks) and Lydia Rodarte-Quayle (Laura Fraser) partner in the meth business. To get the raw materials they need, the men pull off a train heist. Jesse and Mike want to sell their share to Declan (Louis Ferreira), a Phoenix drug dealer, but Walt refuses. Instead, he cooks for Lydia, who distributes the meth in Europe. She is so successful Walt makes more money than he can count. To end the squabble and finally retire from the drug business, Walt kills Mike and hires Jack (Michael Bowen) and his Nazi biker gang to kill Mike's associates. Hank, by chance, discovers that Walt is Heisenberg.

Season 5, Part 2

When Hank confronts Walt, Walt backs him down. Hank then turns to Skyler, but she refuses to betray Walt. Seeing trouble coming, Walt buries $80 million in the desert.

Jack's gang kills a rival gang and takes their meth production gear. Walt tries to negotiate with Jack, but the Nazi gang turns on him, killing Hank, capturing Jesse, and taking most of Walt's money.

Walt tries to get Skyler to run off with him, but their marriage ends when she pulls a knife. At first, Walt hides out, but then he changes course, coercing Elliott and Gretchen into caring for his children.

At Jack's gang's compound, Walt kills Jack and the rest with a remote-control machine gun and frees the imprisoned Jesse. Wounded, he asks Jesse to kill him, but Jesse refuses and drives off. Walt takes a moment to reminisce about his drug empire, then dies.

Cast Design

Third Circle Roles

Third circle characters make no independent decisions. They simply react to other more prominent characters and carry out tasks that assist or resist them. *Breaking Bad* has more than fifty third circle roles. I've grouped some of them around the featured character they serve.

Walt: Carmen, the high school principal; Hugo, the school janitor; Lawson, the gun dealer; Dr. Delcavoli, the oncologist; Old Joe, the junk dealer; Declan, a drug dealer.

Jesse: the Pinkman family, Brock, Combo, Adam, Wendy, Group Leader, Clovis, Emilio, Spooge and his girlfriend, Drew (the kid on a bike).

Skyler: Holly, her baby; Walter Jr.; Walter Jr.'s friend, Louis; Pamela, her divorce attorney; Bogdan, the car wash owner.

Hank: cops and fellow agents Kalanchoe, Munn, Merkert, Ramey, and Roberts.

Gus: fellow criminals Max, Gale, Duane, Ron, Barry, Tyrus, Chris, Dennis, Victor, and Dan.

Hector: fellow gang members Juan, Tuco, Gaff, Gonzo, No-Doze, Tortuga, and Hector's retirement home nurse.

Mike: his daughter-in-law, Stacey, and his granddaughter, Kaylee.

Saul: his staff—Huell, Ed, Francesca, and Kuby.

Screenwriters rarely describe third circle roles in any detail. To make them specific, directors depend on their casting director's guidance, along with the costuming and hair styling that gives each role a specific look. After that, it's up to the actor to make it work.

Second Circle Roles

Second circle characters are not complex, but occasionally their actions send story lines in new directions. The writer gives them specific characterizations, and their actors round them out with intriguing personalities, but their inner natures are without contradiction and therefore dimensionless.

Ted Beneke, for example, starts a love affair with Skyler, who ultimately gives him millions from Walter's stash. Gretchen and Elliot Schwartz make themselves rich after Walter quits their company. Donald Margolis causes a tragic air disaster in the aftermath of his daughter's death. Walter's deeds influence these characters, but they have the final say in the direction their lives take.

The *Breaking Bad* cast has seventeen second circle roles:

1. Steve Gomez (Steven Michael Quezada), Hank's DEA partner
2. Gale Boetticher (David Costabile), Gus's meth cook
3. Eladio Vuente (Steven Bauer), major cartel boss
4. Hector Salamanca (Mark Margolis), former drug kingpin
5. Tuco Salamanca (Raymond Cruz), drug kingpin
6. Leonel Salamanca (Daniel Moncada), assassin
7. Marco Salamanca (Luis Moncada), assassin
8. Krazy-8 Molina (Maximino Arciniega), drug dealer
9. Jack Welker (Michael Bowen), white supremacist gang leader
10. Andrea Cantillo (Emily Rios), Jesse's girlfriend
11. Jane Margolis (Krysten Ritter), Jesse's girlfriend
12. Badger Mayhew (Matt L. Jones), Jesse's crew
13. Skinny Pete (Charles Baker), Jesse's crew
14. Ted Beneke (Christopher Cousins), Skyler's boss and lover
15. Donald Margolis (John de Lancie), Jane's father
16. Gretchen Schwartz (Jessica Hecht), Walter's former lover
17. Elliot Schwartz (Adam Godley), Walter's former business partner

First Circle Roles

First circle characters often become the protagonists of their own subplots. They have the power and opportunity to make decisions and take major actions that affect the central plot and other story lines. *Breaking Bad* has ten complex first circle characters:

Todd: One-Dimensional

Characterization: Todd (Jesse Plemons) is a well-mannered young man who uses violence quickly and efficiently, killing and torturing without hesitation or remorse. He's a Hannibal Lecter without the IQ—creepy, calm, and unnecessarily polite.

True character: the ultimate sociopath.

Todd helps the audience measure the limits of Walt's evil. Sociopathology runs a spectrum of severity from mild to craven. Walt is sociopathic but only to a degree; Todd waits at the dark extreme. Walt takes no pleasure in the suffering he causes; Todd thrives on cruelty. Walt has feelings, even passions; Todd none.

Dimension: Polite/Pitiless.

Lydia Rodarte-Quayle: One-Dimensional

Characterization: Lydia (Laura Fraser) is a tense, aloof, corporate executive.

True character: She steals raw materials from her company and sells them to drug dealers. A thief and loner with no relationships, she will kill anyone in her way.

Dimension: Refined/Brutal.

Mike Ehrmantraut: One-Dimensional

Characterization: Mike (Jonathan Banks) adores his granddaughter as he executes his crime craft with calculated efficiency.

True character: For Mike, breaking the law is just another way to make a living. Loyal to his employer and employees, he never harms innocent bystanders. He's a criminal antihero with a code of honor.

Dimension: Warm-blooded/Cold-blooded.

Saul Goodman: One-Dimensional

Characterization: Saul (Bob Odenkirk) is flamboyant in dress, outrageous in a courtroom, self-marketed in blaring TV commercials. He leverages the ludicrous in desperate situations; his sarcasm provides the show's comic relief.

True character: His real name is Jimmy McGill, but he took "Saul Goodman" because people trust Jewish attorneys. Saul is a skilled lawyer who gives sound advice and finds ingenious loopholes to solve his clients' villainous problems.

He also provides services such as evidence removal, loot stashing, false bank accounts, false documents, bribery, intimidations, relocation, and other crimes-for-hire.

Dimension: Criminal/Lawyer.

Marie Schrader: Two-Dimensional

Characterization: Marie (Betsy Brandt), a medical technician who loves her husband, Hank, her sister's family, and all things purple.

True character: She's a kleptomaniac who fills her empty life with the excitement of petty thefts. She feels dependent on her husband and morally inferior to her sister. When Skyler's crimes are exposed, she glows with moral superiority. When her husband dies, she finds great personal power and independence.

Dimensions: Dependent/Independent, Weak/Powerful.

Walter White Jr.: Two-Dimensional

Characterization: Walter Jr. (R. J. Mitte) is a teenager with cerebral palsy.

True character: Caught between battling parents, the boy's loyalty shifts from his mother to his father and back again. When hit by the discovery that his father is a meth dealer who killed his uncle, he rolls with the shock, then turns it into his moment of maturation and individuation as he changes from protected victim to protector of his mother and sister.

Dimensions: Child/Adult, Protected/Protector.

Skyler White: Three-Dimensional

Characterization: Skyler (Anna Gunn) is an attractive housewife and the mother of a disabled son who earns cash selling items on eBay and working as a part-time bookkeeper.

True character: Some claim that Skyler is a battered wife who's been walking on eggshells throughout her marriage. Others accuse her of abusing, henpecking, and belittling Walt.

I would argue both are true. Like many marriages, Walt and Skyler are mutually abusive and mutually supportive. Secretly, each feels superior to the other; both feel humiliated by life (he more than she); each takes life's disappointments out on the other.

But then comes Walter's cancer, followed by his secret criminal life. Skyler strikes back by seducing her boss. Then, when Walt's crimes bring in millions, Skyler excuses him, rationalizing that he did it for the family. She launders the loot and creates the videotape that coerces Hank into silence.

Some might call her a Stockholm syndrome victim who identifies with her oppressor, but if she were really a battered wife, how did she become the fast-thinking, cool-headed businesswoman who launders millions through her car wash scam?

These contradictions reveal a complex character whose mind can twist negatives into positives, such as "This is bad but not that bad. Walt promises to give up crime, so if I can launder the money, the other problems will disappear, and Walt will be Walt again. It's just a phase."

With the exception of Walter Jr., most *Breaking Bad* characters are either immoral, morally elastic, or, like Skyler, morally split: Intellectually she knows right from wrong, but emotionally she has no center. If she can get away with crime, she's happy to be a criminal. She drifts with her feelings, then acts.

Dimensions: Rational/Emotional, Loving/Punishing, Moral/Immoral.

Gus Fring: Three-Dimensional

Characterization: Gus (Giancarlo Esposito) is a Chilean-born, well-mannered restaurant owner, civic leader, and philanthropic sponsor of an antidrug charity. He's generous, straightforward, and pro–law enforcement.

True character: Gus runs his crime enterprise through the cold-blooded execution of Machiavellian stratagems. The inner force that drives him is revenge for the murder of Max, his lover and partner in crime.

Dimensions: Outer Good / Inner Evil, Low Key in public / High Key in private, Straightforward/Scheming.

Hank: Four-Dimensional

Characterization: To his coworkers, Hank (Dean Norris) radiates the high energy of a boisterous DEA agent. At home, he collects minerals, brews his own beer, and loves his wife.

True character: Beneath this flippant, ill-mannered racist lives a skilled detective. He's strong around men but weak around women, especially his wife. His inner nature pits his courage against PTSD and panic attacks, while he wages a second inner war between his analytical mind and his explosive temper.

Dimensions: Crass/Intelligent, Weak/Strong, Tough/Panicky, Analytical/Explosive.

Jesse: Six-Dimensional

Characterization: Jesse Pinkman (Aaron Paul), Walt's former student and cooking partner, talks in playful slang, wears trendy clothes, plays video games, enjoys parties and techno-toys, listens to rap and rock, and uses recreational drugs. His own family disowned him over his drug use, but he loves his girlfriends and protects their endangered children.

True character: Jesse is the only cast member who sees the moral schism at the heart of *Breaking Bad*. The moment he kills their rival meth cook, he realizes his crimes are not acts of self-preservation. He has tied himself to an evil man, and his series-long struggle to break free arcs him from immoral to moral and from self-destructive to self-possessed.

Dimensions: Undereducated/Street-smart, Impulsive/Cautious, Hedonistic/Stoic, Shy/Bold, Weak-willed/Strong-willed, Risks his life for money / Then throws it away.

A character of this complexity needs a large supporting cast to bring out his multitude of outer traits, plus his six dimensions and arc of change, all told over extensive performance time. The first, second, and third circle characters who surround and interact with Jesse number into the dozens.

Walter White: Sixteen-Dimensional

Characterization: Walt (Bryan Cranston) is a fifty-year-old failed scientist turned high school teacher. He's dedicated to his profession and uses his logical, eclectic knowledge to enrich his teaching. At home, he's a kind husband and father, suffering from lung cancer.

The Six Dimensions of Jesse Pinkman

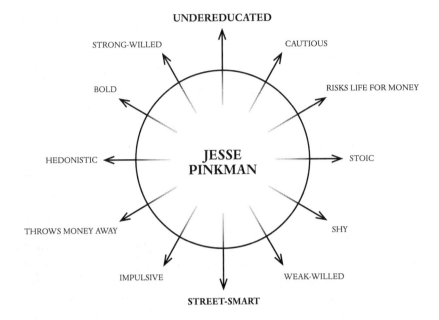

Map of Jesse's Redemption Plot

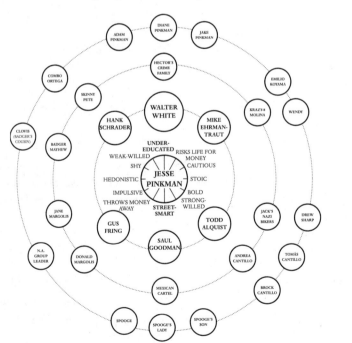

True character: Walt begins as an incomplete character driven by a need for an intense experience at the absolute limits of human possibility. He's a fiercely proud egoist craving recognition. His nonstop lies provide him with rationalizations for the cruelest of actions. In his self-deceived mind, he's an apostle of family values, free enterprise, and scientific progress. In fact, he's ruthless and violent, killing with little regret as he dreams of building his crime empire.

The Sixteen Dimensions of Walter White

Dimensions: Walt's sixteen dimensions divide into contradictions of characterization versus true self and contradictions of true self versus hidden self.

Dimensions: Characterization Versus True Self
1. Family man yet sociopath.
2. Gentle yet violent.
3. Workingman yet entrepreneur. He's a teacher who builds a drug empire worth hundreds of millions.
4. Scientific yet criminal. For some naïve reason, we tend to believe that scientists are moral. Walt is a lethal nerd, the kind of nerd who makes other nerds proud.

5. Apologetic yet never really sorry.
6. He imposes strict rules on others yet doesn't hesitate to break the law.
7. He demands loyalty yet betrays virtually everyone.
8. He demands the truth yet lies nonstop with consummate skill.
9. He idealizes the way science enriches life yet corrupts science to destroy human beings.

These contradictions are not Walter's most profound dimensions because they only contradict his characterization with his true character. The deepest dimensions do not show on the surface of behavior. They can be only implied beneath a character's actions.

Dimensions: Private Self Versus Hidden Self
1. Because he's dying of cancer, he risks his life without hesitation, yet because he's dying of cancer, he loves life and strives to live it to the limit.
2. He's rational yet impulsive; he carefully estimates the odds, then gambles with his life against all odds.
3. He's emotionally cool yet explodes in high anger and grief when he can't get his way.
4. He's self-confident and proud yet self-doubting and humble.
5. He has penetrating insight into other people but virtually no self-awareness.
6. He loves his family and devotes himself to their well-being. Yet to satisfy his narcissistic needs, he constantly puts his family in life-and-death danger, as well as his partner, Jesse, and his brother-in-law, Hank. In the conflict between self and others, he consistently chooses self.
7. Primary dimension: His greatest inner contradiction is between himself and his alter ego, between who he thinks he is and who he really is, between Walt and Heisenberg.

Walt tries to compartmentalize these two guys: the cold, calculating drug dealing Heisenberg on one side, and the well-meaning father and husband Walter White on the other. For example, when he begs Jack to save Hank's life, he's Walt, but when he tells Jack to kill Jesse, he's Heisenberg.

The Walter White side kidnaps Holly because his infant daughter is the only person left in his life who might someday love him, but thanks to her, he finally sees the truth. He realizes that he did not do it for his family; he did it for his true self, for Heisenberg. When he returns Holly to her mother, he throws away his last piece of Walt. From that point on, he's all Heisenberg.

The creation of sixteen dimensions in *Breaking Bad*'s protagonist needed sixty-two hours of constant interaction between Walter White and one of the largest supporting casts in storytelling history. To help make sense of this mass, I've reworked Walter's gangster plot map, putting all the characters who help his enterprise in the first circle, all the characters who hinder his venture in the second ring, Skyler as both in between, and the cops and gangster cohorts in the outer reaches.

Walter's Gangster Plot

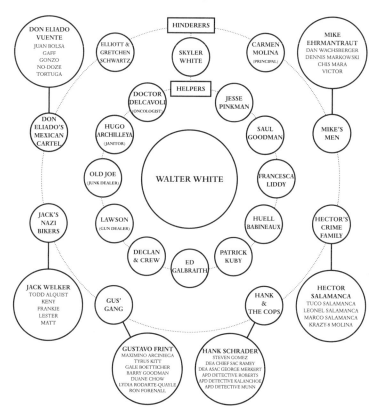

Walter White's Character Arc

I titled the central plot of *Breaking Bad The Triumph of Heisenberg*. Heisenberg is not a new self. Walter has suppressed him all his life. Once he's finally let out with room to grow, Heisenberg takes on a life of his own. He destroys Walt and everything Walt values.

On the surface, *Breaking Bad*'s core story seems to be a Degeneration Plot that arcs Walt from good guy to bad guy. Some, however, would argue that the last episodes redeem him.

After five seasons of revelations, we realize that the shambling classroom nobody he showed his students, the nebbish he was to his brother-in-law, and the milquetoast who shared a bed with his wife were his disguise. Heisenberg, his drug lord nom de guerre, is Walt's true self.

When he cuts the Walter White side out of himself and does terrible things, he's fine. At the Season 1 climax, after he kills for the first time, he comes home to make love to his wife with more passion than he's ever known.

But when he tries to cut Heisenberg out of himself, he erupts with rage.

The *Breaking Bad* climax tilts Walt's Degeneration Plot toward Redemption. It resolves the Walter/Heisenberg contradiction by merging the two into one complete character who does good with the means of evil.

But Walt is not an antihero. He is a Satan-hero who finds fulfillment but with great irony. He loses everything but gains something few of us ever know: life lived to the limit of human experience.

Wrap-Up

Breaking Bad's story-driven meanings and dimensionality of cast are so powerfully human, the series as written would have been a success at any time. But why did the series' stupendous popularity exceed all expectation? Because, I believe, Vince Gilligan said something that needed saying when it was said. Gilligan's *Breaking Bad* satirizes modern entrepreneurial ideology.

In 2008 two things happened: the Great Recession and the premiere season of *Breaking Bad*. In both worlds, real and fictional, some people get a lot; the rest get stiffed. In such times, is it any wonder an audience would empathize with a man who does whatever it takes to win back what he feels should have been his from the start?

Walt was exiled from the hierarchy of science by the treachery of his partners and his bitterly stubborn pride. He knows in his heart that he is superior, and when by chance he discovers his true calling, he fights to claim his rightful place among the world's elite. He is an empire builder out of an Ayn Rand novel, biding his time amid the weaklings, plotting his revenge.

Using superior technical know-how, Walt creates a start-up company that makes a boutique product better than the competition. No easy task. Then this self-made man has to deal with unreliable partners and ruthless competitors. He is constantly beset by raw material shortages on one hand and supply-chain problems on the other. Plus that bane of all entrepreneurs: government regulation. In his case, the U.S. Drug Enforcement Agency.

Like all self-made men, Walt must deal with stupid people who feel threatened by his brilliance and cannot grasp his vision.

In Season 1, everyone was a sinner: Marie steals from stores while her husband bends the law. Virtually the whole cast was composed of criminal businessmen, criminal lawyers, corrupt cops, drug dealers, and drug addicts.

So at first Walt's meth cooking and murder seemed like a matter of degree. But Vince Gilligan made us realize that degrees matter.

Walter isn't just another sinner. From his dark soul he unleashes destruction on the city and his family. He commits multiple murders and creates drug addicts. Anyone, like Jesse, who sees his true face knows that he is Satan.

Yet, the genius of the series is that the audience empathizes. We identify with this Prince of Darkness. Like millions of viewers, Walter bore a lifetime of deep anger and resentment. He screams at his wife that no one respects his greatness. Like all those who have been ground down by the system, Walt's every action cries: "Recognize me!"

Breaking Bad places Walt in the company of other disrupters and innovators who started out in garages, then created products that shook up society. (Not that I'm suggesting Mark Zuckerberg and Steve Jobs are drug dealers—although their products do seem rather habit-forming.)

Walter White became a satisfying character because he takes care of his family, saves Jesse's life, destroys Jack's Nazi biker gang, and ends his empire on his terms, not the law's.

The core genre of *Breaking Bad* is the Evolution Plot, the positive side on a humanity arc. Ultimately, Walt's need for fulfillment of his human potential and completion of his inner nature is met.

CONCLUSION: THE REVOLUTIONARY WRITER

.

The desire to be an artist, to be someone who puts beauty before money, often brings rejection and with that poverty and with that ridicule. These fears have broken the will of many a gifted writer. To face them, an author must become not a rebel but a revolutionary. Rebels resent authority because they feel unloved, unappreciated. A true revolutionary's revolution happens within herself, out of sight and alone. She knows her full worth and needs no one to tell her what it is. Rebels want to overthrow authority so they can put themselves in its place. A silent revolutionary has no such wish; a solitary revolutionary is a humanist.

She's not fanatic, she's independent.

She believes in the centrality of human creativity and the highest values of consciousness, beginning with compassion.

She enjoys good company. In fact, her insights into friends and acquaintances inspired her first fascinations with character.

She's skeptical but not cynical. She distains the lies people believe, the delusions they substitute for reality. Seeing the limits of all groups, all societies, she frees herself from soil and blood, from blind loyalty to nation, class, race, party, religion . . . even family.

She never copies life. Real people may inspire, but they're only a start and never enough.

She works to master her craft, letting instinct and insight show the way.

She never settles for surface characterizations. Instead, she explores the hidden life in ways she never could with anyone she knows to create characters we would all love to know.

She never shows off. She never pens anything that calls attention to her writing as writing.

She knows that eccentricity is not originality.

She knows self-knowledge is her truest source of character, so she spends time within.

She does not limit her sources of inspiration. She pockets ideas wherever she finds them—in happenings, in other people, in herself.

She explores conflict and revels in complexities.

She illuminates the human spirit in wondrous breadths and profound depths.

She never ends the storied paths she gives her characters until they fulfill the promise of their humanity.

The revolutionary writer fills our evenings with delight.

I see the bottom of the last page rising to meet me, so before time runs out, I lift a glass: Here's to you, the writers—navigators of story, explorers of character. May you find your way through the wilds of humankind, unearth buried treasure, then return safely home again.

ACKNOWLEDGMENTS

First drafts are not just rough, they're raw. My thanks to Ashleigh Blake and the members of the Sherman Library Book Club—Andrea O'Connor, Suzanne Ashley, Corinne Kevorkian, Catherine D'Andrea—who explored thick, primitive pages and emerged with idea rescuing insights.

No one has a sharper eye for the flow of logic through a chapter, within a paragraph or from capital letter to full stop than my editor, Marcia Freedman. I am, as always, in her debt.

Equally, I thank design artist Oliver Brown for rendering qualities of cast and character with graphic clarity.

Lastly, if someone reads a first draft and then tells you white lies, it doesn't really help. So with deepest gratitude, I thank my friend Christa Echtle for her immense intelligence and intrinsic honesty.

GLOSSARY

Action: Anything a character does mentally or physically in a purposeful effort to cause change.

Activity: Anything a character does without purpose. Purposeless deeds and thoughts kill time but change nothing.

Agent Self: That aspect of the mind that carries out a character's actions. The agent self does what the core self wants done while the core self sits back, observant and aware. The core self calls its agent self "I" as in "I did that; I'm doing this; I will get that done."

Allegorical Character: A role that represents a specific facet of a universal concept. If, for example, an author wanted to dramatize the idea of Creativity, each cast member might symbolize one of the arts: Poetry, Painting, Dance, Music, Sculpture, Cinema, Theatre, and the like.

Archetypal Character: A role that symbolizes a universal concept. Archetypal characters stand for ideals such as Motherhood, Time, Power, Goodness, Evil, Life, Death, and Immortality, in their purest form.

Cast Map: A display of cast relationships. This graphic maps how characters counterpoint one another's traits and activate one another's dimensions.

Center of Good: A positive quality deep within a primary character. Attributes such as courage, kindness, strength, wisdom, and honesty, usually found in a protagonist, draw a sense of empathy from readers and audiences. This positive center becomes all the more magnetic when it contrasts with negative charges in other cast members or the surrounding society.

Character Complexity: A pattern of consistent contradictions. These dynamic dimensions structure a character's outer personality and inner identity.

Character-driven Story: A story in which the principal characters cause the major events. External influences drawn from physical, societal, or coincidental sources have a minor effect.

Characterization: A character's outer identity. This observable personality combines all of her physical and vocal traits with all the social and personal personae her agent self assumes.

Core Self: The voice of the mind. When asked "Who am I?" this center of conscious answers "Me" as in "It happened to *me*; it's happening to me now; it might happen to me someday." This core of awareness observes the agent self as it carries out tasks, and then judges the results. The observer self also studies the people around it, remembering past events, anticipating future events, and fantasizing about impossible events.

Crisis: A protagonist's final and most powerful confrontation. In this scene, the story's maximum forces of antagonism bear down on the protagonist face-to-face, confronting her with a dilemma of possible actions. What she chooses to do climaxes the story.

Depth of Character: Submerged currents of desire and awareness. A quiet stream of knowing flows through the consciousness of profound characters with even weightier perceptions swirling in the silent fathoms below. When audiences and readers identify with these characters, they feel their expansive awareness, read their unexpressed thoughts, and, deeper yet, sense the subconscious desires that shine from behind their eyes.

Dimension: A living contradiction. Dimensions pivot a character's behaviors between two opposite qualities or traits. For example, a character who is at times wise but then foolish, who does good then evil, who is generous to some but selfish to others, who is strong in one situation but weak in another.

Dramatic Irony: The simultaneous awareness of past, present, and future. As a reader's or audience member's awareness changes from mystery (knowing less than the characters know) to suspense (knowing the same as the characters know) to dramatic irony (knowing more than the characters know), her curiosity shifts from "What will happen next?" to "How will these characters react when they discover what I already know?" When a storygoer knows what's going to happen to the characters before it happens, her curiosity morphs into dread and her empathy deepens into compassion.

Fate: An invisible force that preordains events. Belief in fate arises from the deterministic view that what happens in life is predestined by a godlike power and therefore *has* to happen. Life's events, no matter how complex, take one and only one possible course with one and only one possible outcome. In this view, free will is an illusion.

First-Person Narrator: A voice that tells a fictional story as if it were an autobiography. The author restricts this narrator's knowledge to what one person could know.

Focal Character: The role that draws most interest. A cast's focal character is almost always the protagonist, but in rare cases, a distinctive supporting role can take the spotlight.

Foil Character: A role that illuminates the protagonist. A foil's contrasting qualities help define the protagonist, but when necessary, this character may also explain or interpret a distant or mysterious protagonist.

Forces of Antagonism: Counteractions that block a character's desire. These powers arise from the forces of nature, social institutions, personal relationships, or dark impulses within the character herself.

Hidden Self: The subconscious mind. Silent, often contradictory drives percolate below the level of awareness. These psychic energies fuel an identity (courageous, cowardly, kind, cruel, violent, calm, etc.) and reveal themselves when a character reacts spontaneously to sudden pressure.

Inciting Incident: A story line's first major turning point. *Inciting* means "starting with impact"; *incident* means "event." This event throws life radically out of balance and arouses the protagonist's super-objective—her desire to restore equilibrium.

Motivation: An innate craving for satisfaction. All-encompassing motivations such as the need for security, the drive for sex, and the fear of starvation push a character toward specific desires such as a gated community, a sensuous lover, a filling meal. Gratification of these ongoing passions and appetites rarely lasts.

Object of Desire: What the protagonist wants in an effort to restore the balance of life. It could be something personal or social, mental or physical.

Plot: A story's ordering, linking, and weaving of events.

Plot-driven Story: A story in which physical, social, and coincidental forces cause the major events. Influences drawn from the characters' desires and resources have a secondary effect.

Point-of-View Character: The role that guides the reader/audience through the telling. Most stories follow their protagonist from event to event, but occasionally an author will keep the protagonist at a mysterious distance and narrate from a supporting character's point of view.

Presentational Genres: Story types based on form: differing styles, tones, or media of expression.

Primary Genres: Story types based on content: differing characters, events, values, emotions.

Reliable Narrator: An honest storytelling voice. When authors narrate their stories, they invent a third-person voice with a god-like knowledge of characters and history. When characters narrate, they speak in a first-person voice with knowledge limited to their personal experience. In either case, they are reliable if the reader/audience can trust them not to bend the truth.

Resolution: Any scenes or descriptions that follow the climax of the central plot.

Reveal: The exposure of a hidden truth.

Scene-Objective: What a character wants in the immediate moment that will take her a step toward her super-objective.

Service Role: A character whose actions affect the course of a story's events.

Stock Role: A character who carries out a task according to her profession or social position but does not affect the course of events.

Subtext: A character's unexpressed inner life. Readers and audiences peer through the surface behaviors (text) of a complex character to discover these unsaid and unsayable thoughts, feelings, and drives (subtext).

Super-Objective: The need to rebalance life. From the inciting incident on, a protagonist's super-objective inspires her struggle to reach her object of desire and thus restore life's equilibrium.

Supporting Role: A character who facilitates scenes but does not affect the course of events.

Suspense: Emotional curiosity. A combination of rational interest and empathetic involvement pulls a reader/audience through a story.

Telling: A synonym for story.

Text: The sensory surface of a work of art: words on the pages of a novel, sounds and images on-screen, actors and sets onstage.

Third-Person Narrator: The voice an author invents to tell her story. This voice treats a fictional work as if it were the biography of its characters. Its knowledge ranges from an omniscient comprehension of a story's history, setting, and cast to a limited insight into the inner and outer lives of a single character.

True Character: A character's inner identity comprised of a triad of selves: the conscious *Core Self*, its active *Agent Self*, and its subconscious *Hidden Self*.

Turning Point: An event that changes the value charge in a character's life from positive to negative or negative to positive.

Unreliable Narrators: A confused, ignorant, or dishonest storytelling voice. If an unreliable third-person voice tells a story, he may either warn the reader that he can't be trusted or just let her figure it out for herself. If an unreliable first-person character narrates, she may be sincere but simply biased or blind to the truth.

Value: A binary of charged experience that can change a human condition from positive to negative or negative to positive: Life/Death, Pleasure/Pain, Justice/Injustice, and the like.

NOTES

Chapter One Characters Versus People

1. *Forms of Life: Character and Moral Imagination in the Novel*, Martin Price, Yale University Press, 1983.
2. *Character and the Novel*, W. J. Harvey, Cornell University Press, 1965.
3. *Forms of Life: Character and Moral Imagination in the Novel*, Martin Price, Yale University Press, 1983.
4. *Aesthetics: A Study of the Fine Arts in Theory and Practice*, James K. Feibleman, Humanities Press, 1968; *The Aesthetic Object: An Introduction to the Philosophy of Value*, Elijah Jordan, Principia Press, 1937.
5. *Love's Knowledge: Essays on Philosophy and Literature*, Martha C. Nussbaum, Oxford University Press, 1992.
6. *The Art of Fiction*, Henry James, 1884; repr., Pantianos Classics, 2018.
7. *Forms of Life: Character and Moral Imagination in the Novel*, Martin Price, Yale University Press, 1983.
8. *The Journal of Jules Renard*, Jules Renard, Tin House Books, 2017.
9. "After Sacred Mystery, the Great Yawn," a review by Roger Scruton of Mario Vargas Llosa's *Notes on the Death of Culture*, TLS, November 4, 2015.
10. *Aesthetics: A Study of the Fine Arts in Theory and Practice*, James K. Feibleman, Humanities Press, 1968.
11. *Character and the Novel*, W. J. Harvey, Cornell University Press, 1965.
12. *Aesthetics: A Study of the Fine Arts in Theory and Practice*, James K. Feibleman, Humanities Press, 1968.
13. *Character and the Novel*, W. J. Harvey, Cornell University Press, 1965.

Chapter Two The Aristotle Debate

1. *The Art of Fiction*, Henry James, 1884; repr., Pantianos Classics, 2018.
2. *Wilhelm Meister's Apprenticeship and Travels*, Johann Wolfgang von Goethe, translated by Thomas Carlyle, Ticknor, Reed, and Fields, 1851.

3. *Forms of Life: Character and Moral Imagination in the Novel*, Martin Price, Yale University Press, 1983.

Chapter Three An Author Prepares

1. "Dissociating Processes Supporting Causal Perception and Causal Inference in the Brain," Matthew E. Roser, Jonathan A. Fugelsang, Kevin N. Dunbar, et al., *Neuropsychology* 19, no. 5, 2005.
2. *The Story of Art*, E. H. Gombrich, Phaidon Press, 1995.
3. *The Politics of Myth: A Study of C. G. Jung, Mircea Eliade, and Joseph Campbell*, Robert Ellwood, State University of New York Press, 1999.
4. *Forms of Life: Character and Moral Imagination in the Novel*, Martin Price, Yale University Press, 1983.

Part Two Building a Character

1. *Six Plays*, August Strindberg, author's foreword to *Miss Julie*, Doubleday, 1955.

Chapter Four Character Inspiration: Outside In

1. *My Life in Art*, Konstantin Stanislavski, Routledge, 2008.
2. *Jaws*, Peter Benchley, Ballantine Books, 2013.
3. *45 Years*, film adaptation by Andrew Haigh of "In Another Country," a short story by David Constantine.
4. *On Writing: A Memoir of the Craft*, Stephen King, Scribner, 2000.
5. *Identity and Story: Creating Self in Narrative*, Dan McAdams and Ruthellen Josselson, *The Narrative Study of Lives*, vol. 4, American Psychological Association, 2006.
6. *The True Believer: Thoughts on the Nature of Mass Movements*, Eric Hoffer, Harper Perennial Modern Classics, 2010.

Chapter Five Character Inspiration: Inside Out

1. *The Art of Fiction*, Henry James, 1884; repr., Pantianos Classics, 2018.
2. *Connectome: How the Brain's Wiring Makes Us Who We Are*, Sebastian Seung, Houghton Mifflin Harcourt, 2012; *Networks of the Brain*, Olaf Sporns, MIT Press, 2011.
3. *The Birth and Death of Meaning: An Interdisciplinary Perspective on the Problem of Man*, Ernest Becker, Free Press, 1971.
4. *The Feeling of What Happens: Body and Emotion in the Making of Consciousness*, Antonio Damasio, Mariner Books, 2000.
5. *The Self Illusion: How the Social Brain Creates Identity*, Bruce Hood, Oxford University Press, 2012.
6. *The Concept of Mind*, Gilbert Ryle and Daniel C. Dennett, University of Chicago Press, 2000.

7. *Greek Religion*, Walter Burkert, Harvard University Press, 1985.

8. *Grecian and Roman Mythology*, Mary Ann Dwight, Palala Press, 2016.

9. *Thinks . . .*, David Lodge, Viking Penguin, 2001.

10. *Incognito*, David Eagleman, Pantheon Books, 2011.

11. *The Principles of Psychology*, William James, vols. 1–2, 1890; repr., Pantianos Classics, 2017.

12. *Psycho-Analytic Explorations*, Donald W. Winnicott, Grove Press, 2019.

13. *Consciousness*, Susan Blackmore, Oxford University Press, 2005.

14. *Hamlet: Poem Unlimited*, Harold Bloom, Riverhead Books, 2004.

15. *The Rise and Fall of Soul and Self: An Intellectual History of Personal Identity*, Raymond Martin and John Barresi, Columbia University Press, 2005.

16. *The Principles of Psychology*, William James, vol. 1, chap. 9, "The Stream of Thought," Dover Books, 1950.

17. *The Complete Essays*, Michel de Montaigne, Penguin Classics, 1993.

18. *The Work of the Negative*, Andre Green, Free Association Books, 1999.

19. *Strangers to Ourselves: Discovering the Adaptive Unconscious*, Timothy D. Wilson, Harvard University Press, 2002.

20. Terrence Rafferty on E. L. Doctorow, *New York Times Book Review*, January 12, 2014.

Chapter Six Roles Versus Characters

1. *Character and the Novel*, W. J. Harvey, Cornell University Press, 1965.

Chapter Seven The Outer Character

1. *Philosophical Investigations*, Ludwig Wittgenstein, translated by G. E. M. Anscombe, Macmillan, 1958.

2. *Forms of Life: Character and Moral Imagination in the Novel*, Martin Price, Yale University Press, 1983.

3. Ibid.

4. Ibid.

5. *Theory of Literature*, Rene Wellek and Austin Warren, Harcourt, Brace, 1956.

6. *Character and the Novel*, W. J. Harvey, Cornell University Press, 1965.

7. *The Time Paradox*, Philip Zimbardo and John Boyd, Simon and Schuster, 2008.

8. *Actual Minds, Possible Worlds*, Jerome Bruner, Harvard University Press, 1986.

9. *Dialogue: The Art of Verbal Action for Page, Stage, Screen*, Robert McKee, Hachette Book Group / Twelve, 2016.

10. *Revolutionary Writing: Reflections of the Revolution in France and the First Letter on a Regicide Peace*, Edmund Burke, 1796.

11. Theophrastus's full list of character types: the Ironical Man, the Flatterer, the Garrulous Man, the Boor, the Complaisant Man, the Reckless Man, the Chatty Man, the Gossip, the Shameless Man, the Penurious Man, the Gross Man, the Unseasonable

Man, the Officious Man, the Stupid Man, the Surly Man, the Superstitious Man, the Grumbler, the Distrustful Man, the Offensive Man, the Unpleasant Man, the Man of Petty Ambition, the Mean Man, the Boastful Man, the Arrogant Man, the Coward, the Oligarch, the Late-Learner, the Evil-Speaker, the Patron of Rascals, and the Avaricious Man. For an amusing explanation of each unpleasantness, read *Characters: An Ancient Take on Bad Behavior*, Theophrastus, annotated by James Romm, Callaway Arts and Entertainment, 2018.

12. *The Oxford Handbook of the Five Factor Model*, Thomas A. Widiger, Oxford University Press, 2016.

13. *Story: Substance, Structure, Style, and the Principles of Screenwriting*, Robert McKee, HarperCollins, 1997, pp. 243–248.

Chapter Eight The Inner Character

1. *Nicomachean Ethics*, Aristotle, book 3, chaps. 1–5, SDE Classics, 2019.

2. *Punished by Rewards*, Alfie Kohn, Mariner Books, 1999.

3. *The Denial of Death*, Ernest Becker, Simon and Schuster, 1997.

4. *The Stages of Psychosocial Development According to Erik H. Erikson*, Stephanie Scheck, GRIN Verlag GmbH, 2005.

5. *Man's Search for Meaning*, Viktor E. Frankl, Beacon Press, 1959.

6. *Understanding Civilizations: The Shape of History*, James K. Feibleman, Horizon Press, 1975.

7. *The Science of Logic*, Georg Hegel, translated by George Di Giovanni, Cambridge University Press, 2015.

8. As Claudia Koonz notes in *The Nazi Conscience* (Belknap Press, 2003), death camp commandants suffered sleepless, guilt-ridden nights when their crematoriums weren't running on schedule.

9. *Thinking, Fast and Slow*, Daniel Kahneman, Farrar, Straus and Giroux, 2013; *Subliminal: How Your Unconscious Mind Rules Your Behavior*, Leonard Mlodinow, Vintage, 2013; *Strangers to Ourselves: Discovering the Adaptive Unconscious*, Timothy D. Wilson, Belknap Press, 2004.

10. *How the Mind Works*, Steven Pinker, W. W. Norton, 1997.

11. Jenann Ismael on the nature of choice: "We are shaped by our native dispositions and endowments, but we do make choices, and our choices . . . are expressions of our hopes and dreams, values and priorities. These are things actively distilled out of a history of personal experience, and they make us who we are. Freedom is not a grandiose metaphysical ability to subvene the laws of physics. It is the day-to-day business of making choices: choosing the country over the city, children over career, jazz over opera, choosing an occasional lie over a hurtful truth, hard work over leisure. It is choosing that friend, this hairstyle, maybe tiramisu over a tight physique, and pleasure over achievement. It is all of the

little formative decisions that when all is said and done, make our lives our own creations." ("Fate's Scales, Quivering," Jenann Ismael, *TLS*, August 9, 2019.)

12. *Free Will and Luck*, Alfred R. Mele, Oxford University Press, 2008; *Effective Intentions: The Power of Conscious Will*, Alfred R. Mele, Oxford University Press, 2009.

Chapter Nine   The Dimensional Character

1. "Not Easy Being Greene: Graham Greene's Letters," Michelle Orange, *Nation*, May 4, 2009.
2. BBC Culture Series, April 2018.
3. *The Odyssey*, Homer, translated by Emily Wilson, W. W. Norton, 2018.

Chapter Ten   The Complex Character

1. *The Power Elite*, C. Wright Mills, Oxford University Press, 1956; *Civilization and Its Discontents*, Sigmund Freud, W. W. Norton, 2005.
2. "The Financial Psychopath Next Door," Sherree DeCovny, *CFA Institute Magazine* 23, no. 2, March–April 2012.
3. *Twilight of the Elites*, Christopher Hayes, Random House, 2012.
4. *The Self Illusion: How the Social Brain Creates Identity*, Bruce Hood, Oxford University Press, 2012.
5. *Games People Play*, Eric Berne, Random House, 1964.
6. *The Oxford Handbook of the Five Factor Model*, Thomas A. Widiger, Oxford University Press, 2016.
7. *Personality, Cognition and Social Interaction*, edited by John F. Kihlstrom and Nancy Cantor, Routledge, 2017; *Subliminal: How Your Unconscious Mind Rules Your Behavior*, Leonard Mlodinow, Random House, 2012.
8. *The Private Life*, Josh Cohen, Granta, 2013.
9. *The Courage to Be*, Paul Tillich, Yale University Press, 1952.
10. *Dialogue: The Art of Verbal Action for Page, Stage, Screen*, Robert McKee, Hachette Book Group / Twelve, 2016, pp. 45–53.

Chapter Eleven   The Completed Character

1. *Time in Literature*, Hans Meyerhoff, University of California Press, 1955.
2. *Upheavals of Thought: The Intelligence of Emotion*, Martha C. Nussbaum, Cambridge University Press, 2003.

Chapter Twelve   The Symbolic Character

1. *Man and His Symbols*, Carl G. Jung, Dell, 1968; *Archetype, Attachment, Analysis: Jungian Psychology and the Emergent Mind*, Jean Knox, Brunner-Routledge, 2003.
2. *The Book of Qualities*, J. Ruth Gendler, Harper Perennial, 1984.

3. *The True Believer: Thoughts on the Nature of Mass Movements*, Eric Hoffer, Harper and Row, 1951.

4. *The Origins of Cool in Postwar America*, Joel Dinerstein, University of Chicago Press, 2018.

5. *The Politics of Myth: A Study of C. G. Jung, Mircea Eliade, and Joseph Campbell*, Robert Ellwood, State University of New York Press, 1999.

Chapter Thirteen   The Radical Character

1. *The Principle of Reason*, Martin Heidegger, translated by Reginald Lilly, Indiana University Press, 1991.

2. *Flat Protagonists: A Theory of Novel Character*, Marta Figlerowicz, Oxford University Press, 2017.

3. *On Beckett*, Alain Badiou, Clinamen Press, 2003.

4. "Beckett, Proust, and 'Dream of Fair to Middling Women,' " Nicholas Zurbrugg, *Journal of Beckett Studies* no. 9, 1984.

5. *Civilization and Its Discontents*, Sigmund Freud, Verlag, 1930.

Chapter Fifteen   Character in Action

1. *Childhood and Society*, Erik Erikson, W. W. Norton, 1963.

2. *Love Is a Story*, Robert Sternberg, Oxford University Press, 1998.

Chapter Sixteen   Character in Performance

1. *Aristotle: The Desire to Understand*, Jonathan Lear, Cambridge University Press, 1988.

2. *Language as Symbolic Action*, Kenneth Burke, University of California Press, 1968.

3. "The Myth of Universal Love," Stephen T. Asma, *New York Times*, January 6, 2013.

4. *Actual Minds, Possible Worlds*, Jerome Bruner, Harvard University Press, 1986.

5. *The Better Angels of Our Nature*, Steven Pinker, Penguin, 2015.

6. *Gut Reactions: A Perceptual Theory of Emotion*, Jesse J. Prinz, Oxford University Press, 2004.

Part Four   Character Relationships

1. *The Sociology of Secrecy and of Secret Societies*, Georg Simmel, CreateSpace Independent Publishing Platform, 2015.

Chapter Seventeen   Cast Design

1. *The Birth and Death of Meaning: An Interdisciplinary Perspective on the Problem of Man*, Ernest Becker, Free Press, 1971; *The Denial of Death*, Ernest Becker, Free Press, 1973.

2. *Bloodchild and Other Stories*, Octavia E. Butler, Seven Stories Press, 2005.

3. *The Shifting Realities of Philip K. Dick: Selected Literary and Philosophical Writings*, Lawrence Sutin, Vintage Books, 1995.

INDEX

ABOUT THE AUTHOR

Robert McKee is a Fulbright Scholar and recipient of an International Moving Image Book Award. Programs he wrote and presented for British television have been twice nominated for the BAFTA, and this award was given to *J'Accuse: Citizen Kane*. His pilot screenplay *Abraham* launched the TV series *The Bible*. McKee has lectured on the art of storytelling throughout the world. His former students have won more than 60 Academy Awards, 200 Emmy Awards, 100 WGA awards, and 50 DGA awards, along with the Pulitzer and Booker Prizes.